Construction of Psychological Processes in Interpersonal Communication

Edited by

Maria C. D. P. Lyra
Federal University of Pernambuco, Brazil

and

Jaan Valsiner
University of North Carolina at Chapel Hill

Volume 4 in Child Development Within Culturally Structured Environments

Ablex Publishing Corporation
Stamford, Connecticut
London, England

Printed in the United States of America

Lyra, Maria C. D. P.
   Construction of psychological processes in interpersonal
communication / Maria C.D.P Lyra, Jaan Valsiner.
       p.   cm. – (Child development within culturally structured
environments ; v. 4)
   Includes bibliographical references and index.
   ISBN 1-56750-296-2 (hardcover ; vol. 4.)– ISBN 1-56750-415-9 (pbk ; vol. 4.)
    1. Interpersonal communication in children. 2. Social interaction
in children. 3. Child development–Cross-cultural studies.
4. Child psychology–Cross-cultural studies. I. Valsiner, Jaan.
II. Title. III. Series.
BF723.A33C48 1988 vol. 4
[BF723.C57]   97-20464
155.4'136–dc21   CIP

Ablex Publishing Corporation
100 Prospect Street
Stamford, Connecticut 06901-1640

Published in the U.K. and Europe by:
Ablex Publishing Corp. (U.K.)
38 Tavistock Street
Covent Garden
London WC2E 7PB
England

Contents

Introduction

PROCESS APPROACH IN SOCIOGENESIS

Maria C. D. P. Lyra
Federal University of Pernambuco

Jaan Valsiner
Clark University

FOUNDATIONS FOR CONCEPTUALIZATION OF PROCESSES

This book deals with two related issues. First, it deals with the assumption that all human beings are continuously developing dynamic systems. Although numerous researches on human development in recent decades have emphasized the dynamic nature of developmental phenomena, the full scope of the basic assumption for such an approach—the irreversibility of developmental time (Bergson, 1907/1945)—has rarely been given full coverage. It is particularly the case with the methodological implications of the irreversibility of time. For instances, accumulation of data over time (i.e., accumulation of data into summary indices that eliminate their temporal localization) would be an inadmissible operation, if irreversibility of developmental time is taken seriously. The result would be that developmental methodology steers away from reliance on the statistical methods of inference, and concentrates on formal modeling of time-dependent processes.

One of the main problems in dealing with the process approach concerns the different levels in the dimension of time. For instance, individual psychological processes, phylogenesis versus ontogenesis, and microgenesis versus ontogenesis. Each of those time foci requires its own calibration of the level of details of the process at which the analysis takes place. The microgenetic

1

level of description of dynamic processes (e.g., the description of emergence of novel forms in interaction) does not reflect the emergence of novelty at the ontogenetic level because the microgenetically described novel from can disappear from the person's repertoire, never to return. Furthermore, ontogenesis entails not only formation of novel forms in an individual's life course, but also disappearance of previously established and maintained forms. There is no one-to-one correspondence between microgenetic and ontogenetic domains. A similar lack of isomorphism exists between phylogenesis—ontogenesis is not determined by phylogenesis, nor would and ontogenetic change necessarily lead to a phylogenetic novelty. Contributions to this book focus mainly on microgenetic processes. The other levels of developmental investigation remain underrepresented here.

The dynamic aspect of developmental change, which allows the emergence and construction of novel forms, can be summarized through the ancient Heraclitan problem of being unable to "step into the same river twice." This statement captures the dynamic view of development in irreversible time. However, it overlooks the self-generative nature of psychological (and other open-systemic) processes—the river flows (but does not reconstruct itself), while psychological processes, as they encounter an outside intervening condition (in analogy—the person who steps into the river), become reconstructed by themselves, making use of the intervening condition.

However, even if one accepts the reality of irreversible time, it is necessary that our dynamic developmental models can reflect both the dynamic and (temporally) relatively stale states of the developing system. Instead of viewing the latter as different from the form—in terms of the dynamic versus static opposition—one can describe the functioning of temporarily stable organizations as a case where dynamic processes become relatively stable. This relative stability functions as a background condition for the changeable nature of processes. In the states of stability of a system we can find dynamic processes that have—for a while—become organized into a steady state. That state can become disequilibrated under some conditions, bringing about the change of the system. Alternatively, it may maintain the steady state for considerable time periods. Yet such maintenance itself remains a dynamic process, rather than a static state (which it may look to be, for observers from the outside).

SOCIAL ORIGINS OF PSYCHOLOGICAL PROCESSES

The second area of concentration in this volume is on the dynamic interchange that occurs between the world of social agents and their cultural environments. The latter are considered to be constitutive of—and constituted by—persons. So, the focus is on the dynamic process of negotiations between and within social partners embedded in a cultural environment, and constantly interdependent with it. Different authors in this book deal with the question of how to approach the emergence and construction of psychological processes through the understanding of the dynamics of self-other interchanges. Development of human psychological processes—at least those that entail volitional and sign-mediated (semiotic) functions—are axiomatically assumed to emerge from social interaction. In this sense, they emerge socially; they are *sociogenetic*.

The sociogenetic origin of psychological processes has been claimed by a number of thinkers who have been devoted to investigating and comprehending the social emergence and construction of psychological processes. At the end of the 19th century and the beginning of the 20th century, we can refer to the work of Baldwin, Janet, Mead, Vygotsky, and Wallon as having concentrated on theoretical constructions and investigations of the social embeddedness of psychological development. In the work of those authors, we can identify a constant concern or interest with the dynamic aspects of psychological constructions embedded in a social environment. An instance of this is Mead's (1937) refocusing on Wilhelm Wundt's idea of how the gesture becomes internalized through belonging, at the same time, to the other and to ourselves through exchanges with the social other. Many aspects of Vygotsky's contributions can be taken as demonstrations of his dynamic view of the process of construction of psychological functions. For instance, there is his conception of the dynamic nature of personal sense as the individual side of the constructive nature of the sociocultural environment (Van der Veer & Valsiner, 1991), as well as his focus on internalization. Wallon conceived social interactional dynamics as relying on oppositions between two poles: one of fusion with the social other and another of differentiation from this social other. The tension between those poles allows the emergence of differentiations that constitute the process through which the subjects or persons emerge.

Stressing the personal-mentalistic aspect of the interchanges with the social world, Vygotsky was particularly concerned with the emergence and functioning of the higher mental functions as the core demonstration of the social nature of the individual mind. To Wallon (1934/1973, 1942/1972), by contrast, the dynamics of interchanges with the social world starts from the domain of postures and emotions. At the same time, Wallon conceived of the dynamics of interchanges as the linkage between the social preadapted biological endowment and the sociocultural environment (Lyra & Rossetti-Ferreira, 1995).

In recent decades, psychological discourse has repeatedly emphasized the social nature of the personal psychological processes. Nevertheless, there is a gap between declarations of the social nature of individual minds, on the one hand, and the comprehension of the mechanisms or processes through which those psychological functions emerge and develop, on the other hand. Advancement of theoretical and methodological ways of approaching the question of how the dynamics of the self-other duality allow the construction of dynamic psychological worlds, giving rise to the emergence of individuals, seems to be a major task.

FUSION AND DIFFERENTIATION AS APPLICABLE
TO INTERNALIZATION-EXTERNALIZATION PROCESSES

A directly related issue can be summarized as the degree to which the processes of externalization versus internalization are analyzed and conceived as instances of action or semiotic fields. In other words, the differentiation of psychological processes from the embeddedness in a sociocultural environment requires the conceptualization of both the external dimension of interchanges on negotiations with another and the internal dimension of the individual psychological functioning. Both of these dimensions rely on actions and semiotic devices as the "substance" to which processes apply or from which they are constituted.

Focusing on the microprocesses of sociogenetic development, we can take the fusion-differention dichotomy as encomposing opposed but inseparable poles (Lyra & Rossetti-Ferreira, 1995; Wallon, 1942/1972) of a dialectical dynamics (Valsiner & Cairns, 1992). The reciprocal processes of externalization and internalization can be considered elaborations of the pole of differentiation as it separates individual persons from the external dynamics of self-other relationships. Indeed, considering both processes as reciprocal and cyclical processes, from which novelty is created at individual and societal levels, a process of differentiation is required.

A further point must be raised: How can the integration of the action field and the semiotic field in the processes of internalization and externalization be conceptualized?

At the level of microprocesses of sociogenesis, the idea of *appropriation* (Rogoff, 1992, 1993) of the cultural ways of behaving carries a conception of fusion with the cultural environment, where the differentiated pole of individual subjectivity emerges as an extension of this process of appropriation. The notion of appropriation as fusion is based largely on the pragmatism of Dewey, whose classic work on the reflex circle can be seen as the forerunner of approaches that emphasize person-environment coordination processes.

This notion of fusion with the cultural characteristics or requirements of a cultural environment is also present in the work of Cole (1995), expressed in the idea that the child learns to use existing cultural tools and reconstructs them at the level of psychological functioning. However, the dynamics that guide those reconstructions remain analyzed and conceived in their connection with the cultural environment. Therefore, these dynamics are conceptually mixed with the role of the tools provided by this environment.

Wertsch's (1991, 1995) work can be seen as one step closer to recognition of the process of differentiation from the culture as constituting individual psychological processes. This is achieved through the use of the concept of *voices*—largely based on the ideas of Bakhtin. Two major points can be highlighted in Wertsch's contribution: the fluidity of the appropriated psychological processes and the uniqueness of individual construction of particular narratives.

The process of appropriation can be conceptualized in terms of a reciprocal interdependence of externalization and internalization processes of developmental change, and creation of novelty (Lawrence & Valsiner, 1993). This conceptual extension adds the directionality (inner/outer direction) to the talk about exchange processes between person and environment. The role of the personal agency in these processes is emphasized in the case of use of the internalization-externalization processes.

ACTION AND SEMIOTIC FIELDS: THE DYNAMIC SYSTEMS PERSPECTIVE

Originating in biology (Von Baer, 1828), the idea that development occurs as a system of dynamic relationships—and not as linear exchange of interactions—has contributed as new comprehension of the process of development, opposed to but not separated from its outcome. The two main contributions of this line of reasoning can be summarized as:

1. Developmental systems are inherently dynamic.
2. Novelty emerges from the dynamic pattern of the system as a result of the self-organizing nature of individual and environmental conditions.

These novel organizational forms, which appear as a result of the dynamic patterns of the system, do not need to be planned in advance, nor do they need to be present as structures at the level of the individual or at the level of the environment. Therefore, the dynamic systems perspectives introduces the view that predictability of developmental change and outcomes from simple causal linear precursors is unsatisfactory. The emergence or construction of novelty, resulting indeterministically from change, is the central phenomenon of development (see Fogel, Lyra, & Valsiner, 1997).

However, focusing on the dynamics of the social world, the question arises: What is the nature of these self-organizing characteristics? Which mutual constraints result in the creation of novel forms? From a sociogenetic systemic perspective, we need to explain the dynamics responsible for the functioning of the inter- and intraindividual psychological processes. In other words, the dynamic system conception should account for the processes of externalization and internalization as two interrelated sides of the same developmental phenomenon. Moreover, the dynamic systems perspective should include in its conception of mutually constructed constraints and emergence of novelty both the action dynamic field and the semiotic dynamic field.

The notion of these two fields introduces hierarchical organization into the realm of human development, together with the duality of psychological processes. The domain of human action is regulated by signs, which themselves emerge from the action field and become superordinate to that field, forming the semiotic field. The distinction of the latter from the former creates increased possibilities for the dynamic system to transcend the confines of a particular encounter with the environment. It is through further differentiation of the semiotic field—emergence of new levels of metasemiotic regulatory processes—that the development of the volitional and intentional nature of a person's actions is made possible. This emergence has been elaborated by Bühler (1934/1990) in his notion of presentational fields in his *Sprachtheorie*.

The main implication of this emergence of semiotic (and metasemiotic) fields from the basis of the action field is that the dynamic systems involved in human psychological development become goal-oriented and goal-constructive (teleogenetic). Goal-orientedness is and emergent characteristics of development psychological systems, because through the semiotic (and metasemiotic) field, future-oriented action becomes present in much of the human conduct in any here-and-now setting.

Unlike the analysis of the action field, the semiotic field requires to a greater extent the inclusion of a degree of intentionality or goal-directedness as an element for the analysis and comprehension of the dynamic characteristics of this field. Internalization of psychological processes cannot be describe unless we make use of semiotic devices as constituting those processes and not only as interpreting them, as we do in interpreting the field of action. The difficulty of separating intentionality or goal-directness preexisting (or inherent) in the semiotic field from that which is emerging from the dynamics of the system requires conceptualization at a different level from that required by the field of action. Therefore, the semiotic domain that characterizes the unitary integration of the social construction of psychological processes, highlighted through the mechanism of externalization-internalization, requires a redefinition of some of the fundamental features of the dynamic systems perspective. In other words, if we accept the inherent purposiveness of semiotic functioning, the emergent dynamics that characterize social dynamic systems need to be redefined in order to take into account this emerging intentionality of the semiotic field. However, maintaining the assumption of the dynamic nature of processes and outcomes occurring in irreversible time, the challenge remains how to not attribute or assume that this emerging intentionality has a flavor of preexisting causality, namely a recurrence to some instance of a semiotic and cultural predetermination of psychological developmental processes.

AN OVERVIEW OF THE BOOK

This book brings together the contributions of researches from different sociocultural background and different parts of the world. Different views of the process of how human beings construct their psychological functions through interpersonal processes of communication should emerge from the different sociocultural backgrounds in which these researchers have grown and become adult persons. We accept that different theoretical and methodological analysis perspectives should emerge from researchers who originate from different sociocultural backgrounds. We not only accept, but we aim to stress that we consider them as alternative worldviews, necessary for broadening the relativistic cultural basis of our theoretical and philosophical understanding of the process of construction of human psychological functioning.

Regarding the analysis of the process of communication, we can summarize the dominant difference among the chapters as the degree of stress on the external or internal dimension of this process; in other words, the emphasis on the interindividual versus intraindividual processes and on action versus semiotic fields. Mainly considering the role of actions and semiotic devices, the chapters reflect different assumptions about the idea of developing dynamic systems.

Part I: Historical Introduction

Kojima's Chapter 1 introduces the historical analysis of how cultural ways of childrearing theories evolved and changed through time and in modern Japan. Considering the role of three related groups of participants—layperson, experts, and particular historical time. Having the function of preserving temporarily outmoded ideas through resistance for change, EPI exhibits a dialogue with new existing ideas and practices. Moreover, general core ideas about childrearing theories can be shared by different cultures, at the same time that a diversity of ideas coexists as EPI. The historical analysis guided by this conception shows that many modern principles of contemporary psychology can be found in the writings of our ancestors. As a historical analysis, EPI deals with the more crystallized side of a process through which cultural theories of childrearing practices interact within a society at a particular time.

Part II: Constructions of Psychological Process:
From Infancy to Early Childhood

Holt, Fogel, and Wood (Chapter 2) concentrates on the analysis of a peekaboo game in mother-infant dyads during the first year of a baby's life. Based on the dynamic systems framework, the chapter exhibits the emergence of innovations from the process of dyadic coregulation. From the most simple peekaboo game toward the inclusion of object-in-container situations and the infant's role shifting, new characteristics of the game emerge as a mutual and interdependent co-construction of the partners' dynamic exchanges. Cultural rules as ritualization of the game come to be integrated in the game through the co-regulation and mutual con-creation of the games' tasks through time.

Moro and Rodriguez (Chapter 3) propose a pragmatical interpretation of the infant's construction of the object in the process of communication. Extending Vygotskian social constructionism to the first year of life, the function of the object's usage is analyzed following Peirce's semiotic conception. Beginning by an interpretative process of abduction, the infant slowly constructs the iconic, index, and symbolic dimensions of representing the usages of the object. Empirical examples form 7, 10, and 13 triadic exchanges (two infants and an adult) illustrate the acquisition of those successive dimensions of the semiotic construction of the object by the infant.

Smolka and da Cruz (Chapter 4) analyze the emergence of first words and concentrate on the construction of sense production and signification in the context of the interactive dynamics in a (Brazilian) day-care center. Based on Vygotsky's and Bakhtin's ideas, the authors hightlight the role of a collective movement in the context of the day-care interactions as originating the sense construction. This allows the child's successive construction of a multiplicity of meanings that are appropriated by the child as emergent senses, amplified and restricted as words and gestures embedded in a system of cultural conventions.

Vasconcellos and Valsiner (Chapter 5) focus on a toddler's construction of a personal place through the child's active role and the group canalization of the process of construction. Through imitation, gestures, postural communication, and emotional support, the child constructs a personal place. The authors highlight the role of externalized action as corresponding to internalized elaborations of those actions. Analyzing the process of construction of a personal place by a 18-month child, the authors propose the dynamic nature of a co-constructivistic process of development; the child's active role and the canalization process enhanced by the group interact at the level of actions and are reelaborations at the semiotic emergent level.

Oliveira (Chapter 6) analyzes the construction of gender representation by young children in the context of peer interaction in a (Brazilian) day-care center. She proposes the concept of role taking as allowing the mutual integration of actions and semiotic fields. Considering role taking as mediational instrument, she hightlights the dynamic process of meaning confrontation as realizing a movement of expanding and restricting shared semiotic fields of conduct. Gender representation emerges from the interactional dynamics where those meaning confrontations take place.

Gupta (Chapter 7) discusses the inseparability of language and thought in considering the functioning of social and private speech. She illustrates her point through analysis of 3-to 4-year-old children-adult interactions in a Peabody Picture Vocabulary Test organized as a game Highlighting the role of sense-meaning construction, she argues in favor the merging nature of social speech and private speech. The ontogenetic investigation of both thought and speech needs to cross the boundaries that separate one from the other. Gupta proposes that the comprehension of the dynamic linkages between verbal and motor activities and sense-meaning construction will provide a framework of analysis for approaching the multifunctional role of the complex phenomena of individual mental functioning.

Junefelt and Tulviste (Chapter 8) analyzed the regulative role of American, Estonian, and Swedish mother's discourse with their 2-year-old children in the context of meal time and puzzle solving. Assuming a sociogenetic framework based on Rommetveit's conception of intersubjectivity and Vygotsky's notion of semiotic mediation, they conclude that the mothers differ both in the quantity and the quality of the regulative discourse: Estonians use it the most and Swedish the least. Americans use regulative utterances to elicit verbal communication and use them Estonians to elicit attention. The Swedish use utterances to regulate verbal activity less than Americans, but more than Americans to regulate attention. American and Swedish mothers prefer indirect ways of regulating through questions, whereas Estonian mothers regulate more through imperatives. The semiotical organization of the meal-time and puzzle-solving settings differed. The last were much more regulated than the first.

Part III: Theoretical Elaborations for Sociogenesis

Carvalho, Império-Hamburger, and Pedrosa (Chapter 9) propose a redefinition of interactional concepts through an elaboration of the concept of field of interactions. This is done through the establishment of analogical comparisons between the social-psychological system, conceived as a dynamic system, and the physical system endowed with perennial movement—the Brownian movement. Empirical examples from 2-3 to-year-old children in free play groups illustrate the conceptual elaboration of the concept of social interaction, regulation/co-regulation, and correlation. The emergence of meaning appears from the dynamics of the system. Meanings create a group culture and history through the process of abbreviation, which allows the persistence of meanings in the group as well as its recreation.

Branco (Chapter 10) analyzes the theoretical and empirical status of two ideas: cooperation and competition focusing on the analysis of adult-children interactions in a (Brazilian) preschool setting. Based on Valsiner's conception of the *inclusive separation* of psychological categories and on the co-constructed and cultural canalized dynamics of the developmental process, she proposes a dialectical relationship relating both concepts. The notion of convergence versus divergence of an individual's goal orientations is suggested. The individual active role and the cultural canalization process compose a dynamic system of relationships giving rise to group convergence or divergence of goal orientation.

Litvinic (Chapter 11) theoretically elaborates on the concept of personal culture in order to approach relationship change and identity. Using the symbol as the symbol as the unit of analysis, collective culture, intersubjectivity, and personal culture are pondered as three related areas for understanding the history of relationship dynamics. The tension between individual and relational aspects of relationship development includes a new conceptualization of Vygotsky's *zone of proximal development* (ZPD). More than a social frame for external measurement of development change, ZPD is "the state of potentiality for change within the individual which is opened up by interactive contact" (p. 16).

Lyra (Chapter 12) analyzes the early ontogenesis of the interpersonal process of communication as the "locus" of emergence and creation of meanings. She proposes a mechanism of relational choice among possibilities functioning at two interconnected and interdependent levels; the level that relates the individual and the semiotic-cultural environment and the level that incorporates the specific context of partner's dialogical flow of actions. Assuming the dialogue as the epistemological unit of analysis and based on Bahktin's phenomenological conception of the act of being Lyra proposes that the relational choice among possibilities carries a relational and evaluative the character. This relational-evaluative dynamics creates a historical process that constitutes relationship change and development.

FOCUS ON PROCESSES

The issue of psychological process as unfolding within culturally structured environments has been a general theme around which many of the contributions to the previous three volumes in this series have found a common focus. Nevertheless, one of the previous volumes gave that theme sufficiently concentrated coverage; hence the need for this volume. For various reasons, the preparation of this volume has taken a number of years. We only hope that its long time in the making is compensated for by its comprehensive international coverage of the issues. The later emphasis has been put into practice in the case of previous three volumes, and we are glad to continue in a similar vein. The international readership deserves access to the work of researchers from all countries in which a given topic is currently undergoing serious investigation.

The focus on psychological processes is aimed at reversing the usual tendency in contemporary developmental psychology, where much of the research activity has concentrated on outcomes (e.g., summary scores of tests, accumulated frequencies of observed—and classified—behavior, etc.). The study of outcomes does not allow researchers to get a direct glimpse into the processes that generated these outcomes. In order to study these processes, a careful look at the basic assumptions of developmental research may be necessary.

REFERENCES

Bergson, H. (1945). *L'Evolution créatrice* [creative evolution]. Genève: Éditions Albert Skira. (Original work published 1907).

Bühler, K. (1990). *Theory of language: The representational function of language.* Amsterdam: John Benjamins. (Original work published 1934).

Cole, M. (1995). Culuture and cognitive development: From cross-cultural research to creating systems of cultural mediation. *Culture & Psychology, 1*(1), 25-54.

Fogel, A., Lyra, M.C.D.P., & Valsiner, J. (Eds). (1997). *Dynamics and indeterminism in development and social processes.* Mahwah, NJ: Erlbaum.

Lawrence, J.A., & Valsiner, J. (1993). Conceptual roots of internalization: From transmission to transformation. *Human Development, 36,* 150-167.

Lyra, M.C.D.P. & Rossetti-Ferreira, M.C. (1995). Transformation and construction in social interaction: A new perspective of analysis of the mother-infant dyad. In J. Valsiner (Ed.), *Child development in culturally structured environments. Vol 3: Comparative-cultural and constructivist perspectives* (pp. 51-77). Norwood, NJ: Ablex.

Mead, G.H. (1937). *Mind, self and society.* Chicago: University of Chicago Press.

Rogoff, B. (1992). Three ways of relating person and culture. *Human Development, 35*(5), 316-320.

Rogoff, B. (1993). Children's guided participation and participatory appropriation in sociocultural activity. In R.H. Wozniak & K.W. Fisher (Eds.), *Development in context* (pp. 121-153). Hillsdale, NJ: Erlbaum.

Valsiner, J., & Cairns, R.B. (1992). Theoretical perspectives on conflict and development. In C.U. Shantz & W.W. Hartup (Eds.), *Conflict in child and adolescent development* (pp. 15-35). Cambridge, UK: Cambridge University Press.

Van der Veer, R., & Valsiner, J. (1991). *Understanding Vygotsky: A quest for synthesis.* Oxford, UK: Basil Blackwell.

Von Baer, K.E. (1828). *Über Entwicklungsgeschichte der Thiere: Beobactung und reflexion* [On the history of development of animals: Observation and reflexion]. Königsberg, Germany Bornträger.

Wallon, H. (1972). *De L'act à la pensée* [From act toward thought] Paris: Flammarion. (Original work published 1942).

Wallon, H. (1973). *Les origines du caractère chez l'enfant* [The origins of character in infancy]. Paris: Boivin. (Original work published 1934).

Wertsch, J.V. (1991). *Voices of the mind.* Cambridge, MA: Harvard University Press.

Wertsch, J.V. (1995). Sociocultural research in the copyright age. *Culture & Psychology, 1*(1): 81-102.

part I
Historical Introduction

THE CONSTRUCTION OF CHILDREARING THEORIES IN EARLY MODERN TO MODERN JAPAN

Hideo Kojima
Nagoya University, Japan

INTRODUCTION

This chapter focuses on the construction process of childrearing theories within Japanese society since the mid-17th century. According to my analysis, interpersonal communication, both actual and imaginary, operates in the construction process of childrearing theories. The constructors of theories are mainly adults, and availability of the materials for analysis has necessitated more focus on the prescriptive aspects rather than the actual aspects of childrearing. However, the effects of adults' theories on the child are also considered. In addition, descriptive records by adults are to be involved in the following discussion.

In the first section, I deal with three roles related to the construction of childrearing theories. These are roles of laypersons, expert advisors, and academic researchers. Ethnotheories on childrearing are the second topic. The concept of ethnopsychology as contrasted with commonsense psychology is explained. Then a new concept of an ethnopsychological pool of ideas (EPI) concerning childrearing is proposed and its nature is explicated. The EPI is highly resistant to rapid change and it contains diverse source materials based on which the layperson's, the expert advisor's, and even the scientific researcher's theories across generations are to be constructed. This chapter ends with the discussions of implications for developmental theory and for intercultural and diachronical talks on theories of human development in general and of childrearing in particular.

THREE ROLES RELATED TO THE
CONSTRUCTION OF CHILDREARING THEORIES

The subject of childrearing is not the exclusive domain of experts in psychology, cultural anthropology, medicine, and education, nor do these experts have a monopoly on the discourse surrounding problems such as child development, discipline, and education. In many contemporary societies, there are three social roles that can be identified with regards to childrearing in theory and practice; the layperson, the expert advisor, and the academic researcher (Kojima, 1991).

It is not unusual, of course, for one person to fulfill more than two roles. For example, it is not uncommon for one person to act as both an academic researcher and an expert advisor. It may also happen that such a researcher-expert's ideas, feelings, and behavior in coping with problems of childrearing as a first-time parent may not differ substantially from those of laypersons.

What kinds of relationships hold between these multiple roles? Let us take as an example someone who acts in the capacity of both expert advisor and researcher. When such a person's research findings on child development are publicized, the scholar may be asked by reporters to address the concerns of laypeople and to comment on the implications of their findings for the practical problems of childrearing. It is also conceivable that when a layperson encounters a specific childrearing problem, but has no access to professional advice, he or she may seek out researchers who are considered knowledgeable in the relevant field. In both these situations, the role the researcher is expected to fulfill is that of expert advisor or consultant. Often there is a great deal of difference between the conditions under which the research was conducted and the actual day-to-day conditions under which the process in question takes place. Therefore, the role of the academic researcher and that of an effective advisor or consultant may be partly in conflict with each other. To give one more example, it seems clear that an expert advisor on the subject of childrearing and education is not always successful in raising his or her own children.

These examples suggest that the actual relationships between the multiple roles one performs in a specific domain (in this case, childrearing), are very context dependent and thus cannot generally be defined. Clients seeking childrearing advice are likely to consider more trustworthy an expert advisor who is also an effective parent, or one who is also a prominent researcher. Still, clients can sometimes be aware of a discrepancy between an expert's professional standing and the performance in his or her personal roles, yet not be particularly disturbed by this discrepancy. The Japanese expression "Physicians tend to neglect their own health" has a humorous ring of truth to it, but the saying does not imply that a physician who is in poor health does not effectively treat his or her own patients. Similarly, child psychologists whose own children have psychological problems will not necessarily lose the trust of their clients, unless they dogmatically persist in advocating practices that have clearly failed when applied in their own situations.

Seen from the hypothetical viewpoint of the clients' concerns, we can see that it is possible for an expert advisor to perform his or her role by separating the parental role from the professional role, and the two roles can thus be performed rather independently from each other. On the other hand, it is also probable that performance of multiple roles by a single person often involves some sort of mutual accommodation between the various roles, or else involves some structure of priority that hierarchically organizes the performance of multiple roles. Therefore, I have no a priori conclusions at this point about how mutual relationships would be between the requirements of multiple roles.

Layperson's Role: Direct Involvement

The first role I deal with is that of concerned laypersons, typically parents, who are directly involved in the daily practice of childrearing. Generally speaking, the goal of parents is to have the child become a productive member of society, and they typically hold themselves responsible for the attainment of this goal. Through their experiences in daily interaction with their children, social interaction with other people (e.g., other family members, relatives, peers, and experts), and contact with other sources of information such as the mass media, parents are led to construct a set of working theories of childrearing and development. Parental belief systems (Goodnow & Collins, 1990; Sigel, McGillicuddy-DeLisi, & Goodnow, 1992) at the individual level are the main components of such working theories. Parents' theories of childrearing are motivated by practical questions such as, "Why should I treat my child this way rather than in some other manner? What will the results be if I continue to treat my child in this way? Why has my child come to develop this problem?", and so on.

These questions reflect the parents' need to understand the childrearing process, and to reason about and justify their own childrearing practices. The background knowledge and theories on childrearing brought to bear by laypersons may range from the most unsophisticated and naive to highly sophisticated and well-organized frameworks superior to those of even the so-called experts in the field. Still, whatever their level of sophistication, the parental role is always defined as that of laypersons directly involved in the childrearing process, along with other family members and close friends.

Although parents may have acquired a set of concepts related to child development and childrearing before the birth of their child, typically parental notions and theories are gradually constructed, tested, modified, and verified in the process of actually raising the child. In present-day Japan, parents—especially first-time parents—seek out expert advice on childrearing available from books, parents' magazines, and individual consultation with physicians and public health nurses. Along with these resources, parents are exposed to various other sources of information and advice, including folk wisdom on the subject. For example, if a child's birth weight is slightly lower than the average, one of the parents or a family member will invoke the Japanese proverb "It is better to give birth to a smaller baby and help it to grow larger." If the baby seems inclined to sleep a great deal, the proverb "A baby who sleeps well grows well" will be mentioned. Invoking such proverbs not only serves to relieve the parents of any anxiety about their baby's birth weight or sleep habits, but it also enables them to interpret the baby's state and physical characteristics in a positive light.

In this way, the parents may retrieve notions from the personal pool of cultural ideas that they have accumulated during their formative years when their ideas about parenthood were developing. In addition, their own parents, relatives, and close friends provide them with ideas from the pool of cultural knowledge that they may not have acquired, and all of these ideas are put to use in interpreting and coping with the daily problems of childrearing. It is worth noting that these kinds of ideas are mostly passed from one person to another, being shared by the majority of people in a culture. Thus we have, for example, a set of family diaries exchanged in 19th-century Japan (referred to in a later section) in which we find many examples of sayings about children that adults referred to in order to interpret the changes encountered in different stages of the child's development. These shared notions and interpretive schemas employed by laypersons can be characterized as a kind of commonsense psychology of childrearing.

The Expert's Role: Advisor

The second role I discuss is that of experts in their capacity as advisors on childrearing. This role is that of the socially designated expert who provides advice, suggestions, and directions to specific clients or to the general public through writings, informal and public talks, and in the context of direct consultation. Historically speaking, for thousands of years men and women experienced in childrearing have been called on to give advice to less experienced members of the society. However, this was during a historical period when society recognized a small number of experts whose role was to give childrearing advice to certain selected, privileged members of the society, and only secondarily to the general public. As discussed in a later section, it was in the middle of the 17th century that the role of childrearing expert and advisor emerged in Japan. The activities of these experts became visible to the general public in the 18th century (Kojima, 1990, 1996).

Theories espoused by expert advisors and the practices they advocate are generally more systematic than those of laypersons. Such theories are constructed by individual experts by referring to relevant academic research (if available), the opinions of other experts, the questions by laypersons, and their own personal experience.

In societies in which the scientific study of human development has arisen, the main task of this expert advisor is to act as an intermediary between laypersons and academic scientists in order to convert the findings of scientists into principles and methods that can actually be applied by laypersons. Without the intervention of expert advisors, empirical research findings of the sciences cannot directly be used by laypersons to solve their own problems. These advisors explain the research findings in terms understood by laypersons, and provide advice on how to put these findings into action. As Young's (1990) study on U.S. experts' advice to parents revealed, there will not be a simple relationship between what experts know and what is communicated to parents. Likewise, philosophical theories developed in the insular world of academia are in need of interpreters to communicate theories and related practices to the general public. In this sense, the expert advisors usually represent the interests of academia, and more often than not have the backing or sponsorship of those in power.

If certain theories published by academic researchers are deemed dangerous to the existing social power structure, they are often squelched in one way or another. As a matter of fact, some of the Japanese theorists to be discussed in a later section suffered censure and punishment by the central government (the Tokugawa shogunate). For example, Yamaga was denounced for his heterodox Confucian theory in 1666, and Hayashi was severely penalized by the shogunate for proposing a national defense against foreign countries in 1791, on the grounds that such a proposal would make people puzzled and uneasy.

Thus, the expert advisors on childrearing in early modern (or premodern) Japan functioned in many cases primarily as representatives of the interests of the controlling classes in the society. It is pertinent now to explain the social classes of the early modern period. In the process of unification of the nation in the late 16th century, Toyotomi Hideyoshi took several measures that deeply influenced Japanese society during the next three centuries. In order to establish political stability in the nation, he distinguished four social classes—warriors, peasants, artisans, and merchants—and restricted social mobility among classes. Hideyoshi banned the possession of arms by the peasants. He also ordered that extended families be decomposed to form small families of lineage. The Tokugawa shogunate that established supremacy in 1600 completed the system. The Tokugawa shogunate's ruling system consisted of centralized political power in Edo (later to be called Tokyo) and local control by feudal clans. Under this system, the distinction between the warriors, the ruling class, and the other classes was the most rigid. The artisans and the merchants who lived in towns were virtually indistinguishable as townsmen. The concern of the central and local governments with family life and child care was the chief impetus yielding the various kinds of experts' advice documents on childrearing in early modern Japan (Kojima, 1996). Thus these documents began to be written for the interests of the controlling classes in the society.

The analogous role of expert advisor in present-day society should also be examined from this historical vantage point. I do not mean to exclude the possibility that the expert advisor might also represent the interests of laypersons. It is possible, for example, that experts as intermediaries influence the priorities of scientific research based on the perceived needs of laypersons.

The Role of the Academic Researcher

The third role I deal with is that of the academic researcher. Just as laypersons and healers developed medical practices long before medicine actually became a science, so educational methods of various kinds also predate the educational and developmental sciences. Such empirical research areas as the microanalysis of mother-child interaction and infant development undertaken by developmental psychologists, field study of childrearing practices and related belief systems undertaken by cultural anthropologists, and experimental study on the effects of exposure to children's television programs undertaken by educational scientists, are all examples of the kinds of endeavors currently being carried out by academic researchers. Needless to say, all of these researchers are engaged in the construction of their own theories.

Child development researchers consider themselves engaged in the activity of constructing theories mainly in collaboration with other researchers. Generally such researchers on child development are not aware of, or tend to disregard, the fact that the subjects of their research are also engaged in thinking and even theorizing about child development. Furthermore, child development researchers also fail to recognize that their subjects often hold naive theories concerning the psychology of everyday life (i.e., a kind of commonsense psychology). Therefore, one difficulty for researchers is that their theories must interact with the commonsense psychology of ordinary people.

In actuality, however, the conceptions and theories of researchers are themselves influenced by commonsense psychology (see, e.g., Kelley, 1992). The cultural consensus as to what constitutes academic research may also differ according to society and historical era. For example, until about the end of the 19th century, Japan had no academically organized research activities related to childrearing, human development, and educational processes. However, by the 18th century, Japan had developed intensive studies of Chinese medical theories of human growth and the causes and treatment of pathological cases. Confucian theories of human nature and proposed methods to foster human development were also intensively studied and examined. This no doubt constituted a kind of academic research field in that cultural context.

Incidentally, it should be added that, although I have used the term *development* in the previous paragraphs, the Western concept of the progressive individual and social development did not arise in Japan until the late 19th century (Kojima, 1996). It is reflected in the following fact: A Japanese noun *hattatsu* was a borrowed word from Chinese, originally meaning "social success and prosperity." However, its meaning changed around 1870 when the Japanese began to use the word as translation of development.

Interrelationships Among the Roles

A distinction has been made here between three roles—layperson, expert, and researcher—as related to childrearing, education, and human development. We should note that this distinction is different from that made by the sociology of knowledge. For example, Japanese psychologist Yano (1992) distinguished three kinds of persons in contemporary society as promulgators of views on child development. His categorization was based on the distinction made by Schutz (1964); that is, the distinction between the man on the street, well-informed citizens, and experts. The first two kinds of persons are included in my role category of laypersons (i.e., those who are directly involved in the raising of children), and Yano's "experts" category is subdivided in my scheme into two separate roles: experts as advice givers and as academic researchers.

My classification is different from that of Yano in that (a) no hierarchical order with regard to the quantity and quality of childrearing knowledge is assumed in my classification, and (b) whereas Yano classified persons as ideal types, my classification is based on roles related to the childrearing theories constructed. Despite these differences, both Yano and I consider there to be three kinds of persons or roles sharing some set of mutually interrelated ideas. It should be stressed, however, that whereas Yano assumed a top-down flow of ideas and knowledge in a hierarchical fashion among the three kinds of persons—from higher (expert) to lower (man on the street)—no such top-down flow of information was assumed in my classification. The underlying reason for my characterization of the three roles is explained in a later section.

COMMONSENSE PSYCHOLOGY AND ETHNOPSYCHOLOGY

Commonsense Psychology

Commonsense psychology consists of common people's ideas about their own and other people's behavior, and their ideas about the causes and consequences of that behavior (Kelley, 1992). Commonsense psychology has been contrasted with scientific (or academic) psychology. However, the interrelationships between the two have also been discussed at various times, from Heider's (1958) "naive psychology" to Kelley (1992).

In the domain of developmental psychology, Baldwin (1967) listed three possibilities for the status of common sense in the activity of science. First, common sense may be useful insofar as it actually contains a kernel of truth. Second, common sense may be nothing more than fallacy and myth. The third possible status of common sense pointed out by Baldwin merits more detailed examination. According to Baldwin, what is called commonsense psychology may actually be a set of cultural conventions operating in the sphere of human relations. He argued that commonsense psychology, even if it does not overlap at all with genuine psychological mechanisms, is as important as language itself for purposes of analysis, because people understand each other's behavior in terms of how it accords with commonsense psychological theories. Such theories constitute a system of tacit assumptions that are reflected in the everyday actions of people, and people are led to acquire the commonsense theories of one's society.

If we pursue this line of thinking, we confront a fundamental question; that is, what do the theories and findings of scientific psychology reflect? Do the research findings of scientific psychology reflect an understanding of actual psychological mechanisms, or do they merely represent an understanding of the cultural conventions that are reflected in commonsense psychology?

Take frustration and aggression as an example. Let us assume that, in a particular society, it is recognized or even encouraged as a social convention that a person who has been undeservedly ill treated will direct aggression toward the agent responsible for the ill treatment or its surrogate. Now imagine, in the context of such a society, two situations involving aggressive feelings in a child. In the first situation, the child directs aggressive feelings toward the parents when they abruptly terminate the child's play activity. In the second situation, the child directs aggressive feelings toward a playmate when play activity is interrupted because the playmate suddenly becomes sick. Parents are likely to be more tolerant of the child's aggressive displays in the first situation than in the second. Likewise, a child's acts of retaliation toward a brother will be more readily tolerated or even encouraged by parents when the brother strikes the first blow than when the child initiates the quarrel. Through direct experience of these contingencies, as well as through observing them in other people's interactions, the child would be channeled into behavior patterns that are dictated by cultural convention. It would then become likely that researchers would discover relationships between the children's experience of undeserved treatment and their aggressive tendency.

Are psychologists justified in claiming that they have discovered universal human psychological mechanisms of frustration and aggression as hypothesized by the Yale group (Dollard, Doob, Miller, Mowrer, & Sears, 1939)? Or have they merely observed the effects of certain cultural conventions via scientific methodology? If the latter is the case, it can be said that the science of psychology has merely identified, or unwittingly rediscovered, the culturally defined behavioral conventions of society that were already represented in commonsense psychology and had acted as a constraint on people's daily behavior. In this case, commonsense psychology not only precedes scientific psychology, but also in a causal sense generates the laws of the latter. The replication of common sense by scientific psychology was pointed out in general terms by Smedslund (1978, 1991).

If we admit the influence of the people's understanding of cultural conventions on their behavior, it follows that commonsense psychology, and subsequently the findings of scientific psychology, may differ from culture to culture. Baldwin (1967) noted the possibility that commonsense psychology might be culturally dependent. His characterizations of naive theories of development and change, however, are made in the form of generalizations such as "in every culture" or "of all cultures" (p. 36). It should come as no surprise that discussion of the generic roles of commonsense psychology as contrasted with and related to those of scientific psychology does not specifically take cultural factors into account. It is because the content of commonsense psychology in its social, cultural, and historical contexts has not been the main interest of those who have dealt with commonsense psychology. This tendency is evident in research up to the present day, including that of Kelley (1992).

Ethnopsychology

In contrast with commonsense psychology, the term *ethnopsychology* has been used to describe the psychological theories of everyday life, or folk theories held by a particular culture (see, e.g., Reid & Valsiner, 1986). Traditionally the term has been applied more often than not by Western researchers in describing the folk psychology of non-Western cultures. A database search of, for example, the Library of Congress book catalogs will clearly reveal this tendency. However it is needless to say that non-Western folk psychology is not the only folk psychology worth investigating, and there is clearly no reason to reject the idea that both non-Western and Western folk psychology, in historical and contemporary context, fully deserve to be described and analyzed. An example of this kind of research agenda is the analysis of parents' cultural belief systems as U.S. ethnotheories (Harkness, Super, & Keefer, 1992; Reid & Valsiner, 1986).

Another peculiar aspect of ethnopsychology should be mentioned. In my view (Kojima, 1996), the term *ethnopsychology* has traditionally been employed to denote the folk psychological theory of a particular culture in terms of its modal characteristics. In addition, many descriptive accounts of the content of folk theories are ahistorical; that is, they do not even deal with the historical context in which the accounts were given, let alone aspects of historical change and continuity.

In contrast, my usage of the term here is concerned more with psychological diversity within a particular culture, and, in addition, within-group diversity rather than between-group variation is brought into focus. The diversity of the ethnopsychology of childrearing and development has also been discussed by others (e.g., Lightfoot & Valsiner, 1992; Valsiner, 1989). Psychologists have also dealt with historical changes in representative childrearing conceptions and thinking on child development (e.g., Borstelmann, 1983; Wolfenstein, 1955; Young, 1990). Reading these articles, one gets the mistaken impression that a society's views on childrearing and development constitute a unified and monolithic belief system, evolving inexorably along certain lines, with older views regularly replaced by new ones. Thus, a second feature of my conception of ethnopsychology is that it takes into account the historical dimension, in combination with a view that recognizes the diversity of ethnopsychology. This approach requires the introduction of some new concepts. In the following section, I describe how I arrived at some of these concepts. Readers will notice that the notions I am dealing with are related to the collaborative process of constructing childrearing concepts.

THE CONCEPT OF AN ETHNOPSYCHOLOGICAL POOL OF IDEAS (EPI) CONCERNING CHILDREARING

Actual and Imaginary Dialogues in the Development of Childrearing Advice

In my explorations of Japanese historical childrearing practices (covering a period from the mid-17th century to the present time), I have dealt with prescriptive materials such as experts' advice, as well as descriptive materials such as family diaries. In studying these materials, I soon came to notice a general tendency among historians to emphasize and analyze descriptive data to the exclusion of prescriptive data. In one sense this emphasis is justified, as prescriptive writings should certainly not be used to infer the actual practices of a historical period; these two areas basically involve different sets of data. However, I still believe in the value of analyzing prescriptive materials if one wishes to utilize them in order to construct an ethnopsychology on childrearing. As I have illustrated (Kojima, 1990), the authors of advice documents in 18th- and 19th-century Japan often dealt with points that they knew would be raised by their readers in response to their own views, and thus these documents contain evidence of variation in commonly held notions of the time.

For example, authors who claimed that most children were similar in their innate moral character and intellectual abilities (e.g., Hayashi, 1786/1976; Kaibara, 1710/1976) anticipated in their writings a number of possible responses from their readers. They argued, for example, against a certain view that attributed a son's bad conduct to his innate evil nature. Physician Kazuki (1703/1976) recommended a contingent response on the part of caretakers to the smiling and vocalizing of young infants at 60 days after birth. This recommendation was put forth in a cultural context in which some caretakers were likely to engage in vigorous overstimulation of very young infants, believing this to be advantageous to the baby's development, or simply for fun. By combining classic Chinese theories of development in early infancy with his own experience-based belief in the infant's competence in sensory and cognitive domains, Kazuki tried to discourage potentially harmful treatment of infants based on mistaken interpretations of the infant's responses (e.g., mistaking the infant's distressed reaction to vigorous stimulation as an excitedly happy response). Ohara (ca. 1858/1976), a reformer of farm villages, also advised against certain orally based instruction of children that seemed to be prevalent among the peasants. He maintained that information taught verbally was absorbed by children at the level of verbal responses only, and thus effective teaching should be done mainly through presenting behavioral models, with verbal explanations coming later as a natural part of the process. The advice from these experts could be seen as a communicative attempt to persuade readers, and in this sense the readers—average people of the time—were actually indirect participants in an implicit dialogue in which ideas on childrearing were developed and presented (Kojima, 1990).

This statement is not simply an inference on my part. As a matter of fact, some of the extant advice documents dating from the mid-17th century (Yamazumi & Nakae, 1976) were analects of respected advisors (e.g., Ishida, 1744/1972; Yamaga, 1663-65/1976) compiled by their disciples. Yamaga's message was addressed to warriors, and that of Ishida, founder of Sekimon Singaku (which was an ethical and religious teaching), to the townsmen. Later, Ishida's followers who addressed such everyday problems as interpersonal relationships, family living, vocational life, childrearing, and religion, propagated their beliefs by means of informal lectures. Among these followers, Nakazawa (Ishikawa, 1935) and Shibata (1835-1839/1970) were very effective speakers, and the verbatim records of lectures substantiate, in my view, the notion that such childrearing advice constituted virtual dialogues between the speakers and their audience.

Children were also the object of attempts at moral education by Shingaku scholars. In Kyoto in 1773, Toan Teshima began a series of talk sessions for boys and girls over the age of 7. (Incidentally, the age of the children given here is based on the former Japanese system, which considers the baby to be 1 year old at birth. On the following New Year's Day, which falls on a different day from that on the Gregorian calendar, all the children born in the preceding calendar year were considered to be 2 years old.)

In his book written for merchant families, Gidoh Wakisaka (1803/1976) printed a number of short poems for children and apprentices to instruct them in the principles of interpersonal relationships, and to indoctrinate them with the need for learning the "three Rs" (reading, writing, and arithmetic by an abacus) in addition to a vocation (Kojima, 1996). For these instructions to be effective and persuasive, the author had to take into account views held by children at the time, as well as their actual living conditions. Wakisaka's writings actually did attempt to take readers' perspectives into account, in order to bring them to an awareness of the erroneous nature of their beliefs.

As was reflected in the revisions of official bulletin boards, the shogunate's attitudes toward the commoners underwent a change in the latter half of the 17th century, when commoners began to be seen as intelligent beings capable of responding to rational persuasion. The preceding examples also illustrate that childrearing advisors did not simply attempt in an authoritarian and condescending way to dissuade the ignorant people from their erroneous views. The potential readers and audience were treated as active participants in the ongoing actual and implicit dialogues.

Ethnopsychological Pool of Ideas (EPI)

The awareness of the diversity of childrearing views that became evident from my analysis of Japanese traditional childrearing concepts and theories has led me to a new explanatory concept. In my analysis (Kojima, 1991), both the views promulgated by experts and those of the common people are always drawn from a preexisting pool of folk ideas shared by the members of the society during a particular period. Naive theory, expert advice, and even academic theories from a particular period all seem to be assembled from ideas drawn from this pool of ideas.

Whereas constructed theories of childrearing, whether naive theories, expert theories, or academic theories, are usually internally consistent (or at least locally so), the original pool of ideas from which the elements of each theory are drawn contains a much more diverse set of mutually inconsistent or contradictory notions. The process of constructing a theory is a consensual, collaborative process involving mutual interactions within each group, whether it be laypersons, expert advisors, or academic researchers. In addition, as I have said elsewhere, interactions between the three classes of roles may occur as well, usually with expert advisors serving as intermediaries between academic researchers and laypersons.

Academic researchers are also receptive to information from other cultures. In Japan, a major role of professional academicians has traditionally been to introduce ideas from more advanced cultures (these being mainly China in the past, and, more recently, Western culture). In the domain of childrearing, these professionals in ancient Japan served to introduce into Japanese culture certain medical theories and practices, as well as formal results related to the raising of children. Each wave of wholesale importation of the new theories and practices was usually followed by a more selective assimilation process overseen by the academic community for the purpose of practical implementation by their clients. In ancient Japan, clients of childrearing experts were mostly members of the emperor's family, court people, and aristocrats. Beginning in medieval times, the emerging warrior class also became clients. Finally, as mentioned earlier, early modern Japan witnessed a rise of interest in childrearing theories and practices on the part of the general public.

Generally speaking, the adoption of newly established childrearing practices followed a top-down tendency. New practices were initiated in the emperor's family, from where they spread to the aristocratic class, then to the warrior class, and finally to other lower classes such as urban merchants and artisans and the peasant population. Some aspects of medical knowledge and prescriptions available to the general public in 18th-century Japan had been introduced from China in the late 7th century. At that time, such knowledge was accessible to only a few members of the society. Likewise, some rituals relating to the neonatal period that had been introduced from China before the medieval period became popular among the warrior class and the wealthy merchant class in early modern Japan.

This does not mean, however, that the upper classes in Japan have invariably adopted the newly introduced practices and discarded the older ones. In some cases, the upper class maintained traditional practices for centuries. This is especially the case in families of emperors, who, having been supported by court people, continued to practice centuries-old childraising rituals that the general public had long since ceased observation during the process of Japan's modernization.

In parallel with sporadic introduction of new knowledge from other cultures, the indigenous ideas and practices of a society continually undergo a process of technical evolution and modification. If innovative ideas practiced by certain individuals are able to utilize existing resources and structures in an effective way, these practices will eventually be noticed and will gain the support of either laypersons, experts, or academic researchers, whereupon the practices will be added to the culture's original pool of ideas. The ideas might be recorded and retained in any form, including written records and manuals, transmitted rituals and practices across generations, narrative stories (some of which are might be accompanied by drawings), and children's symbolic play activities.

Not all the notions and practices in the available pool of ideas will remain there indefinitely. Some may fall into disuse for generations due to predominance of competing ideas and practices, or fall into disfavor because of injunctions by religious, political, or academic authorities. Still, I believe that the majority of childrearing practices stored in the cultural pool of ideas has been highly resistant to complete loss. As I have speculated, the expert advice I have analyzed may reveal sets of mutually contradictory childrearing views shared by various subsets of the population. The entire collection of these ideas, along with related attitudes, values, and practices can be characterized as constituting an EPI related to childrearing in the context of a particular society during a particular historical period.

Interestingly, this ethnopsychological repertoire of ideas seems to function so as to preserve temporarily outmoded ideas for possible future use in the society. It is difficult to say whether this future-oriented conservative function of the EPI serves any particular purpose. However, one can imagine that this retaining of unfashionable or temporarily counterproductive ideas and practices has served some adaptive function in a society. Instead of assuming that a society's views on human development evolve in a unified direction, with old views being discarded and uniformly replaced by new ones, I hypothesize that competing views are actually quite robust, and have always coexisted, with their component assumptions and beliefs preserved indefinitely in the pool of ideas. This state of affairs can be characterized as the source-maintaining function of ethnopsychology. At least as far as Japanese documents on childrearing during the past 350 years are concerned, this statement holds. This is illustrated in the beginning of the next section.

IMPLICATIONS FOR DEVELOPMENTAL THEORY

Modern Concepts and Theories in Early Modern Japan

During my rather extensive survey of expert advice on childrearing and various descriptive records in early modern (or premodern) Japan (17th to mid-19th centuries), I was often surprised to encounter certain ideas that were familiar to me from my formative years studying modern psychological theories of human development and learning (Kojima, 1991, 1996). Let me mention a few examples.

Yamana (1784/1976) held the belief that, just as animals such as dogs, cats, and rats can be trained (à la Skinnerian conditioning) to behave in ways quite alien to their innate tendencies, children of the peasant class could be shaped to acquire respectable virtues if they were trained from the time they were young. Yamana, himself a peasant, did not actually advocate training peasant children as one might train animals for street performances. Instead, he stressed the notion of the perfectibility of human beings through continuous behavior modification.

Shingaku scholar Wakisaka (1803/1976) maintained that establishment of close parent-child relationships and parental attitudes that emphasized understanding of the parents' teachings on the part of the children were the prerequisites for the internalization of values. His advice to merchants was as follows.

> Praise children when they do good things rather than physically punish them when they do bad things. Children will be delighted if praised, and, wishing to be praised again, they will spontaneously try to do good things. Trying to do good things will lead them to prefer good things, and this tendency in turn will make them into good persons. Contrarily, if discipline includes only physical punishment for bad acts, the children will not become sincerely devoted to the parents, but will simply become fearful of punishment and thus tend to conceal bad deeds from their parents.

In his book, Wakisaka (1803/1987) also included a number of short poems for children and apprentices to instruct them in the principles of interpersonal relationships, and to indoctrinate them with the need for learning the three Rs and a vocation. Two sample poems follow.

> Like your parents who cherish the deepest affection for you,
> Treat kindly those who work at your house.
>
> Never laugh at the handicapped!
> Your stupidity of laughing at them will be laughed at by others.

It seems to me that these verbal instructions would elicit a form of internal dialogue within the child. In the first poem, the child is expected to project the parent-child relationship onto the relationships between himself or herself and the young apprentices or domestic servants in the home. Thus, the child is induced to make a kind of analogical mapping between the servants and himself or herself as a child on one hand, and between the parents and himself or herself as superiors of the servants on the other. Thus it may happen that paternal or maternal behavior and speech will be invoked within the child when dealing with a servant, with the child thus behaving according to the parental models presented in the home. Note that in the Japanese context, the parents could not directly demand that their children treat apprentices in a kindly, loving way like the parents, for this would be deemed an arrogant attitude on the part of the parents. Instead a third person, a teacher, would instruct the children to treat apprentices as the parents treated them.

A technique to induce the child to take the perspective of others is more clearly represented in the second poem. Superficially interpreted, the poem seems to invoke external control of child's behavior by appealing to the fear of social admonition. My interpretation, however, is that the poem tries to make the child realize the inappropriateness of his or her own actions by seeing the self from the perspective of others. The behavior of the child is thus constrained by self-awareness of his or her own behavior rather than by the fear of ridicule by others.

These interpretations are, in themselves, tightly embedded in Japanese ethnopsychology on childrearing. Kaibara (1710/1976) argued that the foundation of character education should be established during the early period when children still lack proper judgment. According to Kaibara, consistent teaching and modeling based on caring concern for children should begin very early in life, because first habits learned will become ingrained, and once habits become part of the child's character, they are very hard to modify. Kaibara's position is similar to that of his Western contemporary, John Locke, though Kaibara considered children to be more autonomous in their learning, and thus stressed the modeling process more than Locke did.

Yamaga (1663-1665/1976) described a process that we now call *identification*. For example, a son will tend to see his own father as being superior in all aspects—that is, as the richest, noblest, most talented, most knowledgeable, most virtuous, and so on in the world. The son will therefore model himself after his father in all social modalities, and thus it is unreasonable for a father and mother to require their child to behave properly without themselves doing likewise.

Hayashi (1786/1976) even noted the phenomenon of the transmission of improper childrearing practices across generations, attributing a child's problems to the parent, and that of the parents to the grandparents. How shameful it is for two generations of parents, Hayashi argued, that a third-generation child has a problem.

My description of the process of weaning and of changing cosleeping partners in low-ranking Japanese warrior families (Kojima, 1990) might even bring to mind the theories of Vygotsky. Adults in these warrior families, at some point in time began attempts to modify the child's habitual behavior patterns, basing the timing on social norms, or sometimes on their actual needs. The practices employed by these families consisted of a series of social interactions beginning with external verbal suggestions and, through a transitional phase, ending with a stage in which the children were able to regulate their own behavior. The practices of these Japanese families, however, were more explicit than the Vygotskian approach in considering the role of the child's self in regulating his or her own behavior. External verbal suggestions and controls were directed not only to children's behavior and mental and physical states, but also to children's self-concept.

It is worth noting that, especially during the transitional phase from external verbal suggestions and control to self-determined regulation, the children in question seemed to be conversing with the self, trying to modify their habitual behavior. This is inferred from the fact that the children would declare during the daytime that they intend to modify their behavior; for example, to stop sucking the mother's breast (a girl and a boy at 3 years of age), to sleep with grandfather instead of sleeping with grandmother (a boy at 4 years of age), and to stay overnight at a relative's house being separated from this attached grandfather (a boy at 5 years of age). Still, when the critical moment of choice came, the children were unable to actually modify their behavior. At this phase, the children seemed to be conversing with a self that was brought into their awareness through their daily interaction with adults.

Later there would come a point when the children seemed to have finally decided to discontinue the former habit and decisively modify their behavior. At this point the children appeared to try to persuade themselves by making declarations to parents or siblings such as, "I have given the breast to the baby. It is dirty because the baby sucked it," (a girl at 3 years of age) and "I will not sleep with grandmother, because *okanko* (female's sexual organ) smells badly" (a boy at 4 years of age). After this point, the girl in question never again sucked mother's breast, though for a while she regarded the nursing baby enviously. The boy in question also modified his behavior, never again sleeping with grandmother even when the grandfather was not present.

Present-Day Concepts and Theories in Early Modern Japan

These examples show that early modern theories on childrearing and development in Japan are in substantial agreement with their modern Western counterparts. In addition, some Japanese early modern theories closely match very recent theories of human development. For example, the treatment of children by low-ranking warrior families mentioned earlier is in keeping with the basic theme of this volume.

There are other examples of indigenous Japanese childraising ideas of the past that are similar to those of present-day psychology. The awareness of the sensory and cognitive competence of young infants combined with an argument for the importance of responsive caretaking at 2 months of age was explicitly formulated by Kazuki (1703/1976). The need for a balanced development of intellectual abilities and wisdom in young children was stressed by Ohara (ca. 1858/1976). Ohara even argued that intellectual development should actually be restrained in order to facilitate the development of wisdom, although he admitted the close relationships between the two aspects of development. In the realm of aging, acquisition of knowledge, advanced skills, and error-free performance, usually attainable only after 40 or 50 years of age (Kazuki, 1716/1917), can be related to research on wisdom in contemporary life-span developmental psychology (e.g., Smith & Baltes, 1990).

There was a period when modern academic psychology promulgated the concept of the incompetent infant, which downplayed the importance of responsive caretaking from the earliest period of life (because it was deemed useless). At this time, modern psychology also held that there was a rather rapid intellectual decline in human beings after middle adulthood. It seems that during this period, Japanese ethnopsychology as presented in handbooks of child care and health care in the early 18th century actually preserved a record of the opposing views on these subjects, which later proved correct.

It should be recalled that the middle of the 17th century in Japan was the beginning of the period of Great Peace (*tenka taihei*) that lasted for about two centuries. Japan had isolated itself from European countries, both domestic wars and Japanese involvement in foreign conflicts had ended, agricultural production and the overall population were increasing, and economic development and urbanization was proceeding. Japan also witnessed a rapid increase in the number of elderly people in the population compared with the previous period. Under these circumstances, childrearing became one of the chief concerns of the central and local feudal governments. Pregeriatric health care was also an important concern. This era also saw the beginning of a systematic compilation of various documents on health care and psychological development that implicitly represented the diverse views of the period.

I should add that this realization that many modern principles of psychology have precursors in centuries-old conceptions and theories first occurred to me in 1970s. I should admit that, if I had had a chance to read these writings earlier—for example in the 1950s—I would very likely have dismissed them as unscientific myth. What changed was my own conceptual and theoretical framework, which is deeply influenced by the Zeitgeist in which I work. In a sense, my amazement at discovering theoretical insights in 18th-century Japan that predate our own betrays an arrogance typical of present-day psychologists; we all have the tendency to assume that we have progressed to a highly advanced stage, and that there is nothing we can learn from the theories of our ancestors.

Diversity of Ideas and Theories

It should be mentioned that early modern Japanese theories as represented here contained many diverse dimensions, and within each dimension the existence of opposing positions are implied. Thus, for example, a perspective on human nature prevalent at the time took the position that human beings are fundamentally good, and that every child is born with the potential to attain virtue, but this potential will not be actualized without teaching and learning. As illustrated earlier, expert advisors who took this position had anticipated the opposite position, namely that teaching and learning from the early period of life were futile and had no consequences for later personality development.

I am not maintaining that the theories of individual expert advisors and parents in early modern Japan have exact counterparts in modern psychological theory. The Japanese warrior families mentioned earlier never consciously reflected on the behavioral strategy they used in bringing up their children. The sequence of strategies they adopted, however, implies the functioning of certain underlying conceptions and working models, models held by particular individuals and perhaps shared with other members within the family and community. Those conceptions and models, judged in light of present-day frameworks, are partly in agreement with some modern theories. What I am proposing is that there were already present, in the ethnopsychological pool of ideas in early modern Japan, a multitude of divergent notions from which many of the modern Western theories of childrearing and education can be constructed.

I also speculate that this ethnopsychology has helped Japan to selectively assimilate Western theories and methods (Kojima, 1989), and it is this ethnopsychology that constitutes the basic underlying structure of Japanese childrearing ideas, and which explains the overall continuity of these ideas throughout the shifting contexts of the past three centuries (Kojima, 1996).

Contemporary Western theories have certainly been drawn from the Western EPI of childrearing and education. If this is truly the case, then an opposite claim can also be made; that is, contemporary Japanese childrearing ideas and practices can also be constructed from the Western EPI. As a matter of fact, certain remarks made by such researchers of contemporary Japanese educational system as Peak (1986) and Stevenson and Stigler (1992) suggest this possibility. According to these researchers, the basic ideas, methods, and values of Japanese parents and teachers have traditionally been shared by their U.S. counterparts, as well. Therefore, the basic building blocks used to construct the educational methods of the two cultures may not be so different. The differences seem to lie in the construction of actual educational theories and their systems of implementation. Because these depend to a great extent on the indigenous psychological traditions and related folk practices of each culture, the actual educational systems and their outcomes may differ to a large extent from one another.

What constitute the source materials for past and present Western theories on childrearing and human development? How should the relationship between the past and the present be characterized? These are questions for any Western researchers who might find my formulations useful.

GENERAL CONCLUSIONS

One perspective that I believe to be meaningful for such comparative research is that actual as well as imaginary communication occurs between the participants involved in the discourse surrounding childrearing. Childrearing advisors exchanged communication in the process of constructing their theories. In responding to the advice given in order to construct their own personal theories, parents must certainly have engaged in imaginary and actual exchanges with the advisors and with each other. Finally, children, given direct advice by experts and influenced by parental treatment, could also communicate not only with others but also with the self in regulating and changing their own behavior, thought, and attitudes.

Another point to be made is that the diversity of ideas is a fundamental aspect of the communication process. Here an important condition for communication, both at the individual and collective levels, is the commonality of category systems or the dimensions used by the multiple communicators. A simple example of the common category system is the argument as to whether the child's nature is intrinsically good or evil. Arguments as to the relative contribution of nature versus nurture to a specific aspect of child development is an example of commonality of dimensions. This principle applies to intracultural communication as well as intercultural communication.

The actual set of explicit ideas currently or formerly in practice may differ from culture to culture, depending on historical period. Still, the richness of the EPIs of both Japan and the West, along with their basic commonalities, make intercultural communication and mutual learning possible. Needless to say, this perspective may be applied to comparisons involving more than these two cultures.

REFERENCES

Baldwin, A.L. (1967). *Theories of child development.* New York: Wiley.

Borstelmann, L.J. (1983). Children before psychology: Ideas about children from antiquity to the late 1800s. In W. Kessen (Ed.), *Handbook of child psychology* (4th ed., Vol. 1, pp. 1-40). New York: Wiley.

Dollard, J., Doob, L.W., Miller, N.E., Mowrer, O.H., & Sears, R.R. (1939). *Frustration and aggression.* New Haven, CT: Yale University Press.

Goodnow, J.J., & Collins, W.A. (Eds.). (1990). *Development according to parents: The nature, sources, and consequences of parents' ideas.* Hove, UK: Erlbaum.

Harkness, S., Super, C.M., & Keefer, C.H. (1992). Learning to be an American parent: How cultural models gain directive force. In R. G. D'Andrade & C. Strauss (Eds.), *Human motives and cultural models* (pp. 163-178). New York: Cambridge University Press.

Hayashi, S. (1976). Fukei-kun [Precepts for fathers and elder brothers]. In M. Yamazumi & K. Nakae (Eds.), *Kosodate no sho* (Vol. 2, pp. 58-89). Tokyo: Heibon-sha. (Original work published 1786).

Heider, F. (1958). *The psychology of interpersonal relations.* New York: Wiley.

Ishida, B. (1972). *Ishida Baigan zenshu, Jo* [Collected Works by Baigan Ishida, Vol. 1] (M. Shibata, Ed.). Tokyo: Seibun-sha. (Original work published 1744).

Ishikawa, K. (Ed.). (1935). *Dohni-oh dowa* [Moral lectures by Dohni Nakazawa]. Tokyo: Iwanami Shoten.

Kaibara, E. (1976). Wazoku doji-kun [Precepts for teaching children]. In M. Yamazumi & K. Nakae (Eds.), *Kosodate no sho* (Vol. 2, pp. 3-57). Tokyo: Heibon-sha. (Original work published 1710).

Kazuki, G. (1917). Rojin hitsuyo yashinai-gusa [Health-care book for old people]. In K. Shincho Kenkyu-kai (Ed.), *Nihon eisei bunko* (Vol. 2, pp. 1-107). Tokyo: Kyoiku Shincho Kenkyu-kai. (Original work published 1716).

Kazuki, G. (1976). Shoni hitsuyo sodate-gusa [Handbook of child-care and childrearing]. In M. Yamazumi & K. Nakae (Eds.), *Kosodate no sho* (Vol. 2, pp. 287-366). Tokyo: Heibon-sha. (Original work published 1703).

Kelley, H.H. (1992). Common-sense psychology and scientific psychology. *Annual Review of Psychology, 43,* 1-23.

Kojima, H. (1989). Meiji shoki no hon'yaku ikujisho [Translations of western child care books in the early Meiji period (1870s)]. *Journal of Japan Society of Medical History, 35,* 27-44.

Kojima, H. (1990). Family life and child development in early modern Japan. *Zeitschrift für Sozialisationsforschung und Erziehungssoziologie, 10,* 314-326.

Kojima, H. (1991). Kodomo no hattatsu to sono shakai-teki, bunka-teki, rekishi-teki joken [Child development and its social, cultural, and historical conditions]. In H. Kojima (Ed.), *Shin jido-shinrigaku koza* (Vol. 14, pp. 1-36). Tokyo: Kaneko-shobo.

Kojima, H. (1996). Japanese childrearing advice in its cultural, social, and economic contexts. *International Journal of Behavioral Development, 19,* 373-391.

Lightfoot, C., & Valsiner, J. (1992). Parental belief systems under the influence: Social guidance of the construction of personal cultures. In I.E. Sigel, A.V. McGillicuddy-DeLisi, & J.J. Goodnow (Eds.), Parental belief systems: The psychological consequences for children (2nd ed, pp. 393-414). Hillsdale, NJ: Erlbaum.

Ohara, Y. (1976). Bimi yugen-ko. In M. Yamazumi & K. Nakae (Eds.), *Kosodate no sho* (Vol. 3, pp. 108-137). Tokyo: Heibon-sha. (Original work published ca 1858).

Peak, L. (1986). Teaching learning skills and attitudes in Japanese early educational settings. *New Directions for Child Development, 32,* 111-123.

Reid, B.V., & Valsiner, J. (1986). Consistency, praise, and love: Folk theories of American people. *Ethos, 14* (3), 282-304.

Schultz, A. (1964). *Collected papers II. Studies in social theory, applied theory.* (A. Brodersen, Ed.) Hague, The Netherlands: Martinus Nijhoff.

Shibata, K. (1970). *Kyuoh dowa* [Moral lectures by Shibata Kyuoh]. Tokyo: Heibon-sha. (Original work published 1835-1839).

Sigel, I.E., McGillicuddy-DeLisi, A.V., & Goodnow, J.J. (Eds.). (1992). *Parental belief systems: The psychological consequences for children* (2nd ed.). Hillsdale, NJ: Erlbaum.

Smedslund, J. (1978). Bandura's theory of self-efficacy: A set of common sense theories. *Scandinavian Journal of Psychology, 19,* 1-14.

Smedslund, J. (1991). The pseudoempirical in psychology and the case for psychologic. *Psychological Inquiry, 2,* 325-338.

Smith, J., & Baltes, P.B. (1990). Wisdom-related knowledge: Age/cohort differences in response to life-planning problems. *Developmental Psychology, 26,* 494-505.

Stevenson, H.W., & Stigler, J.W. (1992). *The learning gap.* New York: Summit Books.

Valsiner, J. (1989). *Human development and culture: The social nature of personality and its study.* Lexington, MA: D. C. Heath.

Wakisaka, G. (1976). Sodate-gunsa [On childrearing]. In M. Yamazumi & K. Nakae (Eds.), *Kosodate no sho* (Vol. 2, pp. 267-302). Tokyo: Heibon-sha. (Original work published 1803).

Wolfenstein, M. (1955). Fun morality: An analysis of recent American child-training leterature. In M. Mead & M. Wolfenstein (Eds.), *Childhood in contemporary cultures* (pp. 168-178). Chicago: University of Chicago Press.

Yamaga, S. (1976). Yamaga gorui, Fushi-do [Analects of Yamaga, Ways of parents and chld]. In M. Yamazumi & K. Nakae (Eds.), *Kosodate no sho* (Vol. 1, pp. 138-174). Tokyo: Heibon-sha. (Original work published 1663-1665).

Yamana, B. (1976). Noka-kun [Precepts for the peasants]. In M. Yamazumi & K. Nakae (Eds.), *Kosodate no sho* (Vol. 2, pp. 204-222). Tokyo: Heibon-sha. (Original work published 1784).

Yamazumi, M., & Nakae, K. (Eds.). (1976). *Kosodate no sho* [Books on childrearing]. (3 Vols.). Tokyo: Heibon-sha.

Yano, Y. (1992). Jido-kan, hattatsu-kan no kozo to hensen [Structure and historical change of the views on the child and development]. In J. Murai (Ed.), *Shin jido-shinrigaku koza* (Vol. 1, pp. 61-94). Tokyo: Kaneko-shobo.

Young, K.T. (1990). American conceptions of infant development from 1955 to 1984: What the experts are telling parents. *Child Development, 61,* 17-28.

part II

Constructions of Psychological Process: From Infancy to Early Childhood

2

INNOVATION IN SOCIAL GAMES

Susan A. Holt
The University of Minnesota

Alan Fogel
The University of Utah

Rebecca M. Wood
The University of Minnesota

Social games often provide a context for spirited, pleasant interactions (Garvey, 1990; Rubin, Fein, & Vandenberg, 1983; Van Hoorn, 1982). Developmentalists have discussed play in their theories, such as Piaget's suggestion that it is an exercise in assimilation and Bruner's hypothesis that it is useful in language development (Bruner, 1983; Piaget, 1962). The purpose of this chapter is to consider one form of social play found commonly within and across cultures, the peekaboo game, and establish a conceptual framework for interpreting peekaboo and other games, and game innovations based on dynamic systems principles.

The exposition provided here is presented in four parts. First, several basic principles of the dynamic systems perspective are applied to social games. Next, the properties of peekaboo games as described in previous literature are delineated. The nature of innovation within peekaboo games is then discussed and examples of game innovations, drawn from an observational study of mother-infant interactions are provided. Finally, the empirical evidence is considered with respect to both its failure to conform to the hypotheses offered in prior literature and its compatibility with the dynamic systems perspective.

DYNAMIC SYSTEMS AND SOCIAL GAMES

The Participants

Social games involve at least two participants, each of whom is an open, dynamic, self-organizing system. Thus each individual is not an insular, singular unit, but a relational being who processes and acts constantly in relation to the internal and external context. Each participant brings to a social game a range of potential actions, realizes one such action pattern within the game, and in so doing, creates an often salient context for the other to perceive, detect, process, and respond. The actions may change over time, as the range of activities infants may perform in the first year increases due to their emergent capacities for cognition and action (Holt & Fogel, 1993).

Social Interactions

Although the participants are both active, self-organizing, open systems, the actions with respect to the other often form observable, repeated patterns. From a dynamic systems perspective these interaction patterns are thus cocreated by the participants and constitute an active, dynamic, self-organizing system. When the participants have a social interaction history, expectancies about the partner's actions may influence the individual's own actions (see also Fogel, 1993). Thus, in any analysis of social processes, including games, the dynamic systems properties of each of the participants and the properties of their dynamic interrelation must be considered.

Social Games as Dynamic Processes

Games are repeated, patterned, interactive action sequences. As with any behavior on repetition, the action is never precisely the same as it was on a previous occasion, yet discernable elements of similarity are observable across episodes. During subsequent repetitions, the games become smoother in both action and temporal sequence after the first, tentative action interplay (Stern, 1985).

Some games may be common within a culture or across cultures. The peekaboo game, for example, is played in the English, Indian, Japanese, Chinese, American, and various other cultures (Bruner, 1983; Fernald & O'Neill, 1993; Rogoff, Mistry, Goncu, & Mosier, 1993; Van Hoorn, 1982). Some have claimed that the regularities of action in peekaboo games are so rigidly realized as to be considered ritualized (Garvey, 1990; Van Hoorn, 1982).

Games are bound in time. Social interaction is a temporary feature of the individual's everyday action sequences and context relations. Within social interactions, games arise, are repeated, and dissolve. The appearance, maintenance, and disappearance of game may be charted with respect to both real time, a single game, and developmental time, the history of all the games played.

In dynamic systems terminology, simple common patterns that arise in complex systems are conceptualized as attractor states. Systems tend to evolve these attractors or simple patterns from the coalescence of many elements and subsystems. In the study of the dynamic social system of the peekaboo game, particular agency pattens of hiding and revealing may be considered attractor states. The game's agency pattern may become modified systematically, however. Such a reorganization of system elements and subsystems into a new simple pattern is a developmental phase shift. The hiding-revealing pattern, regardless of who serves as agent, is considered a collective variable, a regularity that emerges from the cooperating interactions of many elements (Thelen & Ulrich, 1991).

In addition to the game's agency components, emotional and motivational components occur and contribute to game initiation and maintenance. According to the literature, games are accompanied by the positive affect of both of the participants and each behaves in a way that sustains the action (Bruner, 1983; Garvey, 1990; Rubin et al., 1983). Games have been characterized as focused interactions of mutual interest to both participants (Stern, 1974, 1977). When asked why they played the games, mothers in various cultures replied "to have fun" (Van Hoorn, 1982). The infants' interest and smiles that often accompany peekaboo games can be argued to emerge from the coalescence of the individual processes that occur amid the action and social contexts characteristic of the games. Infant interest and smiles may well function as control variable for the maintenance of the peekaboo game, because their presence may serve as signal to the mother that the game is indeed "fun" and these indications may be used by her in the decision to continue the game if they occur, or suspend the game if they do not.

Variations in Social Games

Those who have categorized games suggest a number of game dimensions that may vary. Game variations may include the nature of the sensory system stimulated: tactual, visual, or auditory (Crawley et al., 1978), whether the game is purely social or incorporates objects, and whether the action involves limb or gross body movement (Rubin et al., 1983).

Part of peekaboo's appeal may be that it commonly incorporates many possible variations in the sensory, motor, and social components. Peekaboo may entail tactual, visual, and/or auditory stimulation and all of these sources of sensory stimulation may vary within and between games. Tactual components include the mother's hiding of the infant's head the infant's hiding objects, or attempting to uncover whatever is hidden by the mother. Visual stimulation varies because an object that is covered becomes uncovered, but it also varies from game to game as different visual stimuli are selected to be hidden. Vocalizations may change from "Peeka peeka peeka boo," or be absent entirely as when two toddlers play without talking but with much laughter. In addition the motor components may vary. Covering requires those gross and fine movements necessary to accomplish the task, such as carefully placing the lid on a pot or a cloth over a doll's face. Uncovering is done by a variety of movements as well. One infant, for example, bends his trunk, turns his head, raises and extends his arm or grasps the lid.

Peekaboo games may be characterized solely by mother infant actions. The agent of action may vary either may participate in the game as the individual who does the covering and uncovering just use one of the actions. The person who institutes the covering action has an additional option, however. Another infant select to cover herself or the social partner, so the object of cover may vary also.

Alternately, toys may be incorporated in peekaboo games. Often a single toy, such as a rattle, is involved in the early games, but several toys are common in later game versions, such as in the object-in-container games when toy food is placed in a pot. Therefore although the cover and uncover elements occur with regularity, game variations abound with respect to vocalizations and among action components, interactions sequences, and objects.

INNOVATION

Games arise as novel patterns within the context of ongoing social interactions. The first peekaboo games are considered a game innovation since the cover-uncovers pattern had not appeared previously in the dyad's social interplay. Which of the possible, simple patterns that peekaboo may assume do occur in these early games? Previous researchers, such as Gustafson, Green, and West (1979), claimed that in early peekaboo games the mother is active and the infant is passive in both the agent roles of cover and uncover. Bruner (1983) considered peekaboo games as strictly circumscribed in format, stressed the formal structures of the games, and stated that in peekaboo games the mother established agency of the cover and uncover action and does so early in the games.

On with repetition, however, peekaboo games do vary in the manner in which they are played. One particular rendition of the cover-uncover pattern occurs late in infancy, the object-in-container game. According to Bruner (1983), the mother serves as the agent of cover in these games and hides objects in containers whereas the infant serves as the agent of uncover and retrieves the hidden objects. If roles within this game changed systematically, a developmental phase shift would occur and the novel pattern that resulted would constitute an *agency innovation*.

EMPIRICAL EVIDENCE: PARTICIPANTS, PROCEDURE, AND FOCUS

The interaction of four mother-infant dyads were analyzed for the occurrence and properties of peekaboo games. The videotaped data were gathered in the first year of a 2-year longitudinal study of spontaneous, mother-infant interactions of 13 participants. The weekly lab visits were conducted in a 12.5-foot square, carpeted, laboratory playroom. Age-appropriate objects were available for incorporation into the interactions.

Games selected for analysis were those of four infant-mother dyads engaged in a face-to-face context during the infant's first year. The face-to-face sessions were 10 minutes in duration and the dyads missed an average of 2.5 sessions during the period of observations discussed here. Cameras were focused on each participants of the interaction and mixed onto a split-screen that also displayed an image of the session's elapsing time.

Since the dyads played the games freely, it was expected that game variations and commonalities would surface across the dyads. Because game features, innovations, and dynamics were primary concerns, games from the developmental histories of the infants were selected that encompassed the periods in which innovations were likely to appear. The first innovation of interest is that of the appearance of the first peekaboo games played since they mark game innovation, a new pattern in the mother-infant interactive repertoire. These games may vary widely in the manner they are played so the dynamic features of these games is analyzed.

As peekaboo is played repeatedly, the games exhibit well-coordinated dynamics. One game type, the object-in-container game, commonly occurs in later infancy. The dynamics of this single game type were selected for comparison across the four dyads to assess the quality of interplay. Because agency has played a central role in discussions of peekaboo structure and innovation, special attention is given to the patterns of agency exhibited by the dyads and whether or not Bruner's (1983) agency predictions are realized in the dyad's peekaboo games. A systematic role shift shown by all the dyads in the object-in-container peekaboo game would constitute an agency innovation.

Game Innovation: The Onset of Peekaboo

Videotapes of the earliest, identified lab visits in which peekaboo games occurred in the mother-infant play of four dyads were analyzed and interpreted. The first dyad followed Bruner's (1983) prescription well. When Ruth was 27 weeks, her mother served as agent of both cover and uncover. The placed her own head on the high-chair tray and said, "Where's mommy? Where's mommy?" Next, the mother lifted her head, looked at the infant and said, "There she is." Ruth smiled and watched. Because the mother provided both the cover and uncover actions, the agency pattern displayed here is defined as that of a single agent.

The second dyad's pattern differed from that of the first and differed also from Bruner's prediction. When Susan was 34 weeks of age, her mother began by acting as the agent of the cover action, and silently covered the infant's hands with her hands. Without prompting, the infant became the agent of the uncover action, and successfully uncovered one of her hands. Her mother then uncovered the infant's other hand. Because the mother and infant assumed the role of agent of the uncover action, but at different points of the game, the pattern is referred to as alternating agents, rather than that of a single, preestablished agents.

The fourth dyad's pattern differed considerably from the others in several respects. First, at 27 weeks, the infant acted as agent of the cover action in different game formats. In the first format, Lewis covered and uncovered himself by looking into a mirror and moving his head or looking away for many repetitions. Then, he shifted cover format as he bent his truck forward and hid his head, face down, on his mother's lap. His mother asked, "Where's Lewis? "Where's Lewis?" but did not physically prompt him as he spontaneously assumed the role of agent of the uncover by lifting his head and raising his trunk. Once up, he turned toward and looked in the mirror as an agent of the other type of uncover action. He then let his body and face plunge into his mother's lap once again. This time she tapped him on the side and raised his arms a bit to prompt his rising. Later in the same game, she took his hands within hers and, while the infant could still view her face quite well over their hands, she brought his hands to midline and apart while repeating "peekaboo." The infant then lowered his head below their hands and she continued repetitions of "peekaboo" as his head was alternately covered and uncovered by their hands.

This example is one in which the infant served initially as sole agent of cover and uncover and then agency was marked by the mother and infant both participating simultaneously as agents of cover and uncover. Because both members of the dyad used the same actions and did so simultaneously, the pattern is referred to as joint agents.

Most of these illustrations, the earliest sessions in which peekaboo games were observed for four infants, offer evidence contrary to Bruner's (1983) view that the mothers establish agency and do so at the beginning of the games. Rather, agency patterns are dynamically cocreated by the participants in the interactive process of the game. Moreover illustrations suggest that the infants are active, rather than passive, even in very early games, a finding not anticipated by the work of Gustafson et al. (1979), who proposed as passive role for infants in early peekaboo games.

As expected, the games varied considerably. Peekaboo games were accompanied by words commonly associated with peekaboo, by words not commonly associated with this game, and by no game-related words whatsoever. Some games involved objects, others did not. The mother or infant or both instituted the cover or uncover actions, and when both performed as agents, different patterns of participation were evident. Thus variation aptly characterizes this sort of interpersonal interaction. No rigid, traditional routine was apparent.

Object-in-Container Peekaboo Games

The early games provide examples of the myriad approaches to playing the peekaboo game exhibited by the dyads, but Bruner (1983) suggested that in the period from 11 to 13 months, infants engaged in a game variant in which objects were hidden inside of containers and retrieved. According to Bruner, during this phase, the mothers hid the objects and the infants retrieved them.

All four dyads whose actions were described in the early games engaged in many game types including several objet-in-container peekaboo games but at ages somewhat younger than those noted by Bruner. The games described here occurred when the infants were between 41 and 46 weeks of age and in a context in which the mothers and infants were seated at a table. The mothers selected objects for the dyadic interactions.

Ruth's mother played the object-in-pot game initially, them verbally encourage, but at times physically discouraged the 46-week-old infant from doing so. The mother began by saying, "Here's a cover to the pot." As she moved the pot closer to the infant, the infant grasped it and the mother continued, "You can put the grapes inside. See, watch." Ruth's mother tried to remover the grapes form the infant's grasp but the infant refused to relinquish them. Her mother then removed the lid, placed as glass inside the pot, and replaced the lid as the infant continued to make manual contact with parts of the pot. The mother queried, "Where'd it go?" then tugged the pot away from the infant, tilted it in the infant's direction, and said "peekaboo" as she covered and uncovered the pot. The mother moved the tilted pot closer to the infant and inquired, "See, where's the glass?" then said, "peekaboo," as she uncovered and covered the pot once again. The infant touched the pot, let it go, and looked away. The mother spoke again, "Punkin, look at," removed the lid and said, "peekaboo," then replaced the lid as the child watched but did not renew the attempt to become manually involved with the game.

The other dyads provided smoothly co-created, object-in-pot games. One game was accompanied by the mother's physical prompting, another by the mother's verbal prompting, and the final game by a combination of physical and verbal prompting.

The second dyad played the pot game when Susan was 45 weeks old. The infant began the game by reaching or and tilting the pot to see inside. Her mother tried to cover the pot with the lid but the infant's grasp, covered it with the lid, slid the pot toward the infant, and tapped it on the table in front of the infant. The infant proceeded to uncover the pot and look inside. In this case the mother supplied no game-related, verbal commentary but did provide a physical prompt.

When Linda (third dyad) was 41 weeks of age, her mother started an object-in-container game by placing toy grapes and apples in the pot. The mother asked, "What's in there, huh? What's in there?" but offered no physical prompting. The infant removed the pot's lid and looked inside the pot.

Another smoothly cocreated instance of the object-in-pot game occurred with the fourth dyad when Lewis was 45 weeks old. His mother hid toy grapes in the pot and covered it. She used physical and verbal prompts by moving the pot closer to him and asking, "Where's the grape?... Where's the grapes? Where are they?" Lewis then removed the pot's lid, lifted the grapes out of the pot, and showed them to his mother as she supplied the commentary, "Peekaboo. There they are."

For each of the dyads, the mothers selected the pot and objects and the infants became actively engaged with the pot and made attempts to locate objects therein. In the first case, Ruth's mother verbally prompted the infant but deprived her of manipulating the pot for an extended period. The infant became far more passive and seemed to lose interest in the game. The three games in which infants successfully retrieved the objects were characterized by mothers' yielding the pot to the infants very early in the games and encouraging infant involvement by simple verbal or physical prompts. The mothers structured the situations similarly and the infants' actions within these situations were similar. Thus, although the mother may set the task, the infant's active involvement and success as agent of the uncover are not mandated by the mother, but rather, are a function of the infant's attention, interpretation, cooperation, and active participation in the game. The mother's actions may facilitate, impede, or have no discernable impact on the infant's actions.

These dyadic interactions were consistent with Bruner's description. The object-in-container games described are structured by the adult who hides the object and the infant who seeks to retrieve it. The infant ages at which the games were played were somewhat younger than those noted by Bruner but similar to those noted by Piaget (1954).

Agency Innovation: The Infant's Role Shift

Appearances are deceiving, however. The dyads continued to play peekaboo after those games described in the previous section. In the very next episode of the object-in-pot game played by each pair, there was evidence contradicting Bruner's contention that these games were characterized by the mothers hiding objects in the containers and infants retrieving them. Each of these games is market by an innovation, a phase shift characterized by the infant's transition to agent of cover in the object-in-pot game.

The transition of infant to agent of cover appeared when Ruth was 50 weeks of age. Ruth's mother started the transition game by inquiring, "Do you want to stir the soup? Can you stir the soup?" The infant continued to mouth a spoon but uncovered the pot. Spontaneously, without prompting, the infant then covered and uncovered the pot twice. The mother commented on the infant's actions after they occurred, "Off. Put it on," and then asked, "Can you take it off?" The infant did not respond and the mother removed the lid. Thereafter, the infant once again became engaged as agent of cover and uncover.

In this episode, the infant's transition to agent of *cover* occurred *spontaneously*, without the mother's physical or verbal prompts. Her mother did prompt other actions and offered a running commentary on the infant's action but the innovation occurred in the absence of prompts. The game's overall agency pattern was one characterized by *alternating agents* for both the *cover* and *uncover* actions and this dyad alternated agency twice during the game.

The agency patterns were quite complex for two dyads in which the infants made the transition to agent of cover in the object-in-pot game. When Susan was 45 weeks of age, the mother and infant began by *alternating agent* roles for cover and uncover. Unlike the previous example, however, the mother provided verbal and physical *prompts* prior to the infant's transition to agent of *cover*. She asked, "Do you want to put that back in the pan? Do you wanna put that back in the pan? There you go. Put that back in the pan," while tilting the pot toward the infant. The infant placed the grapes in the pot. Thereafter, the agency patterns of the game switched to that of *joint agency* of uncover as both simultaneously tilted the pot toward the infant, and finished with *double agency* as the infant reached for the grapes and her mother lifted them toward the infant with a spoon.

Another complex pattern of agency occurred when Linda was 43 weeks of age. Linda's mother began the transition game by covering the pot. The infant then spontaneously uncovered the pot and her mother commented, "You opened the pot up, didn't you?" The infant *spontaneously* began to *cover* the pot and, as the mother tried to assist her, the lid fell. The mother retrieved the lid and placed it on the pot and said, "There you go, all closed up." The infant spontaneously uncovered and then covered the pot again without maternal prompting. Agency continued to alternated: The mother uncovered the pot then the infant covered and uncovered the pot. After her mother helped Linda cover the pot, agency switched back to the infant as she spontaneously made the transition to agent of cover and, once she had resumed that role, she repeated it.

The game's agency patterns were several. The game began with mother and infant *alternating* roles of agent, then they *jointly covered* the pot. Next the agency of cover and uncover *alternated* three times, then both *jointly covered* the pot. Finally, the infant finished the game as agent of both cover and uncover.

Lewis' transition to agent of cover in the objects-in-pot game happened when he was 45 weeks old. His mother concealed objects in the pot and then successively uncovered and covered them several times. She verbally and physically prompted the infant to remove the lid and did so. His mother clapped and said, "Good boy. What's inside there huh?" The infant *spontaneously*, without verbal or physical prompting, *covered* the object. When the action had already commenced, his mother inquired, "You gonna put it back on? Oh, there you go." The infant then continued in the role of agent of uncover and cover. Because agency was established by the mother and switched to the infant, the *alternating agent* pattern was evident here.

In summary, all dyads played object-in-pot games in which an innovation occurred, and the infant became and agent of cover. The transition games had features the violated Bruner's prescriptions that (a) the mother established agency and (b) does so at the beginning of the game, and also that in object-in-container games (c) the mother hid the objects, and (d) the infant retrieved them. All the transition games had alternating agent patterns, two of the games had joint agency pattens, and one had a double agency patterns. Thus the roles of the participants are neither fixed by the mother nor immutable once the game begins, but are cocreated by the participants and emerge from the social dynamic particulars of the game in progress.

Because all dyads managed to create conditions under which the infant emerged as the agent of the cover action, the question arises as to whether the mothers prompted the transition or whether it appeared to be spontaneously initiated by the infants. Once again, the evidence suggest that there are a variety of ways that agency becomes established. Most infants spontaneously assumed the role of the agent of cover without maternal prompting, although one infant made the transition after receiving verbal and physical prompts to do so.

DISCUSSION

The variations in peekaboo games that were expected to occur did occur. Games differed with respect to (a) the sensory system stimulated: tactual, visual, and auditory; (b) being purely social or incorporating, objects; (c) motor system involvement: hands, limbs, or gross body movements, and (d) the dyad member who served as agent of cover and uncover.

Peekaboo games were considered with respect to three dimension: First was peekaboo game innovation, the appearance of the first peekaboo games that constituted for each dyad and innovation in the dynamics of mother-infant interactions. The second was typical games, the presence and features of a single game type, the object-in-container game that occurred across dyads that preceded immediately the games in which the infants became agents of the covering action. The third was agent innovation, the first game in which the infants made the transition to agents of cover in object-in-container games.

Prior to the appearance of peekaboo games per se, mothers introduced peekaboo-related vocalizations in other social contexts. When peekaboo games began, the infants served as agents of cover and uncover. They initiated game-relevant actions sometimes spontaneously, at other times after verbal or physical prompts were offered. Only one game was marked by the single agent pattern, in which the mother was the agent throughout the game. In the other three games, the mothers and infants both participated in agency. In these games, the agency mother and infant assumed the agency role at different times in the game, double agents in which the mother and infant each assumed the role of agent but engaged in different actions, and joint agents in which the mother and infant simultaneously participated as agents with the same actions. Thus, these early game activities did not conform to Bruner's (1983) formula that required the mother to established agency and do so early in the game, nor to Gustafson, et al.'s (1979) contention that infants are passive in early games.

The second aspect of peekaboo studied concerned the dynamic features of object-in-container games as played by all dyads. The infants served initially as agents of uncover in the games described. In the first dyad, the mother verbally encouraged but physically discouraged the infant's active participation as agent of uncover. The infant lost interest, became passive, and was unsuccessful in accomplishing the task of retrieving the object. Games described for the three other dyads were smoothly cocreated: The mothers offered simple verbal and physical prompts and the infants successfully retrieved the hidden objects. These games appeared to follow Bruner's proposition that mothers always hid objects and infants always retrieved them.

The very next object-in-container game that each dyad played, however, violated Bruner's proposition and revealed an agency innovation, that of the infant's transition to agent of cover in the object-in-container game. All the transition games were characterized by the alternating agents pattern and two also exhibited the joint agency pattern. The infant-initiated actions once again showed variation. Three infants realized this innovation spontaneously, and only one may have been inspired by maternal verbal and physical prompts. The transition games once again failed to conform to the suggestion that the mother establishes agency and does so early in the game.

Dynamic Systems

The peekaboo games presented here showed game variability and commonality across dyads. The peekaboo game is composed of a invariant, the cover-uncover pattern that can be considered in dynamic systems terminology a collective variable, regularity that captures the confluence of many elements working together. This collective variable functions at the level of the social system since the game is a product of dyadic interaction and not solely orchestrated by one of the participants.

Bruner hypothesized another invariant pattern, that agency is established by the mother and done so early in each game. The findings presented here argue against this clear formulation. The dyads showed various patterns of agency in both cover and uncover and did so in the earliest identified games and at different points in the games. The appearance of four different agency patterns suggest that the agency patterns are emergent, cocreated by the participants throughout the game and not simply fixed by one of the participants at the onset of the game.

One particular type of peekaboo game, the object-in-container game, seemed to conform to another of Bruner's formulations regarding agency invariance, namely that the mothers hid objets and the infants retrieved them. The games described initially were marked by the presence of maternal prompts. In the first dyad, Ruth's mother appeared to verbally prompt but physically inhibit the infant' activities and the game ended without the infant successfully retrieving the object. For three dyads, mothers offered simple verbal or physical prompts or combinations of these, and the game continued to flow.

Even this simple invariant, (mother-hide, infant-retrieve) is in on sense automatically resultant, but rather is dependent on the specific dynamics of the social interplay. If not smoothly cocreated by the participants, this pattern will not be achieved.

The peekaboo game's essential pattern, cover-uncover, did evidence stability over time in the presence of system variability. An infant sucked on a spoon but her subsequent activity was captured by the game her mother initiated. The game's flow at times was impeded by the infants' resistance to yield objects already grasped, although the mothers attempted to incorporate the objects into game activities. The mothers maneuvered around this infant propensity to retain objects in several ways. They quickly and gently pried the objects away from the infants or substituted different objects, or retrieved objects that had fallen as a result of the tussle. Another potential destabilizing activity in these games occurred when mother began to introduce pretend play games based on conventional, functional uses of the objects. One purported to simmer the pot contents with the lid in place. Others encouraged the infants to stir the pot contents but the infants did not participate in stirring actions when urged to do so. At these ages, the infants continued to be engaged exclusively with the cover and uncover aspects of the game.

Thus, in the context of the peekaboo game, given intrusions to the game's flow, the stability of the game's cover-uncover pattern was preserved by both mother and infant. Because system's pattern was maintained in the presence of variability in the system, the game pattern appears to be a self-organizing activity that constrains the degrees of freedom available in this social system.

Yet the attractor state characterized by the mother-hide, infant-retrieve pattern did yield to another, the agency innovation pattern of infant-hide, infant-retrieve. This innovation of the infant's transition to agent of cover in the object-in-container game is a developmental phase shift, a reorganization of system elements and subsystems into a new stable pattern. It is interesting that in three dyads the infants spontaneously made the transition, without maternal prompts, after they had uncovered the objects. In the fourth dyad, the mother's prompts may have served as an external nudge to encourage the infant's novel agency pattern.

In the dynamic systems view, at the times of the system's transition to a new dynamic pattern, the system is particularly susceptible to external influences. Depending on the qualities of these contextual influences, they may serve to facilitate the system's reorganization and transition to a new pattern or impede the system's reorganization. Note that the new pattern does not supplant the other agency patterns. The mother and infant continue to cocreate games with complex participatory patterns.

Because peekaboo games arise with particular patterns and are maintained although they reorganize over time, questions arise as to the mechanisms responsible for game appearance, pattern, continuation, and innovation. The dynamic systems view suggests that there is no single, underlying cause for a pattern's organization or reorganization. It is necessary to discover the control variables, the factors responsible for marshaling the system's many elements into the constrained, specific, simple innovative pattern that arises without recourse to a reductionist explanation. A confluence of attentional, perceptual, motivational, emotional, cognitive, motor, and social factors may give rise to the emergence of a new pattern, an innovation. Modifications in any of the constituent components may shift the game's pattern from one configuration to another. Indeed, it is likely that different control variables are operative at each different peekaboo game innovation.

Culture

Some have claimed that games are aspects of the culture that are taught to the infant by the mother. She is reputed to scaffold infant action or guide the infant's game participation (Rogoff et al., 1993). The evidence provided here for this view is not compelling. Actions in peekaboo games often appeared to be spontaneously realized by the infants. In the observations presented her, mother did not attempt to teach a culturally correct peekaboo game to the infants from inception. Prior to the appearance of typical peekaboo games, mothers introduced vocalizations commonly used in the North American culture's version of peekaboo during infant engagement in other activities such as thumb sucking or mirror gazing. It is quite possible that the first games played were not demonstrated by the mother to an attentive, passive infant. Because one of the infants spontaneously acted as agent of cover and uncover in the early traditional peekaboo game, it is possible that some of the first peekaboo games played were initiated by the infant's own spontaneous actions and not by maternal modeling, guiding, or scaffolding.

Mothers were noted to introduce (a) culturally specific, game-related vocalizations that may have helped to establish the game's rhythms; (b) agency that assisted in providing the task structure; and (c) verbal and physical prompts that may have facilitated the game's flow. Because the infants were noted to ignore maternal prompts, initiate game-related actions in the absence of maternal prompts, and continue the game in spite of maternal actions not related to peekaboo, these particular maternal contributions are neither necessary nor sufficient for the game's occurrence.

Ritual

In what sense is the peekaboo game "ritualized?" A contemporary definition of ritual includes the ideas of a "sequence of symbolic activities...closely connected to specific sets of ideas that are...encoded in myth" (Schultz & Lavenda, 1990), whereas more traditional definitions of ritual tie the symbolic acts to religion as well (Beattie, 1970; Turner, 1973).

Garvey (1990) provided an unusual approach to the notion of ritual, one in which various types of play can become ritualized providing they exhibit "controlled repetition" (Garvey, 1990, p. 111) with extreme regularity as each participant demonstrates "the precise regulation of behavior" by rigidly "alternating physical gestures" (Garvey, 1990, p. 112). Although the cover and uncover actions of peekaboo do occur sequentially and constituted the task of the game, rigidity in role alternation does not occur. Thus, it appears inappropriate to consider the peekaboo game as ritualized according to the definitions of Garvey or others commonly used in the literature.

Unfortunately, when games are considered as possessing a "fixed" or rule-bound structure, comments such as those offered by Bateson (1972) are made. Games are bounded spatially and temporally and are played "according to a standard set of rules" (p. 191) that governs the participants' activities, whereas other play has paradoxes, "messages untrue or not meant," (p. 183). Games are rigid in contrast to other sorts of play that require communication and an "evolving system of interaction" (p. 192).

The microanalysis of peekaboo games presented here suggests that they are like play, in fact, in that the spontaneous interplay between participants in their cocreation of the game tasks does require consistent communication and interpretation for maintenance of the event. In peekaboo, the task is defined but the manner in which the actions are realized is at the discretion of the participants and invented in the moment-by-moment decisions of each to participate with a game-relevant action. The players create their roles both with respect to the tasks of the game and with respect to the actions of the others. The patterns of agency demonstrated by the dyads were often complex and varied, not prearranged and organized by a stringent code. It is the dynamics of the social interplay that create the game's structure, rhythm, and flow, not the adherence to a predetermine for rigid script. These findings add to the growing corpus of theoretical and empirical work that suggest the dynamic systems approach is a useful framework for the consideration of infant cognitive, social, communicative, and motor behaviors and their development (Eckerman, 1993; Fogel, 1995; Fogel, Nwokah, & Karns, 1993; Thelen, 1992; Thelen & Ulrich, 1991; van Geert, 1991).

Conclusion

A dynamic systems orientation provides a framework by which the empirical phenomena of peekaboo games may be organized and interpreted and periods of game innovation, or phase shifts, have been described. During these innovation periods, the dyads managed to accomplish the game tasks with different patterns of participation. Thus, the peekaboo game is considered and emergent social pattern, cocreated by the participants through constant and active attention, cooperation, and communication.

ACKNOWLEDGMENTS

The authors would like to thank our undergraduate assistants for their enthusiasm, coding, and analyses. This work was funded, in part, by the postdoctoral fellowship MH 15747C to the first author and NIH grant RO1 HD21036 and NIMH grant RO1 MH48680 to the second author. Rebecca Wood is currently at The University of Connecticut.

REFERENCES

Bateson, G. (1972). Metalogue: About games and being serious. In *Steps to an ecology of mind* (pp. 14-20). New York: Ballantine.

Bateson, G. (1972). A Theory of play and fantasy. In *Steps to an ecology of mind* (pp. 177-193). New York: Ballantine.

Beattle, J.H.M. (1970). On understanding ritual . In B.R. Wilson (Ed.), *Rationality* (pp. 240-268). New York: Haper & Row.

Bruner, J. (1983). *Child's talk: Learning to use language*. New York: Norton.

Crawley, S.B., Rogers, P.P., Freidman, S., Iacobbo, M., Criticos, A., Richardson, L., & Thompson, M.A. (1978). Developmental changes in the structure of mother-infant play. *Child Development, 14,* 30-36.

Eckerman, C.O. (1993). Toddlers' achievement of coordinated action with conspecifics: A dynamic systems perspective. In L.B. Smith & E. Thelen (Eds.), *A dynamic systems approach to development: Applications* (pp. 333-357). Cambridge, MA: MIT Press.

Fernald, A., & O'Neill, D. (1993). Peekaboo across cultures: How mothers and infants play with voices, faces, and expectations. In K. McDonald (Ed.), *Parent-child descriptions and implications.* State University of New York Press.

Fogel, A. (1993). *Developing through relationships.* London: Harvester Wheatsheaf.

Fogel, A. (1995). Development and relationships: A dynamic model of communication. In J.B. Slater (Ed.) *Advances in the study of behavior: Vol. 24.*

Fogel, A., Nwokah, E., & Karns, J. (1993). Parent-infant games as dynamic social systems (pp. 43-70). In K.B. MacDonald (Ed.), *Parents and children playing.* Albany: State University of New York Press.

Garvey, C. (1990). *Play: The developing child.* Cambridge, MA: Harvard University Press.

Gustafson, G.E., Green, J.A., & West, M.J. (1979). The infant's changing role in mother-infant games: The growth of social skills. *Infant Behavior and Development, 2,* 301-308.

Holt, S.A., & Fogel, A. (1993, March). *Infant affect as a component of social process: A dynamic systems view.* Paper presented at the meeting of the Society for Research in Child Development, New Orleans, LA.

Piaget, J. (1954). *The construction of reality in the child.* New York: Ballantine.

Piaget, J. (1962). *Play, dreams, and imitation in childhood.* New York: Norton.

Rogoff, B., Mistry, J., Goncu, A., & Mosler, C. (1993). Guided participation in cultural activity by toddlers and caregivers. *Monographs of the society for research in Child Development, 58*(8, Serial No. 181).

Rubin, K., Fein, G., & Vandenberg, B. (1983). Play. In E.M. Hetherington (Ed.), *Carmichael's manual of child psychology: Social development* (pp. 693-774). New York: Wiley.

Schultz, E.A., & Lavenda, R.B. (1990). *Cultural anthropology: A perspective on the human condition.* St. Paul, MN: West.

Stern, D. (1977). *The first relationships.* Cambridge, MA: Harvard University Press.

Stern, D.N. (1974). Mother and infant at play: The dyadic interaction involving facial, vocal, and gaze behaviors. In M. Lewis & L. Rosenblum (Eds.), *The effect of the infant on its caregiver* (pp. 187-213). New York: Wiley.

Stern, D.N. (1985). *The interpersonal world of the infant.* New York: Basic Books.

Thelen, E. (1992). Development as a dynamic system. *Current Directions in Psychological Science, 1,* 189-193.

Thelen, E., & Ulirch, B.D. (1991). Hidden skills: A dynamic systems analysis of treadmill stepping during the first year. *Monographs of the Society for Research in Child Development, 56*(1, Serial No. 223).

Turner, V.W. (1973). Symbols in African rituals. *Science, 179,* 1100-1105.

van Geert, P. (1991). A dynamic systems model of cognitive and language growth. *Psychological Review, 98,* 3-53.

Van Hoorn, J.L. (1982). *Games of infancy: A cross-cultural study* (Doctoral dissertation, University of California, Berkeley, 1982). Ann Arbor, MI: University of Microfilms International. (University Microfilms No. 985-02748, 4012).

3

TOWARDS A PRAGMATICAL CONCEPTION OF THE OBJECT: THE CONSTRUCTION OF THE USES OF THE OBJECTS BY THE BABY IN THE PRELINGUISTIC PERIOD

Christiane Moro
Université de Genève, Switzerland

Cintia Rodriguez
Universidad Autonoma de Madrid, Spain

How does a baby construct reality? How, during the period preceding language acquisition, do children learn about the objects surrounding them and their appropriate uses?

We propose the hypothesis of the social origin of human psychological functions. More specifically, we follow Vygotsky's conception, according to which the relationship between humans and reality is socially mediated. We attempt to show that the learning of object uses through interindividual interaction—which we define as baby-object-adult triadic interaction (Moro & Rodriguez, 1989)— is based on a rather complex construction of significations that is first elaborated within the interindividual interaction and can thus be submitted to semiotical analysis.

INTRODUCTION

In modern psychology in general, the conceptualization of the object during the prelinguistic period does not imply an analysis in terms of signification. The fact that the questions of the sign and the object are often addressed separately confirms this idea (for a review of the literature during the prelinguistic period, see Moro & Rodriguez, 1997).

As psychologists recognize, prior to language acquisition, it is the object that is at the center of the relation between children and their environment. Yet, what is seldom taken into account is the fact that the object itself contains a human dimension and as such constitutes a social object. Through human intervention, molding and using objects, the signs that refer to these objects allow the transmission of their uses.

Following Piaget's lead, which we examine later, the object on which modern psychology focuses is mainly an object cut off from the social world. It is considered by physical, logical, or syntactic aspects but not as the real result of the praxis; that is to say isolated from its rules of utilization and generally depending on a strict subject-object epistemology.

For the child, an appropriate (i.e., conventional) use of the objects in the environmental implies that the child has constructed them in their significations. These significations are based on a system of rules or codes related to cultural conventions. In order to understand the genesis of objects, conventional uses, and thus the signification that subtends these uses, it is necessary to recourse to communication. Indeed, we propose the hypothesis that the conventions pertaining to objects can only be transmitted by communication between people and through the use of signs. The construction of the object and of its meanings depends on these processes.

Therefore, mastering the meaning of objects requires much more than a mere subjective basis, because it depends on the human community as a whole. If one is to comprehend the conventional uses of objects and thereby their significations, the classic dual conception that separates meaning from communication and only considers signification through cognition appears unsatisfactory. Neither the isolated subject nor the isolated object contain any inherent semantic properties when separated from the person using them.

This concept is similar to that proposed by De Mauro (1969) concerning the linguistic sign. This author follows Wittgenstein's lead through his *Tractatus* and *Investigations philosophiques* and outlines the dead ends that result from theories of signification that only take into account the study of the forms by attributing intrinsic semantic properties to them. Such propositions do not only refer to a fixed conception of signification, they also lead to noncommunicability. De Mauro (1969) noted that "on the contrary, only men signify through the use of words and sentences" (p. 28). He also suggested that signification should be based on "an integral theory of communication" (p. 143). This conception emphasizes that "the guarantee of the relation between form and signified in the sign lies only within the use" (p. 193). These considerations established within the field of linguistics are not specific to the linguistics addressed by De Mauro. They also apply to prelinguistic conceptions of the object and of the sign developed in modern psychology (Moro & Rodriguez, 1997).

In order to characterize the issues of what we call the pragmatic approach to the object during the prelinguistic period, we try to show the importance of signification and thus of communication in the genesis of objects' conventional uses. We also show why it seems necessary to develop a new methodology capable of taking both of these aspects into account. To clarify our theoretical position, we first examine two major theories in the field of psychology: those of Piaget and Vygotsky. We then address the questions of object use and of the sign inference that are methodologically unavoidable for a pragmatical approach of the object. We also explain why we believe Peircian semiotics to be most appropriate, from a developmental point of view, to address the questions of the signification of the conventional use of objects in the prelinguistic child. Finally, we illustrate our position with several examples.

THE RESPECTIVE CONCEPTIONS OF PIAGET AND VYGOTSKY

What conceptions of the object, of signification, and of communication have Piaget and Vygotsky developed regarding the prelinguistic child? We refer to these two authors for our discussion because these two giants in the field of psychology, as Bronckart (1985) defined them, have developed quite opposite epistemologies where psychological development and construction of reality are concerned. For Piaget, the construction of intelligence that leads to his conception of the object is individually centered. Subjects construct themselves and also construct the object through their interactions with the physical world, mainly through the innate functional mechanism that constitutes the assimilation process. Communication does not intervene in this construction. On the other hand, Vygotsky put the emphasis on communication and advocates social interaction as a basis for human psychological functions. For Vygotsky, the subject's activity only acquires significance through the influence of other people. Mediation by the use of signs—analyzed by Vygotsky mainly from the language perspective—is of prime importance as the signs are both instruments of communication and of thought.

Piaget and the Construction of the Object as Biologically Based

To date, the most consistent and coherent analysis of the object in the prelinguistic child is probably still that of Piaget. It still inspires much research carried out in individual epistemology-oriented psychology, whether they explicitly refer to Piaget or not (Moro & Rodriguez, 1997). In Piaget's theory, the subject and the object are not present in the beginning. They are constructed correlatively. Therefore, in order to understand Piaget's position regarding the construction of the object, it is necessary to first expose his conception of the development of intelligence.

Piaget demonstrated the existence of a prelinguistic intelligence, which he called sensorimotor intelligence (Piaget, 1936/1977b, 1937/1977a). Intelligence constitutes a particular case of biological adaptation. The child's mode of adaptation to the world—considered only in subject-object terms—is realized through the action whose structure is analyzed in terms of schemes and will allow the coconstruction of the subject and of the object. The scheme results from the exercise of two fundamental mechanisms: assimilation (transformation of the world by the subject) and accommodation (transformation of the subject by the world). The equilibrium between these two mechanisms constitutes what Piaget called adaptation.

Despite his advocating for the interaction between subject and object, Piaget set the emphasis on the assimilation process. Assimilation enables the stability and invariance of the contents (e.g., objects) constructed by the repetitive exercising of the schemes. Assimilation is also the main vector for progress, allowing knowledge of the objects to exist, and constantly increasing this knowledge. Assimilation realizes its two main objectives—stabilization and progress—through its aspects of reproduction, generalization, recognition, and reciprocity. Thus, recognition allows the recognition of certain properties of the object and distinguishing it from others, whereas generalization enables extension of the use of a scheme to objects with closely related properties. Reciprocal assimilation allows for coordinating the schemes on reality, which is major sensorimotor progress. It analyzes common properties and differences between the schemes likely to be assimilated. In so doing, assimilation contributes to the acquisition of more complex object properties by the subject, as it involves interobject relationships. This sophisticated construction depends on the progress observed in sensorimotor Stage IV, allowing for intentional means-goal coordination and the occurrence of intelligent behavior in which the schemes become means for other schemes (goal schemes). A classical example provided by Piaget is that of a child who lifts a screen masking an object and then takes the object.

The major construction at the end of the sensorimotor stage is the construction of the permanence of the object (the stabilization of the object as a content), which depends essentially on the subject's internal capacities. The object only bears consistency in regards to the correlative development of the subject's schematic capacities. The primary role played by assimilation significantly shifts the control process that should be peripheral (somewhere between the subject and the object) toward the interior of the subject. Hence, it is not surprising that in this construction, no place is found for communication.

Furthermore, Piaget did not refer to objects as carrying significations external to the subject himself. Neither did he address the aspect of mediation by other subjects in the transmission of these significations, which refer to the uses as practiced within specific communities. The control of object construction depends mainly on the subjects themselves. The process of assimilation stems from the biological assimilation. On the psychological level, from a strictly functional point of view, it reduces the capacity of signification to a biological basis. Therefore Piaget only considered signification under the aspect of the subject and the exercising of schemes. Knowledge of the object would rely solely on this signification of an individual nature.

The fact that Piaget emphasized the construction of objects as contents and as support for representations shows that the representation aspect, although absent in the sensorimotor stage, overrides the psychological option at this level. The actual occurrence of representation, approximately between 18 months and 2 years, combined with the occurrence of the semiotic function (cf. Piaget, 1946/1978) will only provide an internal version of these "protorepresentations," a type of "enacted representations" of objects constructed during the sensorimotor stage. This conception of the development of the object as first being substantial and then aiming to be represented is at the origin of the consideration prevailing in Piaget of the semiotic aspect as an essentially representational or translation of the world aspect. This rather widespread conception (cf. Moro & Rodriguez, 1997) currently leads to neglect of the communication and inference aspects closely related to the living functioning of the signification processes—for example, the two acceptations of sign equivalence versus inference (Eco, 1988) discussed hereafter as being of prime importance in cognitive functioning even before language is acquired.

Thus, for Piaget, the object is not considered under its pragmatical, historical, or context-related aspects in relation with the uses it elicits. These uses are related to the functions attributed to the object by a community of subjects. From our point of view, this conception is the result of a biologically and logically oriented view of psychology that in fact precludes signification. This Piagetian conception is the consequence of the persistence of dualisms "between subject and object, individual and society, nature and culture, mind and reality" (Sinha, 1988, p. xiii), which, since the time of Descartes, refer the problem of knowledge to the individual subject.

Vygotsky and the Signification as Based on Human Interaction

For Vygotsky (1934/1985), the source of intelligence lies within social interaction. The development of the psychological functions is seen as the progressive appropriation of the culture through social interaction. The sigh is of prime importance in this conception. In this respect, the conception of semiotic mediation becomes essential in the triptic composed by the subject, the other subjects, and the culture. Borrowed from Engels' concept of instrumental mediation and extended by Vygotsky to the psychological tools that are the signs, especially linguistic signs that then become mediators for mental activity, mediation through signs allows both the control of the processes of behavior and the transformation of the subject's mental processes. As was noted by Lee (1985), Vygotsky set the foundations for a functional semiotic psychology.

Yet it should be noted that there is a discrepancy between Vygotsky's methodological propositions for the reconstruction of psychology—mentioned earlier—and the psychological translation of these conceptions (Davydov & Radzikovskii, 1985). Indeed, if one is to consider the prelinguistic aspect, then it appears that development is no longer considered as stemming from culture but is only considered in a dual perspective. Development at this stage is seen as the result of two separate processes. One involves communication and the other involves intelligence, qualified as nonverbal thought and preintelligence language. These two processes merge with the occurrence of language.

The development of nonverbal thought is considered under the aspect of nonsemantic instrumental mediation. In this respect, Vygotsky referred to Köhler's work on phylogenesis. This solely instrumental consideration of mediation during the prelinguistic phase does not explain how the child can use a tool in the absence of signification and thus in a totally separate way from communication. Furthermore, the major reduction of prelinguistic development to its mere instrumental aspect is quite insufficient from the point of view of ontogenesis. It is difficult to understand how the transition from instrumental mediation, involving natural psychological functions, to semiotic mediation, which concerns higher order psychological functions, is carried out.

The opposition established by Vygotsky between sign and tool, the former oriented toward the inside and the latter toward the outside, is to be considered only under the instrumental conception of this first development. The issue of the analogic conception of the sign considered as a psychological tool and of the tool in work (Rivière, 1990; Vygotsky, 1978) further enhances the dichotomy between instrumental and semiotic mediation and between lower order and higher order psychological functions. This separation leads to the disqualification of the object and other people as poles for the construction of semioses in the child.

Yet, a detailed reading of Vygotsky reveals that the question of the independence of the two roots of verbal thought is not quite clear cut. In fact, it appears to be a source of questioning for Vygotsky. Indeed, he asked:

Does it occur [the merging of the two roots with the apparition of verbal thought] at one single point or at several points, does it happen suddenly or is it slowly and progressively prepared to come into existence only later, is it the result of a discovery or of a simple structured action and of a slow functional modification, does it take place when the child is two years old or in school age children? (Vygotsky, 1962, p. 141)

The question of the interpretation of the movement of indication that Vygotsky described as "the most primitive level in the development of human language" (p. 115) also suggests a less dual conception of the period that precedes language acquisition.

In fact, it is at the level of language development that Vygotsky best developed his thesis on the social genesis of human psychological functions and on a mediated conception of consciousness. Semiotic mediation is essential when Vygotsky (1962) addressed verbal behavior:

The word is present in the consciousness, which according to Feuerbach, is impossible for a person alone but quite possible for two. It is the most direct expression of the historical nature of human consciousness [...]. The word with its meaning is a microcosm of human consciousness. (p. 385)

Indeed, the sign is a two-sided entity as an instrument of communication and of thought (cf. also Vygotsky's counterargumentation relative to Piaget's conception of egocentric speech; cf. Vygotsky, 1962, pp. 45-110).

The innovative ideas expressed by Vygotsky on the methodological level and language level show a severe discrepancy with his dual conception proposed for the prelinguistic stage. His appeal for communication, which defines a semiotic conception of consciousness via the mediation through the sign considered as a psychological instrument, needs to be extended to the prelinguistic period. Around the notion of semiotic mediation, Vygotsky set the essential methodological foundations for a complete reconfiguration of psychology including the prelinguistic level. As he emphasized:

From the very first days of the child's development his activities acquire a meaning of their own in a system of social behavior, and, being directed towards a definite purpose, are refracted through the prism of the child's environment. The path from object to child and from child to object passes through another person. This complex human structure is the product of a developmental process deeply rooted in the links between individual and social history. (Vygotsky, 1978, p. 30)

THE USE OF OBJECTS AS BASIS FOR PREVERBAL SIGNIFICATION

A pragmatical approach of the construction of knowledge of objects in the prelinguistic stage necessarily involves usage. As we mentioned earlier, in order to know an object, it is necessary to refer to the uses it has. Thus to use a spoon, to push a toy truck, or as shown in the following examples, to insert various shapes in the appropriate holes, requires not only mastery of the respective uses of these objects, but also a certain knowledge of them. These uses are learned progressively during the development. The examples of work presented at the end of this chapter show this slow construction.

Usage is where communication, cognition, and signification meet. Thus at all times, the object is defined in relation to the human community through its use. Through this usage, the child can appropriate the object and its significations. In order to better understand the notion of reference to objects in the human community, it is necessary to understand that the different possible uses of objects are based on conventions. Indeed, objects are not constructed randomly by humans; they are built for the specific purpose of fulfilling a function or even several functions. In the previous example, the holes are to be filled with specific pegs.

Usage—the manner in which an object is used to fulfill a need—refers to human communication. The rules for the use of the object depend on communication but also on cognition, as they are constituted into signification systems internal to the subject. When these rules—related to conventions— are mastered, they allow the carrying out in an ordered sequence of the different actions aimed at carrying out the practice on the object. They are also closely related to categorization and conceptualization. The object conceptualized by the child over time is the result of the uses that have been applied to it.

In this respect, the object is not only a solid mass with its own unity and independence—a definition with which Piaget could agree—but it also fulfills a purpose in relation to its use. The knowledge of the object (i.e., the definition that the subject can acquire of it during his or her development) is correlative to the appropriation of its uses. Thus, it could be said that the object or the comprehension we have of it is situated at the end of its uses.

Hence we propose the hypothesis that in order to understand the object and the manner in which it is constructed by the subject, it is necessary to set a methodological distinction between the object and its usage. The uses— resulting from conventions—involve communication and signification in an intimately related manner. The study of the uses that the child acquires during his or her development as well as the study of the transmission of these by the adults close to the child allows us to better understand the levels of object conceptualization that are reached by children.

As we have sought to show, communication is of prime importance for the construction of object uses and for their appropriation by the child. The human community intervenes in both of these processes. Therefore, the construction of the uses is strongly related to the sign. The study of this construction allows rehabilitation of the semiotical aspect during the crucial period of development, that is the prelinguistic phase. The sign is a perfectly two-sided entity. Through uses, it refers to communication but also to thought as it allows access to the different levels of conceptualization reached by the child during his or her development. Through the explication of the two levels—sometimes characterized as intersubjective and intrasubjective—and through the sign being constructed and conceived as an inference that constitutes the semiosis, a semiotical analysis (cf. Peirce, 1931-1958) will allow a better understanding of the knowledge the child has concerning the object.

Peirce's Inference Conception of the Sign

Unlike the conception of the sign seen as a resemblance or an identity (Kristeva, cited by Eco, 1988, p. 33) in Piaget's sense, which implies a form of status quo of signification, Peirce's conception is essentially dynamic. It aims at describing "the semiosis, that is the process through which signification occurs for an interpreter in a given context" (Everaert-Desmedt, 1990, p. 39). For Pierce, "a sign is something which once it is known allows to know something more" (Peirce, cited by Eco, 1988, p. 33).

The triadic conception of the sign according to the three terms of *representamen, object,* and *interpretant,* which constitute the foundations of Peircian semiotics, appears as essentially dynamic through the inferential process that subtends it. It appears to us quite adequate for the analysis of online interaction processes such as we propose to address them. Thus:

> A sign, or representamen, is something in some respect or capacity. It addresses somebody, that is, creates in the mind of that person an equivalent sign, or perhaps a more developed sign. That sign which it creates I call the interpretant of the first sign. The sign stands for something, its *object.* It stands for that object, not in all respects, but in reference to a sort of idea, which I have sometimes called the *ground* of the representamen. (Peirce, p. 33)

We discuss later the signification of these different concepts for the purpose of analysis. The sign conceived as inference is particularly useful for the description of development processes. Indeed, in a mere equivalence ratio, knowledge is already present—and to temporarily borrow a terminology used by Saussure, the signified of the sign is already known—it can be reached by a deductive process: "⌐ is always used for |a|; yet we have |.⌐|; therefore |a|" (Eco, 1988, p. 50).

What happens when the signified is not known and needs to be constructed? This is the case when a baby has not yet constructed the conventional use of the object. In this case the interpretative process employed by the subject is abductive. The subject must extract the rules from elements in the context.

> Therefore, abduction represents the sketching or a random attempt for the elaboration of a system of signification rules which will enable the sign to acquire

its adequate signified. [...] As soon as the rule is coded, any successive occurrence of a same phenomenon becomes a more and more "necessary" sign. (Eco, 1988, p. 51)

We add to Eco's remarkable explanation that, for the baby in the situation of appropriating the object's uses, the attempts are much less random as the child interacts with adults. The adult possesses the rules for the use of the object and strongly guides the child in the elaboration of his or her "hypotheses." For instance, the adult may emphasize the result of an adequate practice so as to encourage the elaboration by the child of specific hypotheses relative to the uses of a given object. Indeed, as the sign implies a reference to something external, the link is not given but is to be constructed. Children do not construct themselves alone, they need to be helped by adults. The significations thus elaborated enable children to access the conventional uses of the objects.

In the examples proposed at the end of this chapter, we examine how the different inferences involved in semiotic processes at key points in development are elaborated. These inferences will allow the child to progressively acquire the significations necessary for mastering the canonical uses of objects.

Therefore, through inference we can better understand how signification and knowledge of the objects it entails occurs in the child at a given point in development. The semiotic theory will allow us to follow nearly online the various inferential movements at play at the child during the construction of his or her knowledge relative to the object.

DATA COLLECTION

As we have already mentioned, in order to master the uses of objects, the child must interact with adults. The resulting child-object-adult unit, called triadic interaction, will constitute the basic unit for the observation and analysis of children's behavior.

The situations we propose involve the object as well as the mother (privileged adult partner). The adults are given the following instructions: "Play with your child as you usually do." To remain as close as possible to everyday life situations, the dyads are filmed within their home environment. Only one camera is used and the subjects are informed that the dyad will be filmed during 5 minutes and that if they wish (if they are tired) the session may be interrupted at any moment. The dyads are free to use objects as they wish. The recorded sessions are transcribed second by second using a timer and following a transcription method devised specifically for this purpose.

The object used for this study is a toy truck. It has four wheels and the back of the truck supports six holes of various shapes into which six pegs of different colors and shapes can be inserted. The back of the truck can also be tipped by using a lever located on top of the truck's cabin. The truck also has a back door that may be opened by pulling a handle located in its lower part. The canonical use of inserting the pegs into the appropriate holes—hereafter "put into"—is at the center of the analyses presented at the end of this chapter.

The age range of the children observed here was determined following two criteria. The lower limit was that the child must be able to be interested by the object and act on it with a certain ease. The higher limit was that the child was at a stage before language acquisition. The babies studied were 7, 10, and 13 months old.

Semiotic Analysis Using Peircian Concepts

The construction of the conventional uses of objects is not instantaneous; it requires a lengthy temporal process. These uses—as we have proposed—are constructed by using signs. Through a semiotical analysis of the baby-object-child interaction, we illustrate how this progressive construction of use is elaborated. During development, before actually acquiring the conventional use with the appropriate significations, children use objects in many different ways according to the signification they attribute to them. The semioses or inferential significations that the child produces throughout his or her development are milestones on the path to the appropriation of the canonical uses of the object that is reached between 7 and 13 months old. These semioses are detectable through the different functions attributed by the child to the object either under the influence of the signs emitted by the adult or directly to the object itself when it becomes the sign of its use.

We strive to show that, although Peirce's semiotics was not developed in a communication or developmental perspective, it can prove to be a valuable tool in this context. Indeed, it allows one to understand the establishment of object uses via the signs displayed in the interactions with others and also enables one to apprehend the subject's cognitive development at different stages of the construction of an object's canonical uses.

Prior to the presentation of the examples, it is necessary to clarify some of the aspects of Peirce's semiotics that have guided our analysis. As mentioned earlier, for Peirce the semiotic process is triadic. It is defined as the relating of three terms, the representamen, the object, and the interpretant. The representamen or sign is something that represents something else, called its object. Everything can become a representamen if it becomes part of an interpretation process. In other words a, thing becomes a representamen when it is included in a triadic process. The object is what the sign represents, either a physical or a mental entity. It should be noted that the object Peirce referred to is the object of the semiosis and not the real object. As for the interpretant, it operates the mediation between the representamen and the object. This general definition of the semiotic process shows Peircian semiotics to be a particularly valid tool for the analysis of prelinguistic phenomena.

Aside from his definition of semiosis as a triadic process, Peirce considered that all phenomenon relative to human experience can be expressed according to three fundamental philosophic categories: firstness, secondness, and thirdness. These categories define three types of relations between the representamen and the object: the icon, the index, and the symbol.

The first level of interpretation is called *iconic* and it constitutes the basis for later semiotical constructions. As Peirce stated, the icon is first: "The icon is a representamen that represents its object according to its specific characteristics, whether the object exists or not. The icon as its name indicates is an image of its object, it resembles the object" (cited by Deledalle, 1990, p. 127). For instance, in the situations we propose, the child's interest in the real object presented to him or her in the use demonstrated by the adult, can by qualified as iconic in the sense that the child's interest refers to the object. As a source of attention, it constitutes a first semiotic process that will later subtend more complex processes. The function of an iconic sign, within the baby-object-adult triadic interaction, is to capture the child's attention and to focus it on the object itself or on its characteristics. When the adult succeeds in directing the baby's attention to the object, the child may react in a number of ways such as turning his or her gaze toward the object, trying to catch the object, and so on. From an intersubjective point of view, there is an agreement between the sign produced by the adult and the understanding the child has of it. As far as the knowledge of the object is concerned, the sign allows one to refer to the object itself, or to its characteristics. Thus it highlights a specific object among other objects available in the environment, which is a prerequisite for the object's conventional use to be acquired.

The index is second: "The index refers to its object: it indicates [...] The index refers to an object different from itself" (Peirce, cited by Deledalle, 1990, p. 127). Although remaining faithful to Peirce's definition of the index, we add the following aspects: In the situations we propose, we define the indexical or transition toward the rule level as an entry into "conventional use." It occurs only sporadically as if the child suddenly realized the inference relative to the whole or part of the exercise of canonical use. This is illustrated in the examples at the end of the chapter in which the child suddenly grasps the relation between the peg and the hole. Yet this inference remains relatively basic (in the sense that the peg-hole relation is global) and unstable. At this stage, the child does not take into account the corrective signs given by the adult (e.g., pointing to indicate the adequate holes). At this point, exploration behavior, such as the insertion of fingers in the holes in an attempt at understanding directly through the body some characteristics of the object or some phenomena, is frequently observed and indicates that conventional use is only under construction.

It should be noted that the very first manifestations of indexical relations—prior to those already exposed—emerge from iconic signs. For example, when the adult shows the appropriate use, the child can follow the adult's actions with his or her hands and come closer to the part of the object that the adult is manipulating. These relations will hereafter be called *iconico-indexical* throughout our analyses. This behavior occurs when the adult maintains the child's interest while using the object in a conventional manner (ostensive value of the conventional use made by the adult). The child follows with is or her hand the whole or part of the adult's action within close range of the parts of the object manipulated by the adult.

The symbol is third: "The symbol 'stands for' its object: it defines" (Deledalle, 1990, p. 128). Peirce's conception of the symbol should not be interpreted in the classical psychological sense. "All 'conventional sign' (C.P. 2.297) or law 'normally established by men' (C.P. 2.246) is a symbol" (cited by Deledalle, 1990, p. 128). Again, in the situations we propose, when the child has mastered the conventional use of objects and when the object as it is seen becomes a sign of its use, then the use can be considered to be symbolic. Generally at this moment, the child is capable of understanding the signs the adult produces to correct an erroneous practice. The child who has attempted to insert a peg into the wrong hole can modify his or her action in the direction indicated by the adult (comprehension of the pointing).

Behaviors related to the appropriation of objects' canonical use can be classified according to the three types of semiotical relations defined by Peirce. According to Peirce, these three types of relation refer to hierarchically more and more complex levels of semiotical interpretation—all the way up to the conventionality with the symbol, each time including the preceding levels. Peirce's indication in this respect is, "No matter how indirect the symbolic relation proves to be, it presupposes the relations of indexicality and iconicity and no matter how direct the indexicality relation is, it presupposes the relation of iconicity" (cf. Peirce C.P. 2.304) (Deledalle, 1990, p. 86).

Peirce's theory can prove most interesting for a better understanding of the baby's semiotic behavior within the triadic baby-object-adult interaction during development. It allows comprehension of the basis on which object-related knowledge and conventional use is constructed. Peirce's semiotic triangle enables access to the interpretative or inferential processes that take place within each sign through the intervention of the interpretant. It is thus possible to have access to the significations that the child progressively constructs during his or her development. The analysis of the components of semiosis (in terms of representamen, object of the semiosis, and interpretant) makes it possible to take into account the interpretation processes formulated by the child concerning the object, either through the adult's mediation or directly relative to the object itself when it becomes a sign of its use.

Peirce described this entirely fallible interpretative process as an abduction process comprising four major phases. The first three phases appear particularly relevant for the developmental characterization of object use construction in children.

The first three phases of the abductive process have been summarized by Everaert-Desmedt (1990) and can be described as follows:

In the first stage, the child is faced with an unexpected fact, unexplainable within the frame of his or her previous knowledge. In our interaction situations, the occurrence of the unexpected event is represented by the fact that the child shows interest in the object presented by the adult.

In a second stage, the child formulates hypotheses relative to the unexpected fact or event. In our interaction situations, the child attempts to relate peg and truck or peg and hole under the adult's incentive.

In a third stage, the hypothesis is applied by deduction: the behavior adopted conforms with the hypothesis. In our situations, the term *deduction* is not to be understood in its mathematical meaning, but rather as indicating that the child follows a rule that allows him or her to deduce the use *put into* from the mere sight of the pegs and truck.

An analysis of our interaction situations according to Peirce's semiotic model reveals that 7-, 10-, and 13-months-old children pass through the different levels just described. These levels allow identification of different developmental steps in the construction of conventional object uses.

Presentation of the Examples

The extracts presented here are parts of triadic interaction sessions that lasted 5 minutes and were video-taped. The data come from a longitudinal study involving 6 female dyads and 6 male dyads filed at age 7, 10, and 13 months in Geneva and Madrid.

These sequences allow us to grasp the different stages in the semiotical construction relative to the acquisition of objects' conventional uses and that the children go through at 7, 10, and 13 months.

Still in reference to Peirce, we called the first level *iconism*, the second level *level of transition toward the law*, and the third *level of the convention* or law. These levels refer to the three phenomenological Peircian categories described previously. Peirce's theoretical formulation relative to these different steps has demonstrated its heuristic use in the identification of the various moments in the construction of objects' canonical use in children between 7 and 13 months old. Each analysis of the different sequences illustrating the levels already mentioned will be preceded by a brief analytical summary of the sessions from which the examples are selected. Then the examples more specifically aimed at illustrating each of the major steps of semiotical construction are described.

These reflect the main moments during the development of the construction of the conventional use *put into.*

ANALYSES

The Iconical Level: Julia, 7 Months

Presentation of Sequences 1.1 and 1.2

At 7 months Julia does not yet have any knowledge of the object's canonical use "put into" nor even an approximation of this use. In fact, at 7 months, none of the children observed presented such knowledge, nor were they able to understand the conventional signs such as pointings produced by the adults. Nevertheless, they react in an adequate fashion: that is, in accordance with certain types of signs produced by the adults such as ostensive signs (the adult shows the object and shakes it or uses it in the complete canonical manner). In this case, the children react by demonstrating interest; they wave their arms, and so on.

The highest level of object use reached by the child is described in Sequences 1.1 and 1.2. In these sequences, despite the little knowledge Julia has of the object, she comes close to the canonical use under the incentive provided by the adult's use. Her action is more the result of what we could call a *magnet effect.* Julia acts on the object close to the area manipulated by the adult. Although this behavior is a step toward canonical use, it does not imply a comprehension of what is to be done with the pegs and the holes. This is confirmed by the fact that during the 5 minutes of observation, those are the only two times when the child displays such behavior, always under the adult's influence.

Sequence 1.1

Description of the use:

Julia holds two pegs in her hands and watches the adult's actions. The adult inserts a peg in the appropriate hole without dropping it—ostention. Julia places one of her pegs on a hole close to the location the adult acted on.

Description of the semiotical process:

Representamen: Insert the peg in a hole without dropping it.
Object: Follow the adult's action and drop the peg at the same location.
Interpretant: Level 1 of abduction: Unexpected event. The adult acts at a given location therefore "go toward this location."
Relation between the representamen and the object: It is of an iconico-

indexical type (i.e., that beyond the initial interest for the object elicited by the adult—iconicity—the child begins to grasp the relation between the peg and the truck although it expressed quite roughly indexicality).

Sequence 1.2 (continued From Sequence 1.1)
Description of the use:

Julia takes the peg again, sucks on it while watching the adult's action, the adult inserts the peg in the hole. Julia then "applauds" using the pegs against the truck.

Description of the semiotical process:

Representamen: Introduce the peg in the hole.
Object: "Applaud" with the pegs against the truck.
Interpretant: Level 1 of abduction: unexpected event. The adult acts on the truck, therefore applauding with the pegs against the truck.
Relation between representamen and object: Iconico-indexical (see previous explanation).

In Sequences 1.1 and 1.2 the child is faced with an "unexpected event" comprising the object and the adult's action. This event attracts the child (magnet effect described earlier), who reacts by moving toward the location of the adult's action. From the point of view of object use, this constitutes an iconico-indexical semiotical manifestation, as it is still similar to the displays of interest that are the very first iconical behaviors. It nevertheless constitutes a starting point toward the construction of the peg-hole relationship during the display of interest.

This iconico-indexical semiotical manifestation that can be reached through the interpretant (which allows grasping of the sign during its implementation in action, nearly online) stems from the very first semiotical manifestations that are of iconical type.

Level of Transition Toward the Rule: Julia, 10 Months

Presentation of Sequences 2.1 and 2.2
At 10 months, the situation changes. The child "starts" to give a conventional value to the object; this was not the case at 7 months. The specificity of the transition toward the rule level lies in that the conventional construction aspects are unstable. Most of the children use objects as Julia does in Sequence 2.1 described hereafter, and then return to a utilization of the object displaying a more iconic type of relation (when the adult presents the peg to the child he or she might take it to his or her mouth and suck on it, throw it away or shake it, etc.). At this moment, large variations in object utilization can be

observed. Children also have a better understanding of the conventional signs produced by the adult (e.g., pointing). These progressively become mediators toward a change in utilization, although without enabling a complete correction (i.e., inserting the peg into the adequate hole).

Sequence 2.1
Description of the use:

Julia takes a peg and brings it close to the truck. She then places the peg over the wrong hole.

Representamen: To see the peg and the truck.
Object: Place the peg over the wrong hole.
Interpretant: Level 2 of abduction: Beginning of the hypothesis on the peg-hole relationship.
Relation between representamen and object: Near-symbolic (peg-hole relation globally understood but not yet specified according to the respective characteristics of the peg and the hole).

Sequence 2.2 (*Continued from Sequence 2.1*)
Description of the use:

Then the adult takes the peg and moves it towards the appropriate hole (ostension), places it over the right hole without making it fall (ostension) and, inserts it into the adequate hole. Julia looks at the hole and puts her fingers into it.

Description of the semiotical process:

Representamen: Successive ostensions and insert a page in the hole.
Object: Watch and put fingers in the hole the adult acted on.
Interpretant: Level 2 of abduction: Search for an explanation..
Relation between representamen and object: Indexical (carried out with the body-hand-indexical relation with the hole with the objective of exploration, and search for an explanation).

In this example, we see how Julia initiates a canonical use of the object from the mere sight of the truck and the peg. Although she does not correct her use beyond her first action, the peg and the truck present a more complex signification than at 7 months, as a relation is made between the two objects even though this relation remains elementary and does not yet lead to the proper utilization. Sequence 2.2 confirms that construction of objects' canonical uses is still a subject of questioning on the part of the child.

Level of the Convention or Rule: Julia, 13 Months

Presentation of Sequences 3.1 and 3.2

Finally at 13 months, the signification *put into*, which implies the peg-truck or peg-hole relation becomes more stable. The children also understand the conventional signs, such as pointing, produced by the adult and use them correctly. The following example illustrates this progress in the understanding of the conventional use as well as of the signs produced by the adult. At this point the objects truck and pegs can be considered signs of their utilization.

Sequence 3.1

Description of the use:

The adult shows the peg to the child. The child takes the peg, brings it close to the truck, and tries to insert it into the wrong hole.

Description of the semiotical process:

Representamen: Peg.
Object: Put into wrong hole.
Interpretant: Level 2 of abduction: The use is deducted from the sight of the peg and the truck: If peg then *put into*.
Relation between representamen and object: Near symbolic (see Sequence 2.1).

Sequence 3.2 (Continued From Sequence 3.1)

Description of the use:

The adult indicates the appropriate hole. The child changes toward another wrong hole, then places the peg over the correct hole, and finally inserts the peg correctly into the hole.

Description of the semiotical process:

Representamen: The adult indicates the correct hole.
Object: Change the location of the peg for another hole.
Interpretant: Level 3 of abduction: If the adult indicates another hole, then change for the other hole and insert peg into the appropriate hole indicated by the adult.
Relation between representamen and object: Symbolic (the child can take into account the adult's instructions and successfully carry out the conventional use).

In the first sequence, the child makes a global elementary peg-hole relation: Julia takes the peg presented by the adult and tries to insert it into a wrong hole. In the second sequence, Julia correctly interprets the adult's pointing: She changes the peg's location and inserts it into the right hole as signaled by the adult. The adult's pointing is correctly understood and constitutes an indication of the change in the utilization concerning the objects truck and pegs. At this stage the truck and the pegs actually become signs of their utilization.

The analysis of the triadic interaction situations according to Peirce's semiotical model reveals that between 7 and 13 months, children go through several steps of semiotical elaboration that correspond to the progressive construction of objects' conventional utilization. Hence, at 7 months Julia presents no expertise of the canonical use of *putting into* concerning the truck and the pegs, whereas at 13 months she has become an expert or near expert at it. Through the interpretant, these different levels of semiotic construction allow access to the developmental steps in the subject's inferential process.

CONCLUSION

Throughout this chapter we have tried to show that the consideration of the object in its significations through its uses—what we called a pragmatical conception of the object—still remains to be investigated. Referring to two major theories in the field, those of Piaget and Vygotsky, we have positioned our approach by stressing the importance of communication in the construction of object signification and utilization in the prelinguistic child. Taking communication into account implies a reconsideration of the classical psychology paradigm. Indeed, a nondual conception of knowledge is necessary, which implies that the subject-to-subject interaction and the subject-to-object interaction be merged into one single process. Peirce's semiotics offers the possibility of investigating all significant fields and provides appropriate tools for the reformulation of object analysis in its pragmatical aspects in the prelinguistic period.

REFERENCES

Bronckart, J.P. (1985). Vygotsky, une oeuvre en devenir [A becoming work]. In B. Schneuwly & J.P. Bronckart (Eds.), *Vygotsky aujourd'hui* [Vygotsky today] (pp. 1-21). Neuchâtel-Paris: Delachaux & Niestlé.

Davydov, V.V., & Radzikhovskii, L.A. (1985). Vygotsky's theory and the activity-oriented approach in psychology. In J.V. Wertsch (Ed.), *Culture, communication and cognition*. New York: Cambridge University Press.

Deledalle, G. (1990). *Lire Peirce aujourd'hui* [Reading Peirce today]. Bruxelles, Belgium: de Boeck.

De Mauro, T. (1969). *Une introduction, à la sémantique* [An introduction to semantics]. Paris: Payot.

Eco, U. (1988). *Sémiotique et philosophie du language* [Semiotics and the philosophy of language]. Paris: Presses Universitaries de France.

Everaert-Desmedt, N. (1990). *Le processus interprétatif. Introduction à la sémiotique de Ch.S. Peirce* [The process of interpretation: Introduction to Ch.S. Peirce semiotics]. Liège, Belgium: Mardaga.

Lee, B. (1985). Intellectual origins of Vygotsky's semiotic analysis. In J.V. Wertsch (Ed.), *Culture, communication and cognition* (pp. 66-93). New York: Cambridge University Press.

Moro, C., & Rodriguez, C. (1989). L'interaction triadique bébé-objet-adulte dans la première année de la vie de l'enfant [Baby-object-adult triadic interaction during the first year of life]. *Enfance, 42*(1-2), 75-82.

Moro, C., & Rodriguez, C. (1997). Objet, signe et sémiosis. Fondements pour une approche sémiotique du développement préverbal [Object, sign and semiosis. Ground for a semiotical approach of preverbal development]. In C. Moro, B. Schneuwly, M. Brossard (Eds.), *Outils et signes. Perspectives actuelles de la théorie de Vygotski* [Tools and Signs. New perspectives in Vygotsky theory]. Berne, Switzerland: Peter Lang.

Peirce, C.S. (1931-1958). *Collected papers.* Cambridge, MA: Harvard University Press.

Piaget, J. (1952). *The origins of intelligence in children.* New York: Ballantine.

Piaget, J. (1954). *The construction of reality in the child.* New York: Ballantine.

Piaget, J. (1962). *Play, dreams, and imitation in childhood.* New York: W.W. Norton.

Rivière, A. (1990). *La psychologie de Vygotsky* [The psychology of Vygotsky]. Liège, Belgium: Mardaga.

Sinha, C. (1988). *Language and representation: A socionaturalistic approach to human development.* New York: Harvester Wheatsheaf.

Vygotsky, L.S. (1978). *Mind in society: The development of higher psychological processes.* Cambridge, MA: Harvard University Press.

Vygotsky, L.S. (1962). *Thought and language.* Cambridge, MA: MIT Press.

4

GESTURES, WORDS, AND OBJECTS: AN ANALYSIS OF POSSIBLE CONFIGURATIONS WITHIN INTERACTIVE DYNAMICS

Ana Luiza B. Smolka
Maria Nazare da Cruz
Universidade Estadual de Campinas, Brazil

INTRODUCTION

The moment a child begins to talk is taken as a turning point in development, both by parents, relatives and educators in their daily practice, and by psychological theories. Yet, one of the most intriguing questions within the scope of developmental studies concerns the configuration of first words by the young child and the functioning of language in the interactive movement.

Depending on the assumed theoretical framework, the emergence of the first words is interpreted and explained in different ways: derived from symbolic function, proceeding from the transformation of act ion into representations, as for Piaget (1975); necessary support for representation, as for Wallon (1979); indispensable and constitutive in mental organization and mental functioning, as for Vygotsky (1987).

We can say that each of the these theoretical positions imply distinct ways of conceiving the nature of human development and of considering thinking and speech relationships.

73

The undoubted importance of language, related to the diversified attempts to describe and explain the emergence of first words in ontogenesis still raise many questions concerning signifying processes and the locus of language in developmental psychology. Thematized within a historical-cultural perspective (Vygotsky, 1987; Bakhtin, 1981), in which the sign and symbolic activity acquire a central status, such questions become specially relevant. Our research work is developed in this perspective.

In this study, we raise the problem of sense production and signifying processes emergent in the interactive dynamics that happens in the daily routine of a day-care center. Assuming that the child is immersed in a human universe, in a cultural ambience, in a system of social relationships that sustain and support the organization and the meanings of his or her actions, we focus on movements and processes shared among adults and children, analyzing and discussing how words, gestures, and objects in the world become configured as such.

Taking as theoretical and methodological points of reference assumptions and constructs made explicit by Vygotsky and Bakhtin—as semiotic mediation and dialogical principles—we highlight from our weekly video-recordings in a public day-care center three situations for the analysis of signifying processes and sense production.

On two of these situations, we discuss the configuration of the Portuguese word *ai*, uttered by adults and children. This word (seen as an articulated, meaningful sound) is an interjection that primarily expresses pain, but it might carry such different meanings as discomfort, reproach, and protest, among others, and it might also be eventually related to assertions and reflexions in conversations. Because of such features, the word *ai* is distinct from other words that are usually focused on psychological and linguistic studies of young children's early language development that characteristically have a concrete object as referent. As the word *ai* can be related to sensations, emotional states, and motivations, it does not have an explicit object relatedness or referent.

In a third situation, we raise the issue of object relatedness and referent, discussing aspects of word-object relations in the dynamics of interactions.

Theoretical and Methodological Assumptions

We start our considerations by briefly highlighting and commenting on Piaget's (1975) and Vygotsky's (1987) perspectives, because they talk about the child's first words, analyzing data of 12-month-olds who designate different objects by the same word. Both of them are concerned, in their analyses, with logical processes and, more specifically, with concept formation. Their analyses allow us to establish some counterpoints and to raise some questions concerning sense production and the configuration of meanings and first words in the context of their occurrence.

In his explanation about the child's use of the word *au-au* to indicate different objects, people, and animals, Piaget considered the child's action as criteria for the grouping made under this word. Piaget understood that the term *au-au*, in the case analyzed by him, designates for the child not only dogs and everything that, is similar, but also everything the child sees from the balcony.

Piaget considered the child's first words as verbal schemas and, therefore, as generalizable ways of action. That is to say that the young child's words designate systems of possible actions and not objects. But generalization itself *proceeds* from the point of view of the subject, of his action, leading the child to establish between things designated by the same word "some kind of kinship subjectively felt" (Piaget, 1975, p. 283).

Vygotsky (1987) considered that the child establishes this kind of relationships between objects, according to the principle of associative complexes and syncretic images. An associative complex may rest in any relationship between objects perceived by the child, the relationship being a similarity, a contrast, or a simple spatial proximity. A *syncretic image* is an agglutination of a "vague and syncretic conglomeration of isolated objects" (Vygotsky 1987, p. 134), resulting from a tendency to compensate for the insufficiency of objective connections by the abundance of subjective connections.

Although both Vygotsky and Piaget acknowledged the diversity of meanings that the young child's first words may assume on different situations, they explained this fact in different ways, and they did not describe or analyze the interactive dynamics in which the word's uttering occurred. In short, these analyses on child-object interaction and not on social interaction.

Vygotsky, however, assumed the fundamentally social nature of children's mental functioning and first words and conceived of word meaning as a unit of generalization and social relationship. For him, social interaction presupposed generalization at the same time that generalization is only made possible in and social interaction. Hence, word meaning is understood as historical production, implying that it is not given, finished, and immobilized. On the contrary, "word meaning is inconstant. It changes during the child's development and with different modes of the functioning of though" (Vygotsky, 1987, p. 244).

This conception of the word meaning's production and transformation is related to the conception of generalization, given that, in his perspective, it is not only the content of the word that changes, but the very mode of reflecting and generalizing reality in the word.

Vygotsky's formulations can be articulated to Bakhtin's (1981) conceptions because, for the latter, "a multiplicity of meanings is the indicator that makes a word a word" (p. 130). In Bakhtin's perspective, meaning is understood as belonging to a word not in itself, but as a trace or feature of the interlocutor's possible communication and mutual understanding. Therefore, meaning is an effect of social interaction, and the organizing nucleus of any enunciation is external to the individual: "The most primitive human enunciation, even made by an individual organism is, from the point of view of its contents, of its meaning, organized outside of the individual by the extra-organic conditions of the social environment (Bakhtin, p. 121).

These statements by Vygotsky and Bakhtin constitute the theoretical and methodological anchor points from which we have been focusing signifying processes and the child's first words, emergent in the interactive, discursive dynamics. This focus marks the specificity of our study.

The research was carried out at a University day-care center, in Campinas, São Paulo Brazil, where periods of the infants' daily routine in a naturalistic environment were videotaped weekly for approximately 40 minutes. The group was composed of 25 children and 9 adults who took turns in such a way that at least four of them were caring for the children at each turn. The group of children changed periodically (approximately every 3 months); as the older children were transferred to other groups. Due to this institutional way of functioning, the total number of children participating in the study was 45.

The weekly recordings, during a continuous 6-month period, focused on 9- to 18-month-old children. From the tapes, we selected and gave priority to multiparty interactive episodes, not necessarily dyadic, with the purpose of identifying and relating indicators of children's appropriation of their experiences in a cultural matrix. The methodological option was for microethnographic and microgenetic analysis, which allow for description and interpretation of refined details.

Assuming that signifying processes emerge in cultural practices, we take the episodes as an empirical and methodological instance of occurrence of such practices in which sense and meaning are being produced. The identified processes in our analyses are not seen as given or inherent to the empirical material, but are considered as resulting from a theoretical and interpretive work that goes beyond that empirically observable. In this sense, the analytical procedure is conceived as a construction, a "constructive method" (Vygotsky, 1989, p. 55).

Signifying Processes in Interactive Dynamics

Episode 1.

The caregiver, Rosa, places a large pillow on the floor, close to the wall, and sits on it.

Natalia (15:6), Tais (16:11), and Jonathan (116:17) get close to her. As she sits, the caregiver stretches her legs. (At this same moment, another caregiver starts calling the children to the external area).

Rosa places Tais on her lap, and holds Jonathan's arms, making him sit on her knees.

As Jonathan sits;
Rosa: Ai!
Natalia (passing through on her way out): Ai!
Thamara (13:23) from farther: Ai! (coming closer)! Ai!
(Thamara gets close to Rosa.)
Rosa (liking at Thamara): Ai!
(Thamara starts to give Rosa soft pretend slaps.)
Bia (16:03), who is around, takes a look, gets closer, and also starts giving Rosa
soft slaps.
Rosa: Ai! Ai, ai, ai, ai!
(Bia and Thamara stop slaping, and look at Rosa.)
(Bia goes out.)
Thamara tries to give Rosa another slap.)
Rosa: Ai, ai, ai, ai!
One child (not identified in the tape): Ai!
(Thamara slaps Rosa once more.)
Rosa: Ai, ai, ai, ai!
Other children: Ai, ai! Ai, ai! Ai, ai!
(Children start leaving the room.)

We could say that the first *ai* heard in this episode can be taken as an
expression of pain and discomfort when the child sits on the adults' knees.
This *ai* echoes, however, in may different ways among children and adult, while
configuration an interactive dynamics.

Natalia says *"ai"* as she goes out, Thamara says *"ai"*, and repeats the ai,
as she approaches the scene. We could speak about the establishment of a
mimetic game, which stays on the borderline between accompanying gestures
that re-echo among participants and actual imitative gestures.'

Rosa goes into the game as she repeats and responds to the children, imitating
them. The word provokes slapping gestures from Thamara, and those are
imitated by Bia. The adult's pain expression and the children's (pretense)
slapping gestures get articulated in an ai that then turns into a motive for
playing. In this interplay, the ai gets transformed, impregnated by other
meanings in the interaction. The word gets new contours: the intonation, the
pitch, and the frequency of the ai change as it acquires different meanings.
When Rosa says ai, ai, ai, ai, for example, this "ai" condenses multiple
meanings: the pain, the discomfort; the very echoing, imitating game; the
eventual, playful reproaching.

Ai has no specific referent or explicit object relatedness, although it carries
multiple references in instantaneous and confused focuses of attention. As an
uttered word, the ai might become a certain focus of attention by and itself.
As such, it gets spread among the children, but in this very movement, it also
gets dissolved in the many different uttering mouths.

Our analyses point to diversified movements in the interactive dynamics that are interchangeably initiated by adult and children *in improviso*: At first, the word spoken by the adult and repeated by Natalia and Thamara transforms itself in its very echo. Then, Thamara's gesture—provoked by the word—is interpreted by the adult as an invitation to a playful activity. As the adult again utters the word ai, now in a different rhythm and intonation, in reply to Thamara's gesture, a new meaning pervades this gesture.

The child's gesture is form of reply to the adult's word, which seems to give it certain meaning. The gesture is thus brought up and signified by the word at the same time that it delineates a possible meaning for the word. As such, the gesture indicates the child's appropriation of socially conventionalized meanings.

In discussing the modes of apprehension of linguistic forms by the speaker, Bakhtin (1981) stressed that the important aspect in the interlocutory process is that which permits the linguistic form to become a suitable sign in a given concrete situation. Also for Vygotsky, the child's appropriation of socially conventionalized signification involves the apprehension and construing of relationships within the context of their occurrence.

As we assume the same perspective in relation to the gesture, the child's slapping in the episode can be interpreted as movement of appropriation of conventional meanings, because it shows itself appropriate and adequate to the context of its emergence.

The child slaps, and if this gesture is related to the word ai, it is by the adult answering to the gesture that the playful activity with the word gets structured. The speech and voice of the adult sustain and condense possible meanings— pain, echo, play and reproach.

We could say, then, that in the interaction with the adult whose interpretations are socially circumscribed, diverse moments of meaning stabilization become configured, as the child turns into his or her own (appropriates) something that is pertinent and proper to the situation from the point of view of the social group.

Episode 2.

After a brief dispute around a cup of water, involving five children, Jonathan (16:24) and Gisele (12:28) hold Natalia's (15:13) arms and t-shirt. Jonathan goes away and Gisele holds Natalia's arm and shirt from the back.

Natalia, walking forward as Gisele holds on to her: aie, aie! (an intonational variant of *ai*) ai! ai! aie!
Rosa: Gisele! Careful there, uh? You two!
(The girls stop, take a short look at Rosa.)
Natalia, taking Gisele's right hand off her shoulders: aie! ai! ai! (while Gisele, still holding Natalia with her left hand, places her right hand again on Natalia's

shoulder). ai! (walking forward and leaving Gisele behind). Gisele tries again to hold on to Natalia's shoulders at the same time when Natalia leans forward saying: ai!
(Gisele falls on her knees.)
(Natalia turns back, sees Gisele on the floor, stretches her right arm to pull Gisele's hair, and pulls Gisele's hair with both hands): ai! aie!
(As Natalia pulls Gisele's hair, Gisele holds on to Natalia's shirt pushing herself to stand up. Gisele stands up at the same time Natalia stops pulling her hair. Gisele holds on again to Natalia's shirt as Natalia utters some unclear word with the same intonation. Natalia walks forward muttering, Gisele holding her shoulder.)
Rosa: Gisele!
Natalia (walking): ai!
(Gisele goes away.)
Natalia (walking): ai!
(Natalia stops and looks at Gisele going away.)

In this episode, the ai expression spoken by Natalia on a certain rhythm—ai, ai, aie—seems to bring the meanings of complaint, fight, discomfort, protest, and so on. In 36 seconds, Natalia utters ai 14 times. In fact, she is the one to say ai during the hole event, while suffering some actions (having her arms and t-shirt pulled), or while acting on the other (pulling Gisele's hair).

Examining the girls' interactive movements, we observe that they change positions: In a first moment, Gisele is the one to provoke Natalia's discomfort; later, Natalia might have provoked Gisele's pain.

It was expectable that, when Gisele falls down and Natalia pulls her hair, Gisele would cry or complain. Actually, Gisele does not say anything and does not cry. The adults in the room are busy and seem not to pay attention at this moment (except for the research who is recording), so they also do not say anything. Thus, it is Natalia who speaks, who still has and keeps the word, whether suffering the action of the other or acting herself and provoking sensations.

Natalia's utterances become significant as they may acquire different functions and multiple meanings: They may express, designate, signify, and concentrate actions, emotions, sensations, relations, and positions, in the whole event.

What Natalia says is quite appropriate to the situation, carrying diverse meanings as well as a synthesis of social positions—she speaks for herself and for the others: discomfort, protest, pain, and even reproach might be condensed in her speech.

We could interpret Natalia's utterances as instances of appropriation of cultural experiences she makes or transforms into her own the words of others in different positions. In theoretical terms, this appropriation movement seems to imply the idea of pertinence, acceptability, and adequacy concerning social practices and norms.

Episode 3.
   Marina, the caregiver, is sitting on a bench singing a children's song and a child calls her when the scene begins to be focused by the camera.

Marina: Yeah! The little stick!
(Ééé. O pauzinho!)
Look the little duck, look, look! (placing a little duck with wheels on the floor)
O o patinho ó, ó!)
   Breno (13m;29d) and Carolina (15m;26d), who are standing beside Marina sitting on a bench, look at the toy on the floor. Marina pushes the toy that moves forward. Carolina points to the toy (with her pointing finger straight).
Marina: It is the little duck!
(É o patinho!)
Look there!
(O lá!)
Carolina walks to the toy with her finger still pointing. She picks up the duck and gives it back to Marina. Breno tries to get the little stick Marina holds in her left hand.
Marina: Look there, the little duck!
(O la, o patinho!)
Look there!
(O la!)
Carolina walks to the toy with her finger still pointing. She picks up the duck and gives it back to Marina. Breno tries to get the little stick Marina holds in her left hand.
Marina: Look there, the little duck!
(O lá, o patinho!)
Marina looks and smiles to Danilo (16m;8d) who approaches the scene also holding a little stick and making sounds.
Marina: Hi! (getting the duck from Carolina)
(Oi!)
Hi! (looking at Danilo and putting the duck on the floor.
(Oi!)
Marina pushing the little duck imitating the noise and the honk of a car): Ooonn!
Bi-bi!
Marina leans back on the bench, looks forward and turns to Danilo: Look the little duck!
(Olha o patinho)

   The adult and children get involved with a toy, a little wooden duck with wheels. The adult says "little duck" (patinho) many times. At the beginning, she names and pushes the toy. As she speaks and acts on the object, Marina also calls the children's attention to the toy and to her own action. Hence, her speech condenses reference to an object, reference to her own action, and establishing and maintaining contact with the children.

When Carolina points to the object, Marina names it and also points to it, interpreting the child's gesture and sustaining the interactive dynamics. As she names the object, saying: "It is the little duck," Marina assumes that the child's gesture (pointing) is referring to the object, and that in this same gesture is implied a sort of interrogation. So, she states, she repeats, and she confirms.

The pointing gesture was taken by Vygotsky as mediator in the configuration of the child's first word meanings, as a transition between a purely affective expression and objective speech. This conception is related to the way he considered the child's first words, as initially having only a nominative function and, semantically, an objective reference. For Vygotsky, the pointing gesture was the precursor of this capacity of objectively referring to something through speech. However, in his own perspective, the very reference function does not happen on a direct relation between the word and the object, but on a mediated path, which implies the interaction with the adult. Just then, through mediation, the word of the other acquires meaning (for the child).

In our episode, Carolina does not only point to the object; she gets it and turns it back to the adult, producing a certain (re)action, a new reply, from the adult: The adult repeats the action and renames the object, establishing a sort of interplay among the participants based on the repetition of the interactive sequence developed with and around the object.

This leads to some questions concerning the child's understanding of the adult's words, because we suspect that the word (or word's functions) is (or are) not limited to a link between word and object, but is related with the many different perspectives and orientations and many possible meanings that circulate in the interactive dynamics.

Luria (1988) mentioned that the nominating function of the word—called *object reference*—develops in the child and becomes sufficiently stable around 4 years of age. Referring to data collected on research about the understanding babies have of adults speech, he showed that, at an early age, the object reference is unstable, depending on the context of the words uttered the concrete conditions, such as who speaks, the intonation, and even the spatial position of the child. Luria, however, talked about experimental situation and did not approach this question from the point of view of signifying processes and sense production in daily interlocutory movements.

In our studies, we have been trying to approach the child's possible comprehension and participation in sense production not only in relation to a given and fixed meaning, but in relation to senses and meanings built in everyday interactions, and in informal, daily discursive dynamics.

From the last episode, it becomes particularly interesting to raise this issue, due to the specificity of the objected being manipulated and referred to: It is a toy duck with wheels; it is not a "real" duck; it is not a copy or reproduction (such as stuffed animal). The fat that it has wheels, easily allowing for pushing and pulling, is highlighted through the adult's actions and speech.

As she pushes the duck, by the end of episode, Marina imitates the sound of a car and a honk, thus expanding possible meanings related to the object. In her way of acting and speaking, the wooden duck's movement is linked to the movement and sound of cars; her action of pushing is also related to pushing toy cars.

In this way, Marina's speech highlights her own action and the effect of such action on the object, not referring here to the object as such. Her speech is invested with a multiplicity of meanings: More than the name of an object, more than the simple establishing of an objective reference, the multiple sense of the word condense culturally determine and possible actions and interactions, becoming configured in the interactive dynamics.

In such interactive dynamics, the adult points, names, highlights objects, action, and relationships: The child's appropriation and signification of objects always implies the word of the other. The act of nominating an object through a word seems to imply a cultural mode of identifying, understanding, and inserting it in a certain system of social relationships. However, one object can be identified in many different ways through a word, given that there is always a point of view, a referential perspective (Wertsch, 1985) involved in any act of reference. We could say that as word always generalizes, it also allows for a particular version and vision of a concrete object in a certain meaningful context. If mediation by the other, by the word, is inescapable or is a condition to make an object meaningful, it implies, at the same time, the impossibility of a direct apprehension (of the object) by the child.

As we have already pointed out the adult's speech condenses reference to the object and other culturally determined possibilities of action on it. As she says "Ooonn! Bi-bi! / Look the duck!," the adult highlights specificities of the object and of (her own) actions. This opens multiple possibilities of signification and meaning; at the same time that circumscribes actions and relationships.

What we still want to point out (although this needs further elaboration) is that in this very interactive and complex dynamics a word begins to become configured as such. Studies on psycholinguistics, semantics, and pragmatics have been thematizing this issue. From our perspective, at this moment, it is sufficient but important to call attention to a simultaneous movement of delineation, configuration, detaching, or *crafting* of words and objects in and from the continuum of experiences.

In the episode, if the word *patinho* (little duck) is recurrent and appears many times, it is immersed in the continuum of the adult's speech—as other words and sounds: "eee/o/o; o la/olha"—and can become discrete, relevant, and meaningful in the many different forms of saying, referring, assuring, confirming, calling attention, and relating:

Ééé. O pauzinho!
O a patinho, ó, ó!

É o patinho
O lá!
O lá o patinho!
Õõõnn! Bi-bi! Olha o
(Yeah! The Little stick)
(Look the little duck, look, look)
(It is the little duck)
(Look there)
(Look there the little duck)
patinho! (Õõõnn! Bi-bi! Look the
little duck)

From this situation, we would point out that recurrence and diversity of sounds and intonational nuances get configured and established within interactional movements in which multiple sense might be produced. In the dynamics of sense production, the adult's speech seems to sustain and condense the (conventional) nucleus of meaning stabilization as well as possibilities of transformation. Hence, we could say that the same movement that expands and opens multiple possibilities of senses and meanings is the very movement that allows for and makes viable social convention, stabilization, and precision.

FINAL CONSIDERATIONS

As we centered our analyses on the empirical material, we primarily aimed at inquiring about and exploring possibilities of seeing and highlighting the emergence of first words in the social dynamics of sense production.

In a first moment, we focused on some movements in which the word of the adult echoes among the young children and provokes a gesture, becoming delineated in a process that involves multiplicity and dispersion of meanings, as well as moments of meaning stabilization.

Then we focused on the word uttered by a child in an appropriation movement—adequability, pertinence—of words, and voices of others. In such a movement, the word emerges—polysemic, polyphonic—condensing meanings and synthesizing social positions.

In a third moment, we discussed aspects implied in word-object relations, pointing out that in same process in which the adult's speech and the continuum of the child's experience and productions become somehow delineated or highlighted in the interactive dynamics, the possible emerging senses become, at the same time, amplified and restricted, configurating, in may different ways, objects, actions, and relationships, and constituting meaningful words and gestures in a system of cultural conventions.

This mode of considering signifying processes, of giving priority to the collective movement of sense production, leads to the questioning of conceptions that attribute to the individual the origin of meaning, as well as those that assume the object reference as the main feature of the child's first words. We think that this way of approaching the issue might contribute to the (re)dimensioning of the locus of language in developmental psychology

ACKNOWLEDGMENTS

This research work was sponsored by grants of FAPESP—Fundação de Amparo à Pesquisa do Estado de São Paulo. A preliminary version of the study was presented at the Vygotsky and the Contemporary Human Sciences Conference, Moscow, 1994.

REFERENCES

Bakhtin, M. (1981). *Marxismo e Filosofia da Linguagem* [Marxism and the Philosophy of Language]. São Paulo, Brazil: Hucitec.
Luria, A.R. (1982). Language and Cognition. New York: John Wiley & Sons.
Piaget, J. (1975). *Play, dreams and imitation in childhood*. Rio de Janeiro, Brazil: Zahar.
Volshino, V.N. (1973). *Marxism and the philosophy of language*. New York: Seminar Press.
Vygotsky, L.S. (1989). Concrete human psychology. *Soviet Psychology* 27(2), 53-77.
Vygotsky, L.S. (1987). *The Collected Works of L.S. Vygotsky, Vol. 1, Problems of General Psychology*. R. Rieber & A. Carton (Eds.). New York: Plenum Press.
Wallon, H. (1979). *Do Ato ao Pensamento*. Lisbon, Portugal: Moraes Editora.
Wertsch, J.V. (1985). *Vygotsky and the social formation of mind*. Cambridge, MA: Harvard University Press.

5

MAKING OF PERSONAL PLACE
AT 18 MONTHS OF AGE

Vera M.R. de Vasconcellos
Universidade Federal Fluminense, Brazil

Jaan Valsiner
Clark University

Persons constantly enter new environments and reorganize them so that they become "their own." Furthermore, existing environments change as novel objects are introduced into them. Persons who inhabit these environments adjust their personal sense system to incorporate the newly introduced objects, and to make use of them in their conduct.

In this chapter, we examine the microgenesis of the construction of personal place in the course of one child's play in the context of a day-care center. Within the center's playroom, children's peer group activities abound. In play, a child is always involved in both intrapsychological and interpsychological processes of transformation of experience into semiotically encoded means for future encounters in the life world (Mead, 1910, 1912, 1913). We are interested in the complexity of these transformations in a child's play and their role in the emergence of the child's personal place-the structure of the child's environment constructed by the child in the given immediate context, under episodic inputs from peers and adults.

Research on sociogenetic origins of personal cognitive phenomena has largely overlooked the intensive constructive activity that goes on in everyday settings. Using traditions of "participatory observation" (Rogoff, 1990) and contemporary interest in "socially situated activities" as relevant contexts for cognitive development, this research orientation has successfully focused the attention of psychologists on the contextual embeddedness of cognitive development. However, what has been overlooked (as a result of discovering the intricate connection between the child and the socially organized environment) is the child's constructive action, by which new psychological phenomena come into existence. Although the epistemological perspectives of Wallon, Piaget, and Vygotsky have emphasized the idea of construction in human development, the discipline of developmental psychology has rarely used its methodology to explicate construction in process, or to specify the essentially social nature of the individual human being, whose actions are continually being confronted with those of others, and redefined by the confrontation. The goal of this chapter is to apply the notion of construction to a concrete real-life episode of child-environment interaction.

THEORETICAL UNDERPINNINGS

We believe that children create what is necessary for reaching their personal goals through social mediation in their interpersonal relations with peers. In turn, the goals are, through social mediation, changed dynamically and replaced by new personal interests. New general interests are enabled and bound to personal goals. The possibility for real conflict arises, based on new individual interests. During this process, the peer relationship can be transformed into an "instrumental relationship." The peer could be utilized by the target child as a resource to build up and reach personal goals. The other child is a condition for the target child to achieve his or her own aims. The play activity is constructed both by coordination of an individual's goals or interests and perseverance in the construction of common goals among preferred peers. The former tend to be brief alliances and the latter are more persistent alliances with greater emotional content. The understanding of social interaction as a mechanism to achieve personal goals is here related with the possibility of seeing it as a way of achieving goals. Social interaction becomes not only a goal in itself, but a meaningful process for the creation of new goals. It can be seen as a means to an end, rather than being only an end in itself.

A Coconstructionist Stance In Developmental Psychology

The present orientation is an elaboration of the sociogenetic theories of Vygotsky (Van der Veer & Valsiner, 1994) and Wallon (1942, 1945). The social world in which a child is embedded presents her or him with meaningful constructions made by the previous generation, in anticipation that the child will build one's own meaningful world on this basis. The child is independently dependent in relation to her or his social environment (Winegar, Renninger, & Valsiner, 1989) and, indeed, utilizes the collective culturally meaningful surroundings to build his or her personal understanding of the world. Yet the ways in which the latter is constructed are the child's own-each child creates a unique personal world. The individual child is dependent on the social group for continued personal development, but is at the same time prepared to change that group in a creative way. The process of construction of individual subjectivity is understood here as the simultaneous construction of subjective agency and intersubjectivity. It can be argued that individual development is the development of individuals within—and through—social relationships. The creative action usually takes place under circumstances in which there exists a temporary convergence of individual and collective goal orientations (Branco & Valsiner, 1992; Fogel & Branco, 1997). However, given the redundancy of developmental processes, the construction of personal place (and sense) is also possible in purely individual conduct. Children can construct their own development via interaction with peers and more experienced social others, as well as in play. Development of culturally guided subjective constructions of personal sense (intrapsychologically) and personal place (in the sphere of socially shared environments) is guaranteed in human ontogeny.

Dynamic Views on Person-Environment Relations in Environmental Psychology

Despite a number of traditions in child psychology that have attempted to address the issues of children's relationships with experienced environments (e.g., Lewin, 1927; Muchow, 1931; Muchow & Muchow, 1935; see also Wohlwill, 1985), contemporary developmental psychology has been remarkably inefficient in taking the child's perspective and making sense of the heterogeneity of the world (Valsiner, 1989). However, in contemporary environmental psychology it is possible to locate a number of efforts to conceptualize the relationship of a person with his or her immediate sociospatial environment (Altman, 1993; Altman & Gauvain, 1981; Altman & Lowe, 1992; Bonnes-Dobrowolny & Secchiaroli, 1978; Lawrence, 1981, 1985; Saile, 1985; Werner & Altman, 1996; Werner, Altman & Oxley, 1985). Most of the efforts in environmental psychology have focused on how adults subjectively relate to either their immediate environments (spatial arrangements within the home) or to their macroenvironments. In those cases, the specific forms of relationships are already established, rather than in the process of formation. These relationships may be maintained by a dynamic (or dialectical—see Altman & Gauvain, 1981; Werner & Altman, 1996) process.

Undoubtedly the most dynamically oriented general scheme that has been generated within environmental psychology, and that has potential for the developmental study of children's construction of personal place, is Altman's dialectical perspective on personalization of space. This perspective has grown out of Altman's interest in adult privacy issues, as those are dynamically regulated by environmental structures. Hence two pairs of dialectical opposites have appeared in Altman's work as major creators of tension in person-place relationships: identity <—> communality and accessibility <—> inaccessibility (Altman & Gauvain, 1981, pp. 316-317; see also Altman, 1993). Research on the social organization of home spaces in different cultures has indicated the presence of such tensions (Lawrence, 1981, 1985) and the construction of ritualistic forms for overcoming them (Saile, 1985). Furthermore, the temporal aspects of events-in-environments have been given relevant attention (Werner, at al. 1985). The existing environmental context sets up (affords) a range of possible actions by the persons (of given age and cultural backgrounds), which then unfold at a specific pace and are rhythm-bounded by the actors' cultural conceptualization of time in respect to their actions. Altman (1993) conceptualized dialectical processes in person-environment relationships as taking place in parallel at three levels: intraindividual, interpersonal, and intergroup processes, looking for his basic dialectical oppositions at each level.

The Present Focus

The focus on dialectical tension between opposites fits well with our developmental co-constructionist emphasis (Vasconcellos & Valsiner, 1993, 1995). However, differently from the traditions of environmental psychology, where the person-environment relationships can be posited to exist in some (dialectical) form, developmental research is interested in the emergence of such oppositional organization in child-environment relationships. Our analysis of young children's construction of personal place in a creche environment allows us to concentrate on the two types of interaction as a way to achieve goals or a way to create shared goals together with a peer. The younger the child the more difficult it is to make a distinction between these two types of peer interaction, because they have not yet become differentiated.

Place-Making as Externalization.   Children's construction of personal place in a peer group setting can be viewed as the externalization process of intrapersonal semiotic construction of the given setting. The intramental processes remain inaccessible in any observational study of children in peer groups, yet their externalized products can be observed in the course of the unfolding of the child's actions. By creating new rules (for oneself, and insisting on peers' acceptance of they) for actions within (and with) certain spatial conditions (and objects), the child gives us a glimpse of the dynamics of the intrapersonal semiotic construction process. Usually, it is within the realm of children's interaction with others where such semiotic creativity has been noted by investigators (e.g., Lyra & Rossetti-Ferreira, 1995). However, human beings are known to fill all of their relations with the whole environment with specific personal-cultural meanings (see Csikszentmihalyi & Rochberg-Halton, 1981, for adults' personal-cultural construction).

We are interested here in looking at similar co-constructive processes in the case of young children. As we show, Altman's dialectical oppositions are not there within the children's environments in a creche, but come into being as a child acts to delineate the specific place (in a location and using resources that defy adults' expectations). Once this step of differentiation of the personal place from general communal space has taken place, the child constructs for it specific forms of solutions for the dialectical oppositions at the interpersonal level: the individuality of the constructed place and the child's autonomy within it become continually asserted, with selectivity for closedness to (and connectedness with) specific peers becoming a corollary to the constructed personal control of personal place.

The Meaning of Personal Place and Its Construction.   From the general perspectives already outlined we examine the microgenesis of the construction of personal place, and the structure of the environment constructed by the child in a given immediate context, with episodic input from peers and adults. The psychological organization of personal place simultaneously entails internalized (meaning-based emotional reflection upon the place) and externalized (purposeful actions to organize, expand or constrict, defend, use, and eventually abandon the constructed personal place). As pointed out earlier, the resources for the child's construction of his or her personal place are social (that is, adults' arrangement of the environment, their direct or indirect social canalization of children's actions within it, likewise children's peer relationships based on action strategies) yet the child as a co-constructive personal agent constructs the actual personal place within the ongoing flow of conduct.

MAKING A PLACE AT AGE 18 MONTHS

Among toddlers all social alliances are temporary. They normally appear in situations where similar meanings are about to be shared by peers, on the basis of their simillar developmental levels. The alliance is constantly reevaluated within conflicts. The child acts in specific ways, which may be confronted with the other child's action plans, or trigger associatively determined processes (Basov, 1931/1991) of a contradictory kind in the others. Each one of these expressions portrays the shape of real personal (individual) interests in the making. Negotiations occur within the conflicts that happen as part of play activities. In order to retain the association between peers, the alliances produce a power-based emotional affiliation between the children, which makes it possible to identify the "preferred peer" status (Vasconcellos, 1986).

The emotional affiliation exists in a constant state of tension in relation to the other children who are present in the same group, as well as in relation to the caregivers' action plans. The other children's conduct is a constant reason for the disintegration of the peer alliances, because the emerging personal sense systems and goal orientations between the pairs are not shared. Young children's apparent cohesion with peers' interests has to be based on concrete external elements (objects or features) that hold the dyad together. The regulation and integration of interests for each other or for a common object occur in an emotional and cognitive disequilibrium. This unequal but proximal distribution of emotional and cognitive power in peer relationships exists not only among preferred peers, but also with the whole group. This imbalance affords an opportunity for the child who is being used as a means to construct personal goals. These two kinds of relationship present in children's interaction, that is, the instrumental relation (goals attempted to be reached through interaction) and the relation of intersubjectivity (goals reached through joint negotiation of personal senses) exist in parallel in childen's play activities. In order for a single child to build up his or her own place to play, he or she makes use of the other child (or children) in play, as well as sharing the uncertainty of his or her interests and goals in the action of constructing together the meanings of activities.

Studies have demonstrated the importance of spatial arrangements as a support for peer interaction among children younger than 3 years old (Campos de Carvalho, 1989, 1990; Rubiano & Rossetti-Ferreira; Campos de Carvalho, 1989: Campos de Carvalho & Rossetti-Ferreira, 1993; Legendre, 1983, 1987, 1989; Legendre & Fantaine, 1991). These studies are based on the belief that the spatial arrangement of environments for children in a peer group expresses the educational philosophy as well as the quality of day care (Campos de Carvalho, 1990). It has been demonstrated that the establishment of special "circumscribed zones" in children's group environments promote specific ways of social interaction within these zones, as well as lure the children away from other areas in the available spatial structure. When these zones begin to suggest to children specific meaningful objects, this promotion is especially enhanced (Campos de Carvalho, Meneghini, & Mignorance, 1994).

Hence we look at a specific context in a children's peer group, in which adult caregivers introduce a spatial novelty.

The Subjects and Context

The empirical material used here is taken from the play behavior of an 18-month-old girl in an infants' peer group in a Brazilian day-care center, in

Rio de Janeiro. Most of these infants' families live in slums or very poor suburbs. The data were obtained by the first author from the video recording of free-play sessions (12 weekly observations) of a group of eight infants and toddlers. Episodes of constructive play involving joint actions of the target girl with two or more other children are analyzed, with the focus on the microgenesis of the personal place of the target child in the given socially organized physical environment.

On the day of the reported observations, the creche's caregiver and the researcher discussed the role of spatial arrangements in free activities, which has the objective of promoting good developmental conditions for children through interactive situations among peers. The understanding shared between them included the following: (a) children explore, discover and initiate actions in a familiar environment by selecting partners as well as objects and places for play; to carry out their play activities, some changes in the environment according to their goals are necessary; and (b) adults organize the environment in accordance with their personal or pedagogical goals, and these plans are based on their anterior knowledge of children's abilities in their age group.

The Example

The caregiver and the researcher organized the environment with a new colorful cloth tunnel, a new decoration for the baby's room, in order to see how the children organized themselves to explore the new toy. In the very beginning the caregiver suggests to the group of children how to play with the new toy. The group of young children play around it, with their attention divided between the new toy and the caregiver, who embraces some of them.

The target girl of this episode, Pamela, is hugged (with another child) by the caregiver, after being criticized for hitting a friend. Meanwhile, a second child, Bruna, has found a doll and is walking around carrying it. Most of the other children are going around the novel object (the tunnel), episodically exploring small objects, abandoning them and going to others, without an apparent interest in any of them in particular. We analyze the episode by looking at a sequence of scenes in the children's play.

Scene 1: New Toy: A Colorful Tunnel

1.a— (4 min. 59 sec). Pamela is in the middle of the room; she turns around, wandering toward the tunnel. When she comes close to the tunnel, she turns right, looking at it, and sits inside a semicircle made by the long toy tunnel. She is inviting someone to sit with her, as well as calling the videotape operator to sit beside her.

1.b— (5 min. 45 sec change scene). She is fiddling around with the toy tunnel. Another child, Bia, comes to sit by her side. Pamela messes her friend's hair and clothes, while talking with the third child. This is not the child that she at first invited.

1.c— (6 min. 17 sec). Pamela leaves her companion and returns to tap the tunnel. The child that had sat beside her comes to do the same thing she is doing (imitates her actions).

The researcher's intention in bringing this tunnel into the children's group environment was to make a new arrangement for the children's room, in order to see how they organize themselves to explore the new toy. In reality, the tunnel did not attract the group in the manner expected by the caregivers. It was used in exploratory activities by the children only in the presence of the caregiver. Children rarely persisted in acting on it after she left. They explored the external features of the tunnel, but rarely did the children use the rest of the possibilities it afforded (exploring the interior of the tunnel).

1.d— (6 min. 32 sec). Suddenly Bruna, a girl with a doll, appears from the toy tunnel. The target girl goes through the tunnel to its end, imitating Bruna but going in the opposite direction from that taken by Bruna with her doll. The third child tries to imitate the first. Pamela reaches the end of the tunnel, continues to crawl and goes to see the third child who is still trying to go into the tunnel, without success.

Pamela is ready to crawl through the tunnel, repeating Bruna's action. It could be more than imitation of a peer's action, a search for a friend who has the doll. Bia, the youngest among them, has insufficient motor coordination to crawl as quickly as the others. She tries, but gets stuck in the tunnel's entrance. Bia is always following Pamela, who does not pay too much attention to her. Pamela is busy wondering what to do next.

Scene 2: The Box: A Topographical Feature

2.a— (7 min. 17 sec). By accident, Pamela discovers an empty box close to the tunnel and hops into it. Bia goes to join her. Pamela reacts with ambiguity, pushes Bia away softly and does not help her to get into the box, but when Bia succeeds Pamela hugs her while calling another child.

If the tunnel entails the suggestion of "going into it," the unexpected object (the box) was a closer object that could give the same suggestion without being predesignated to do so. The child (Pamela) transfers the idea of going into, being in, and playing on, from the tunnel to the box. The box-a circumscribed area different from the tunnel-allows the child to play in a bounded, secure place with a clear view of the entire room.

Being one of the oldest in the group, Pamela promotes an imitative affiliation with the younger (Bia) around the same action (going into) and the same object (the box). Anything in the room could be transformed into a place to join and play. Some places, such as the box, are more suggestive by their structure (Vasconcellos, 1993). The process of play is formed in the beginning from several distinct casual actions, which have nothing in common and are related in the child's play only in time. The previous facts can not be suggested as the reason for any further development but the child's construction of meaning is dependent on them as well as the interpretation of these facts from his or her social environment (the other children). The construction of meaning is a nonstop process in the entire group.

2.b— (8 min. 43 sec). Pamela calls the caregiver who comes close, followed by a child, who had been called by Pamela. This girl brings a piece of a puzzle to give to the caregiver, who does not realize the girl's intention, because she is busy justifying to Pamela the impossibility of her going into the box. Pamela takes the piece of the other girl's puzzle and gives it to the caregiver.

Pamela could have called the caregiver in order to complain about Bia's persistent presence and invasion of her box, but the adult understands it as an invitation to join her in the box. It is interesting to note that the semistructured area formed by the box evokes the adult's attention as well as the children's. The adult seems to respond more to the people in the box in comparison to children from less defined spaces in the same playroom.

Scene 3: The Doll Comes to the Scene

3.a— (9 min. 23 sec). Bruna, who has the doll, also comes to see the scene. She pulls the tunnel to have more space close to the box. She is looking around, following the caregiver with her eyes. She looks at Pamela, as if to ask if she may climb into the box. Pamela nods her head. Pamela invites Bruna to join them inside the little box, by waving her hands and head and holding Bruna's hand.

3.b— (9 min. 45 sec). Bruna tries to go into the box by pushing Bia. Bia rejects her entry by pushing her away. Pamela holds Bruna's legs, and hits Bia twice and tells her to leave ("go away" = "vai embora"). While being pulled by Pamela, Bruna drops the doll and looks at it while moving away. Immediately, Pamela picks up the doll and puts it into the box.

The doll is dropped on to the floor when Pamela tries to help Bruna climb into the box. Pamela picks it up, and then the doll becomes the center of her play. This is not necessarily perceived or shared by the other two girls (Bia and Bruna). It becomes Pamela's individual focus.

3.c— (10 min. 49 sec). Bia leaves the box by herself and Pamela is moving around inside the box, holding the doll. Then the second girl (Bruna) comes to join Pamela in the box. Then Bia comes back to see the other two, and continues looking at them, while scratching her belly for long time.

Pamela and Bruna begin a harmonious joint life by sharing the small space of the box. In contrast to her previous actions toward Bia, Pamela now takes the initiative in joint activity, and Bruna passively participates in it.

Bruna's activity, like that of other children in the earliest stages of development, has a general lack of clear purpose. Her action is simple movement from one place to another, wandering until another child's interest in her affects her and pulls her into a simultaneous construction of intersubjectivity.

The box starts to be a clear topographical feature (using Legendre's term; see Legendre, 1987), an enclosed area that modifies the physical spatial arrangement and provokes intrapersonal semiotic construction of this given setting.

Scene 4

4.a— (11 min. 27 sec). Bia moves away. Pamela calls the caregiver, who comes back followed by a number of other children, including one girl who is there as an observer. Before leaving, the caregiver suggests to the fourth girl that she go into the tunnel and she obeys.

The caregiver comes to the scene, and with her a dispersed group of young children, who tend to remain near her, moving with her from place to place.

The interaction between Bia and John, the strongest boy of the group, takes place by way of short expressions and signals, and sometimes a few words. To an adult observer, making sense of communication in this age group is a considerable task. Bia, who is being pushed away, persists in her effort to stay.

4.b— (12 min. 24 sec). Bia comes back and picks up a small piece of wood from Pamela's box, and moves away again. Pamela shouts for her toy, and the caregiver asks Bia to give it back to Pamela.

Bia's personal interest is created through tension with Pamela's interests and her emerging differentiation from Pamela. Bia does everything to keep Pamela's attention, including taking the toy from her. Meanwhile, she is creating common goal orientations with John in another moment of affiliation or fusion of intentions.

4.c— (12 min. 43 sec). Bia obeys, but starts to exchange shouts with Pamela. Meanwhile, Bruna moves away and John comes to look at them (Bia and Pamela), and starts to hit Pamela, after she has snatched his stick toy.

The emotional tone present in Bia's and Pamela's actions are observed to be particularly intense at that moment. Bruna, John, and the other children give the impression that they are a group of observers confronting and expecting the end of the dispute between Pamela and Bia.

Bruna, who usually tends not to fight, moves away. The negotiation of fused interests in play activities is full of alternation, confrontation, and successes.

Scene 5: Peers' Affiliation With a Common Goal

5.a— (13 min. 31 sec). John starts to hit Pamela on the head. She does not react but only shouts at him, while he keeps hitting her. He hits her several times, moves away and comes back with a big plastic ball to continue hitting her (14 min. 1 sec). He tries several ways of hitting Pamela's head. Bia (the third girl) joins him in hitting Pamela with a plastic train.

Another interesting affiliation to be noted is the link created by Bia and John. When Bia was pushed out of the box by Pamela, she went to complain about her lucklessness to John, the strongest boy in the group. Back with John as her new companion, Bia could use her physical force against Pamela. Together with him she can be very abusive to her old companion (Pamela).

5.b— (14 min. 10 sec). Pamela does not cry or shout, and continues to play busy, with the doll and the stick toy inside the box.

Pamela is handling the problem of being hit without crying or screaming for adult help. After several attempts, she finally succeeds in staying alone in the place that she constructs for herself and with an object (the doll), which is the center of her interest.

Pamela first shares the box with Bia in an ambiguous pushing and cuddling manner. With Bruna she is different. Pamela calls her, looking forward to playing with her or looking at her doll. Bruna is the child who has possessed the focus object, the doll, since the beginning of the episode. The regulation between these two girls of their mutual interest in sharing a place to play could be motivated by Pamela's personal interest in having the doll to play with. Bruna might be being used as an instrument for Pamela's achievement of her personal goal.

5.c— (14 min. 30 sec). A much younger girl, who has been an observer, tries to play with Pamela and the doll. She tries to hold it, and drops it on the floor while Pamela shouts at her. Pamela moves swiftly, moving her body out of the box to bring the doll back to her place. She does it by keeping one leg inside the box, showing a clear intention of saving her own place to play.

Pamela does not react. The young child carefully observes this and her continuous and serious construction of her own play activity. Pamela's grimace has been remarkably effective in keeping her away. The young girl is a busy observer of the dyadic affiliation of John and Bia.

5.d— (14 min. 49 sec). John and Bia find a similar box full of small toys and tip it over throwing all the toys on the floor. But the noise made by the small toys keep their attention away from the box, leading John and Bia to explore and play with the small toys together.

In a constant interaction or friendly affiliation, John and Bia find another box like Pamela's. They are taken by the small objects that fall out of the box. Their attention moves from the box to the small toys. As has been said before, the young children's apparent cohesion with peers' interests had to be based on concrete objects or a clear common goal. In this dyad the common goal is hitting Pamela as well as finding another box to go into, or play with the small toys that come from it.

Scene 6: Building One's Own Place to Play

6.a— (15 min. 25 sec). Now, Pamela is quietly playing by herself, inside her box with her small doll, as well as with other small toys.

Finally, Pamela builds her moment of increased self-other distinction; she differentiates herself from the whole context. Now she can be involved with the construction of her understanding of the symbolic aspects of her own actions.

6.b— (15 min. 58 sec). John moves back and forth, hitting Pamela several times, and throws a big plastic train at her. She throws it back, paying no attention to him. He hits her again and is imitated by another boy, who was passing by. Pamela reacts, but without leaving her place.

John is persevering and tenacious in hitting Pamela. He is motivated by her nonreaction and the persistent activity with which she is concerned, that is playing with the doll. By simple contagion and imitation of John's actions, the other boy acts against Pamela. This exemplifies how the whole group is emotionally and cognitively contaminated by their fighting.

6.c— (16 min. 16 sec). At this point, a small boy tries to get into the box but Pamela hits him, keeping him away from her place.

6.d— (16 min. 58 sec). Pamela still plays in her box, cleaning it by throwing out small toys that John and Bia had thrown at her. Suddenly, she gets out, carrying her doll in her hand, and heads to the nurse's room.

In sum, we observe the following sequence in Pamela's construction of her own personal place to play in a peer group setting: (a) in the beginning she wanders around, doing nothing in particular, not paying attention to anything or anybody (Scene 1.a); (b) after a brief individual exploration of the new toy (Scene 1.c), she suddenly pays attention to Bruna, who is walking from one place to another holding a doll in her hand; Pamela starts to establish some personal links with the other children in the group and the new toy is used as a central place for their meeting (Scene 1.d); Pamela sits in a semicircle formed by the tunnel, starts calling Bruna to sit with her, and Bia sits at her side (Scene 1.b); (c) by chance, a box was left close to the tunnel (Scene 2.a); it just happened to be there, giving the opportunity for the toddlers to perform on it the activities suggested by the tunnel (at least from the adult's perspective); (Scene 2.b); it starts to be a suggestive object, a resource for the child's play situation; (d) Pamela gets into it, a second child (Bia), and a third (Bruna) join this interesting activity of meaning construction; for a short period Pamela shares with Bia (thanks to Bia's interest; Scene 2.a) or with Bruna (thanks to Pamela's interest; Scene 3.b) a common circumscribed place that divides the locale from the room surrounding it into a private area to play; (e) the box allows the children a physically close relationship (Scene 3.c); this object, during the ongoing episode, acquires a jointly constructed meaning, which makes the other children and adults attentive to what is happening in it (Scene 4.c); (f) the alliance formed by Bia and John is marked by two different personal interests, which by the circumstances are found connected by their actions (Scene 5.a); the effect of combining activities in a dyad reinforces the pleasure of satisfying individual interests; their affiliated activities appear to have a more intense emotional and playful tone (Scene 5.d); and (g) in the end Pamela is identified as someone who finds her place (Scene 2.a), chooses her companion (Scenes 3.b, 5.c, 6.c), and creates her play activity (Scene 6.a), which she ends by taking her doll to the doctor (nurse's room; Scene 6.d); in doing this she externalizes in her actions what she often sees, as an everyday routine in the creche.

The episode shows a number of strikingly rich affiliations among peers, marked by tensions with the other children in the group. The scenes point out the dynamics of the process of switching from one action to another, which are seemingly unrelated, but actually function to form affiliated relations (construction of common interests) or instrumental relations between peers. These shifts of action are possible mechanisms used by young children to achieve the construction of their own place to play in the course of social interaction.

GENERAL DISCUSSION

Starting from a sociogenetic theoretical perspective our aim was to analyze, through an episode of children's play occurring in a group of toddlers in a day-care social context, the role of peers in the process of building up a temporarily stable personal place to play. Our unit of analysis was the specific structure of the child's active construction of personal place, while being surrounded by the emergence of collective attention that was given to the process in a peer-group setting.

The children in this group were clearly active participants in a purposefully prestructured environment, which had been prepared by adults to provide for the children's assumed individual social, cognitive, and emotional needs. They are, at the same time, independent actors of, and subordinate (dependent) performers in, this social world. They are producers and products of this environment. As actors or observers, children build, in a unique and creative way, their collective and individual understanding of social meanings. In spite of limitations in the verbal domain in this age group, interpersonal communication functions through gestures, simple signals and a rich expressive body (postural) language (Wallon, 1942). The children communicate by a constant process of building a sharing experience with other members of the social group, both caregivers and peers. They also create personal places to play within the group, sometimes with a peer and sometimes using peer interaction as an instrument to achieve personal goals. The active child is simultaneously an autonomous actor and participant in a social group.

Our main empirical interests in this chapter were: (a) how does an 18- month-old child construct and change his or her personal world by acting and communicating with adults and peers?, (b) how does the group work as a resource and means for canalizing the child's play situation? Our focus has been on defining and illustrating the basic factors in the process by which a child moves from uncertainty of actions to a clear (that is, persevering) personal interest, through emotional affiliation and separation, and the imitation of others' actions. A child's personal conduct is coconstructed in conjunction with peers' actions. In the episodes described in this chapter, the environment was organized by adults to set boundaries to the children's actions. These boundaries are redefined by the child across time, by a process of building interpersonal actions, by establishing an internal coherence composed by single apparently isolated actions. The children in a toddlers' group are always involved with internal and external changes in play situations, constructing their images and representations of the world by imitation, gestures, and postural communication (Wallon, 1945). The transformations in the children's play are multiple and complex, ranging from an awareness of an isolated play setting where they are fused with peers, to more persistent alliances where they become aware of their similarities and differences, back to being either alone or alternating from one place to another. This process includes the construction of the individual's capacity to internalize the social world, transforming it by playing and externalizing this understanding in moments of sharing meanings. In order to be personal, a person needs to be social. In other words, individual development is the development of individuals within and via the social group.

ACKNOWLEDGMENTS

An earlier version of this chapter was presented at the Jean Piaget Society annual meeting, Philadelphia, June 3/5, 1993. The preparation of this work was made possible through a fellowship from the Brazilian Ministry of Education (CAPES branch), a warded to the first author for a research visit to the University of North Carolina at Chapel Hill in the 1992/1993 academic year. Special thanks are due to the staff of *Freelandia*, a creche located in a supermarket in Rio de Janeiro.

REFERENCES

Altman, I. (1993). Dialectics, physical environments, and personal relationships. *Communication Monographs, 60*, 26-34.

Altman, I., & Gauvain, M. (1981). A cross-cultural and dialectic analysis of homes. In L.S. Liben, A.H. Patterson, & N. Newcombe (Eds.), *Spatial representation and behavior across the life span* (pp. 283-320). New York: Academic Press.

Altman, I., & Lowe, S.M. (Eds.). (1992). *Place attachment*. New York: Plenum.

Basov, M. I. (1991). The organization of processes of behavior. In J. Valsiner & R. Van der Veer (Eds.), *Structuring of conduct in activity settings: The forgotten contributions of Mikhail Basov. Soviet Psychology, 29*(5), 14-83.

Bonnes-Dobrowolny, M., & Secchiaroli, G. (1978). *Space and meaning of the city center*. Paper presented at the 19th International Congress of Applied Psychology, Munich, Germany.

Branco, A.U. & Valsiner, J. (1992, July). *Development of convergence and divergence in joint actions of preschool children within structured social contexts*. Poster presented at the 25th International Congress of Psychology, Brussels, Belguim.

Campos de Carvalho, M.I. (1989). Organizacao espacial da area de atividades livres em creche. In *Anais da 18 Reuniao Anual de Psicologia da Sociedade de Psicologia de Ribeirao Preto* (pp. 305-310.) Ribeirao Preto, Brazil: USP Editora.

Campos de Carvalho, M.I., Rubiano, M.R.B., & Rossetti-Ferreira, M.C. (1989). *Spacial characteristics of the setting and day care children's use of space and social state*. Paper presented at the 10th Biennial Meeting of the International Society for the Study of Behavioral Development, Jyvaskyla, Finland.

Campos de Carvalho, M.I. (1990). *Arranjo espacial e distribuicao de criancas de 2-3 anos pela area de atividades livres em creche*. Unpublished doctoral dissertation, Instituto de Psicologia de Universidade de Sao Paulo, Brazil.

Campos de Carvalho, M.I. & Rossetti-Ferreira, M. C. (1993). *Importance of spatial arrangements for young children in daycare centers*. In Children's Environments, 10 (1)10-19.

Campos de Carvalho, M.I., Meneghini, R., & Mingorance, R.C. (1994, October). *Arranjos espaciais e formacao de pares entre criancas de 2-3 anos em creches*. Paper presented at the 24th Reuniao Anual de Sociedade Brasileira de Psicologia, Ribeirao Preto, Brazil.

Csikszentmihalyi, M., & Rochberg-Halton, E. (1981). *The meaning of things: Domestic symbols and the self*. Cambridge, UK: Cambridge University Press.

Fogel, A. & Branco, A.U. (1997). *Meta-communication as a source of indeterminism in relationships*. In A. Fogel, M. Lyra & J. Valsiner (Eds.), Dynamics and indeterminism in developmental and social processes. Hillsdale, NJ: Erlbaum.

Lawrence, R.J. (1981). *The social classification of domestic space*. Anthropos, 76, 649-664.

Lawrence, R.J. (1985). *A more humane history of homes*. In I. Altman & C.M. Werner (Eds.), Home environments (pp. 113-132). New York: Plenum.

Legendre, A. (1983). Appropriation par les enfants de l'environment architectural. *Enfance, 3*, 389-395.

Legendre, A. (1987). Transformation de l'espace d'activites et echanges sociaux de jeunes enfants en creche. *Psychologie Francaise, 32*, 31-43.

Legendre, A. (1989). Young children's social competences and their use of space in day-care centers. In B.H. Schneider, G. Attili, J. Nadel, & R. Weissberg (Eds.), *Social competence in developmental perspective* (pp. 263-276). Dordrecht, The Netherlands: Kluwer.

Legendre, A., & Fantaine, A.M. (1991). The effects of visual boundaries in a two-year-olds' playroom. *Children's Environments Quarterly, 8*, 2 16.

Lewin, K. (1927). Kindlicher Ausdruck. *Zeitschrift fur Padagogische Psychologie, 28*, 510-526.

Lyra, M.C.D.P., & Rossetti-Ferreira, M.C. (1995). Transformation and construction in social interaction: A new perspective on analysis of the mother-infant dyad. In J. Valsiner (Ed.), *Child development within culturally structured environments: Vol. 3. Comparative-cultural and constructivist perspectives* (pp. 51-77). Norwood, NJ: Ablex.

Mead, G.H. (1910). Social consciousness and the consciousness of meaning. *Psychological Bulletin, 7*, (12), 397-405.

Mead, G.H. (1912). The mechanism of social consciousness. *Journal of Philosophy, 9*, 401-406.

Mead, G.H. (1913). The social self. *Journal of Philosophy, 10*, 374-380.

Muchow, M. (1931). Zur Frage einer lebensraum und epochaltypologischen Entwicklungspsychologie des Kindes und Jugendlichen. *Beihefte zur Zeitschrift fur angewandte Psychologie, 59*, 185-202.

Muchow, M., & Muchow, H. (1935). *Der Lebensraum des Grobstadtkindes.* Hamburg, Germany: M. Riedel.

Rogoff, B. (1990). *Apprenticeship in thinking.* New York: Oxford University Press.

Saile, D.G. (1985). The ritual establishment of home. In I. Altman & C.M. Werner (Eds.), *Home environments* (pp. 87-111). New York: Plenum.

Valsiner, J. (1989). Collective coordination of progressive empowerment. In L.T. Winegar (Ed.), *Social interaction and the development of children's understanding* (pp. 7-20). Norwood, NJ: Ablex.

Van der Veer, R., & Valsiner, J. (Eds.). (1994). *The Vygotsky reader.* Oxford, U.K.: Basil Blackwell.

Vasconcellos, V.M.R. (1986). *Social Interaction in a creche.* Unpublished doctoral dissertation, Sussex University, Sussex, U.K.

Vasconcellos, V.M.R., & Valsiner, J. (1993, April). *From imitation to symbolic construction: elaborating sociogenetic perspectives in developmental psychology.* Unpublished paper presented at the 5th Conference of the International Society for Theoretical Psychology, France.

Vasconcellos, V.M.R., & Valsiner, J. (1995). The co-constructivist Perspective in Psychology and Education. Porto Alegre, Brazil: Artes Medicas.

Wallon, H. (1942). *De l'act a la pensee.* Paris: Armand Colin.

Wallon, H. (1945). *Les Origines de la pensee chez l'enfant.* Paris: P.U.F.

Werner, C.M. , Altman, I., & Oxley, D. (1985). Temporal aspects of homes: A transactional perspective. In I. Altman & C.M. Werner (Eds.), *Home environments* (pp. 1-32). New York: Plenum.

Werner, C.M., & Altman, I. (1996). A dialectic-transactional framework of social relations: Implications for children and adolescents. In D. Gorlitz, H.J. Harloff, G. Mey & J. Valsiner (Eds.), *Children, cities, and psychological theories: Developing relationships.* Berlin: Walter de Gruyter.

Winegar, L.T., Renninger, K.A., & Valsiner, J. (1989). Dependent independence in adult child relationships. In D.A. Kramer & M.J. Bopp (Eds.), *Movement through form: Transformation in clinical and developmental psychology* (pp. 157-168). New York: Springer.

Wohlwill, J.F. (Ed.). (1985). Marta Muchow, 1892/1933: Her life, work, and contribution to developmental and ecological psychology. *Human Development, 28,* 198-224.

6

PEER INTERACTIONS AND THE APPROPRIATION OF GENDER REPRESENTATIONS BY YOUNG CHILDREN

Zilma de Moraes Ramos de Oliveira
University of São Paulo, Brazil

The call for a comprehension of human action as socially and historically embedded (Bakhtin, 1986; Baldwin, 1895; Janet, 1929; Mead, 1934; Vygotsky, 1935/1986; Wallon, 1942, 1959) is not new but has been reemphasized in present research in Development psychology (Berger & Luckmann, 1966; Bronchart, 1992; Cole, 1985; Doise & Mugny, 1984; Du Preez, 1991; Levine & Resnick, 1993; Mugny & Carugati, 1985; Newman, Griffin, & Cole, 1989; Rogoff, 1990; Shotter, 1992; Wertsch, 1991). That emphasis has stimulated the study of how meanings are generated and modified by sociopsychological processes according to concrete historical circumstances.

From a theoretical perspective based in the work of Vygotsky and Wallon, the human's self and consciousness are constructed through social life. In it, the cultural forms of organizing the situations in which the individuals are involved give to each one of them the means (knowledge, abilities, values, motives, etc.) for their actions. Human psychism is especially developed through the many social relationships in which individuals are involved daily, by a continual confrontation of interpersonal boundaries (Oliveira, 1997). This standpoint invites us to pay attention to the persons' activities in concrete situations, with historically meaningful ways of acting.

In light of these conceptions, most studies have focused on the adult-child interaction, the adult being considered as a more experienced partner. The underlying paradigm considers that the asymmetry of adult-child relationships guarantees the presence of external constraints and the transference of social material into the child (Bruner, 1975). However, this emphasis on adult-child interaction as a unidirectional process, linked with the idea of socialization (Lawrence, Benedict, & Valsiner, 1992), created has a bias toward the idea that the child does not play an active role in the dyadic interaction (Elbers, Maier, Hoestra, & Hoggsteder, 1992). The acknowledgment of these criticism led some researchers to a recognition of reciprocal activity in adult-child interaction (Fogel, 1992; Lyra & Rosseti-Ferreira, 1995; Winegar, 1994). The study of the developmental process has to focus not only on adult-child interactions (O'Connell & Bretherton, 1984; Valsiner, 1987), but also on child-child interactions (Camaioni, 1980; Dubon, Josse, & Vazine, 1981; Musatti, 1986; Nadel-Brulfert & Baudonnière, 1982; Tudge, 1990).

A special problem for the investigation of human interactions, however, concerns the unit of analysis that is used. Avoiding an individualistic and historical perspective, I have recovered the concept of *role* elaborated by the sociogenetic tradition (Baldwin, 1892, 1895; Bergson, 1889/1948; Guillaume, 1926; James, 1890; Janet, 1929; Mead, 1934), and also present in Vygotsky's and Wallon's works, and use it to discuss human interactions (Oliveira, 1988; Oliveira & Rossetti-Ferreira, 1993, 1994; Oliveira & Valsiner, 1997).

I consider human development as a joint and reciprocal task occurring in contexts in which certain forms of social relationships and sign use are present. In these contexts, both the individual and his or her environment are constantly changing and creating singular situations in which individuals' actions are negotiated and defined in their interpersonal experiences. In the dynamic situations that are created in the social matrices in which the child is inserted since birth, some meanings are attributed to his or her actions by his or her partners' actions as they interpret the situation as having certain goals, and/ or different intentions and representations. These framed behaviors constitute roles that are assumed, denied, and recreated by the child in the interactional process. The child is thus in a constant process of transformation and development, through imitation of the partner's roles together with role-counterrole oppositions.

This perspective fosters some challenging reflections about the concept of social interaction and its function in promoting the child's development and cultural novelty and, as such, can contribute to the study of social representations. Social representations are signifiers that regulate people's actions and their construction of reality, as they constitute the world in a certain form and attribute some identities to the individuals in it. They are expressed through discourses and historically vary with social concrete experiences (Farr & Moscovici, 1984).

Social representation establish a semiotic encoding not only of objects, events, and objectives but also of behavior styles and social positions related to them (Lloyd, 1987; Lloyd & Duveen, 1992). The study of the ontogenesis of social representations is required for a better comprehension of the area, being central to the understanding of the psychological development of the child (Moscovici, 1990). How social representation become psychologically active for individuals (Duveen & Lloyd, 1991a).

From a Piagetian perspective, the young child's capacity for representing something is related to the development of the symbolic function, and his or her gestural evocations are seen as evidence of the child's growing representational ability (Bretherton, 1984; Galifret-Cranjon, 1981; Piaget, 1945). My personal perspective, however, is closer to Vygotsky's and Wallon's positions. Focusing on the semiotic nature of every human action, this position highlights the interpersonal units as the locus for representational behaviors even before any special intraindividual psychological function responsible for it can be advocated. The difficult task of detaching something of an usual meaning and using it as substitute for an absent object occurs as the same young child takes someone else' role, reproducing its gestures, postures, and verbalizations, as in pretend play.

AN EMPIRICAL STUDY

After studying, young peers interactions, especially when they create pretend play using a role perspective, I became interested in analyzing the evolution of children's gender roles. Since very early, through the many situations in which the child is involved, especially through his or her interactions with adult members of his or her culture, he or she constructs an individuality. This is supported, among other things, by some historically defined gender identifications that are observed in adults' processes of shaping masculine and feminine actions, processes that are more conservative in some communities than in others. As the child develops, he or she becomes increasingly immersed in schooling and in the mass media processes of transmission of social representations that amplify the forms through which his or her family presents the world.

For Duveen and Lloyd (1990b), the adult structures the semiotic field of gender and amplifies the gender marking available to children. First the child cognitively can only handle signals that allow an immediate engagement in some action scheme or in our words, in a certain script. Afterwards with development the child is used to establishing a relationship with objects and situations more mediated by signs. In their study of gender representation among 18-to 48-month-old children through different modalities of gender regulation—play, language, and problem solving—Duveen and Lloyd analyzed very interesting data and concluded that although boys and girls develop similar representations of gender in many ways, they not behave in similar ways. Especially in mixed pairs but also in same-gender pairs, boys choose more masculine toys than the girls choose feminine toys, both in mixed or in feminine dyads. The ability of young children to control a set of signs related to gender depends on the context of the activity. However, the difference between the social identities displayed by girls and boys in their play cannot be ascribed to a difference in their knowledge of social markings. It seems, rather, that the arena of toys is one in which it is imperative for boys, but not for girls, to use their knowledge to mark a difference.

These interesting conclusions must be followed by new investigations in different cultural settings to further illuminate the social construction of gender representations. The process by which gender representations are appropriated by the children must also be investigated.

The aim of this study is to discuss the process of construction of gender representation from a developmental perspective, through the investigation of join play of young Brazilian children in day care based on the concept of role. With that purpose, a qualitative, contextual, and transactional analysis of 20 free play session of two groups of 2-and 3-year-old children[1] videorecorded in a 12-month period in a Brazilian day-care center for children from low-income families presented. Episodes frame from ongoing situations were analyzed for a comprehension of the process of role coordination in which, among others, some roles related to gender were played by the children. This analysis gave us support for the elaboration about the appropriation of gender social representations by day-care children from some Brazilian low-income families.

WHAT IS GOING ON IN YOUNG PEER INTERACTION?

The analysis of our data indicated that self-differentiation, in terms of gender, appears in the child's development in every interesting ways. Around 2 years of age, the child acts more fused with the situation, and has great difficulty in differentiating his or her actions from the partner's actions. The differentiation of gender roles is not so clear, as can be seen in the following episodes:

Episode 1: John (25)[2] holds a toy dog and walks around the playroom, while three other children are playing with some objects: cars, dolls, and so on. He looks at the researcher and shows her the dog, saying: "Olha o bebê!" (Look at the baby!). He sits on the floor, puts the dog to sleep like a human baby, holds it up in his arms, and brings the dog's mouth to one of his nipples, in a breast-feeding gesture.

Episode 2 (9 months later): Vivi (32) says to John (34), who is playing with a doll in the playroom: "Põe aqui, mãe. Mãe, aqui!" (Put it here, mother. Mother, here!).

In these episode, the peers create their make-believe play through a process of unification of fragments of their experiences in a here-and-now frame. In the created scenes, the reproduction of the mother's gestures by the children seems clear. Her role is clearly expressed by these young children, who easily adopt a complementary role to it, even when the child who is enacting the mother's role is a boy. However, some questions come to mind: Why is there this incongruent choice of gender role?

One possible answer is that, in fact, mothering scripts are very often played by these children, partially explained by their prevalence in the daily routine at traditionally oriented homes and day-care centers, where female figures are more easily seen as caregivers. These experiences for long periods each day in an institution more concerned with physical care than with the enrichment of the child's experience may be responsible for the many imitations that are seen among the children.

Another possible answer, more related to the development process according to a sociointeractionist paradigm can also be presented. For Vygotsky and Wallon, the interpersonal activity in shared situations is so integrated that the individuals, especially the young children, have some difficulty perceiving their actions separate from those of their partners. The child's development is thus created through a dialectical movement of fusion with the partners and differentiation from them. That movement involves alternation, confrontation, and overcoming of social personal positions. After a first phase of being completely fused with the social world, when responsiveness to the partner's behavior is a more tuned process, the child becomes aware of the similarities and differences between him or her and the other persons and things, as well as of the characteristics he or she attributes, by his or her actions, to each one of them. The child becomes acquainted with the changes in the roles that can be assumed according to these situation, and is very ingenious in passing alternately from one role to another, especially in his or her make-believe play. The syncretic relationships that the young child forms with these situations lead him or her to assume different characters or parts of them in a motor-expressive way of meaning elaboration through role imitation. That process occurs together with the I-other differentiation.

Vygotsky and Wallon were specially interested in the adult-child dyad and how the child adopts the adult's role; that is, the manner through which he or she incorporates culture as a means to transform his or her own psychological functioning. Vygotsky emphasized the child's growing capacity to take the adult partner's speech to orient himself or herself, creating a discursive mind, whereas Wallon stressed the I-other differentiation leading not only to the emergence of thought but also to self-formation. For both of them, pretend play is seen as privileged arena for taking the partner's role. For the young child, however, that partner is his or her mother or another caregivers and to reproduce their actions does not indicate a confusion of identities, as identity is always being formed, but is an indicator of the developmental processes in operation that are providing the child with opportunities to work on the mother-child relationship.

Finally, if we carefully analyze the episodes, it is possible to assume that the submission of the child to every event and its roles in the episodes is total and linked to the basic behavioral aspects of the character performed rather than to the characteristics of the actor that gives life to it. It seems as if the reproduction of some well-known scenes is an irresistible force, from which the children cannot escape.

Some developmental changes will alter this last possibility. Although the 2-year-old children of Group A are often seen taking some elements—like sounds, movements, clothes, and objects—as support for their actions (thanks to their culturally attributed characteristics and based mainly in perception), the 3-year-old children's reproduction of past experiences becomes less memory in action than rule-based behavior, as it can also be noticed in the next episode.

Episode 3:   In his group's playroom Fábio (46) examines an empty plastic bottle of shampoo Vanessa (37) tells him with a threatening posture and intonation; "Vai virar mulher!" (You'll turn into a woman!). Then she asks him, "Dá o shampoo?" (Give me the shampoo?). Fabio replies, loud and briskly, "Não!" (No!). Vanessa manipulates some objects for a whole and once again asks him, in a humble posture: "Dá o shampoozinho?" (Give me the little shampoo?). Fabio asks her, "O quê?" (What?) and continues to play with the empty battle of shampoo. Vanessa, with her right hand very extended toward him, firmly demands, "Dá o shampoo?" (Give me the shampoo?). Fabio replies, "Não vou dar não!" (No, I won't give it!) and places the empty bottle inside a big toy car. After staring at Fabio for some seconds, Vanessa takes some other objects to play with.

Episode 4 (3 months later): Four children inspect some empty bottles of shampoo, deodorant, creams, among other objects such as a wooden bus, a doll, some handbags, a hat and son on. Daniel (38) offers an empty shampoo bottle to Vanessa (40) saying. "Tó!" (Take it!). Fernando (38), passing by, takes the bottle from Daniel's hand. Vanessa chases Fernando and, pointing to him, says, "É minha! É p'a mim! Ele deu p'a mim!" (It's mine! It's for me! He gave me it!), and adds, pointing to him as in a menace, "Vai virar mulher!" (You'll turn into a woman!). Fernando keeps the bottle with him and plays with it, observed by Vanessa, who after some seconds, goes to play with other toys.

The partner's actions create a field of interpersonal activity as they take some roles that continuously structure the situation in new ways. Gestures and intonations bring some ideologically shaped attitudes—violence, roughness, humidity, firmness—to create the ongoing situations, as shown in Episode 3. In Episode 4, more semiotic mediation can be noticed in the children's relations with the objects, as well as in the intentions or objectives associated with the roles assumed in the interpersonal relationships.

The girl's speech in both episodes is related to the social meanings she is building up through her daily experiences at home and at the day-care center. Maybe because in her low-income traditionally oriented community, shampoo is an expensive object in relation to the family's low income and is more associated with women, culturally more interested in beauty, in the girls's discourse, to use shampoo is a woman's thing and she tells that to her male playmate. Her information comes as a form of advice or threat in the same way as she and her peers used to be informed by their caregivers of many cultural interdictions. Therefore the girl's statement to the boys on the two occasions (you will turn into a woman) refers to an element of a social representation circulating in the children's culture and expressed by their discourse. Besides that, at that age there is an increase in interpersonal competition in the older group, providing more differentiation among the partners.

That verbal marking, although prejudiced or even because of that, remains obscure for the children as they try to figure out what is masculine or feminine using some cultural indices, as in Episodes 5 and 6.

Episode 5 (Approximately 3 minutes after the end of Episode 4): Wellington (45), who entered the room after Vanessa and Fernando's dialogue, gets a belt from the floor, puts it on, and looking at Vanessa, who is playing with a doll, says, "Isto é de homem, não?" (It's a man's thing. Isn't it?). Vanessa looks at him and nods affirmatively.

Episode 6 (3 months later): Vanessa (now 40) gets a cap from some clothes left by the caregiver in the playroom and puts it over her head. Fabio (49) tells her, "Mulher não usa. Só homem" (Women don't use it! Only men!). Vanessa replies, "Usa!" (They do!). Later on, David (42) puts on the cap that Vanessa had used and states, "Coisa the homem!" (It is a man thing!). Vanessa approaching David and taking the cap from him, says, "É meu chapéu! Me dá meu chapéu!" (It is my hat! Give me my hat!).

Episodes 5 and 6 show the children classifying objects according to a criterion of gender. "These are women's or men's objects." This distinction helps the process of role differentiation as an attribute of the child—that is, to be of the male or female gender—is used to scaffold the construction of roles in their pretend play that also has a dimension of reality (Forbes, Katz & Paul, 1986). That this is a major concern in Group B more than in Group A is agreement with Duveen and Lloyd's (1990b) conclusions about the increasing ability of the children to respond to the gender marking of the toys.

In the episodes, existing interdictions related to objects ("men do not use shampoo," "women do not use hats") are brought to the situation as parameters to regulate the children's interactions. Nevertheless, the division of the objects according to the gender of its owner also constitutes a tactic that the child uses to dispute an object. Vanessa is often seen using this tatic, sometimes with success, although generally with failure, as in Episodes 3, 4, and 7.

> Episode 7: Fernando (42) is pretending to give some food to a doll using a cap and a spoon. Vanessa (42) comes near him, looks at him for a while and says, painting to him, "Me dá pá mim! Vai virar mulher!" (Give it to me! You'll turn into a woman!). Fernando, continuing to feed the doll, replies, "Então vou virar mulher!" (Then I'll turn into a woman!). Vanessa looks at him for a while and goes to play with other objects in the playroom.

As Moscovici (1990) said, the way we justify or mask the arbitrary aspect of the essential constraint on our thought still remains unknown. However, the analysis of the previous episode provides some interesting cues. The contradictions involved in the arbitrariness of the always changing social representations ("to feed a baby is a woman's task, although many men are doing this") mediate the boy's actions, showing their unstable aspects. More research is necessary for a better distinction of the complex and dynamic gender features by the children. The steps that were already taken in that direction show them to be active actors appropriating historical scripts.

SOME CONCLUSIONS: FROM THE GIVEN TO THE CREATED

Human interactions are conceived in this study as a dynamic process of expanding or constructing shared semiotically organized fields of conduct. In other words, interactions are seen as role taking by active persons with different needs, intention, and personal charateristics. As the concept of role is related to different mediational instruments that are built up in certain economic-political-ideological moment of a given society, it provides further comprehension about the appropriation of social representation of gender or other topics by the young children.

Our analysis has taken into account the historical period in which the observations were taking place (the second half of the 1980s in a developing country) with its antagonist values in dispute, as well as the day-care educational philosophy, the social representations of the untrained caregivers that worked with the children in day-care, and fact that the children's families were part of a traditionally oriented illiterate community in which the masculine figure is central. However, these cultural constraints interacted with the capacities the children had already constructed.

Our analysis allowed us to notice that the children's social interactions evolve through meaning confrontations regarding present objects and situations or compared with past experiences. As the scenes constituted by the children's role confrontations are always changing, an appropriate conduct has to fit with the variability of the here-and-now situations. Sometimes it seems that the child precociously, found out that it is strategic to preserve a social norm even if it expresses his or her own figure in a subordinate way. Other times, to break and change the norm is the child's main rule.

Especially through play, children become able to assume different role in order to construct and attain their goals and motives while interacting with peers that have their own and frequently opposite intentions (Giffin, 1984; Oliveira, 1997; Ortega, 1994). Children's pretend play in naturalistic situations with an "as if" atmosphere allows for the examination of internalized rules and images related to the partner's roles. These rules and images are modified through the partners' interactions, in order to fit to the changing aspects of every situation enacted in pretend play.

The challenge created by the children in their play is related to the need to take some roles as systems that canalize their possible actions through the negotiation of the rules involved in a situation and creating it. Playing them in the situation obliges the individual to follow, in a not necessarily conscious manner, some ways of acting that involve complex abilities. At the same time, the very fact of having to coordinate the assumed roles leads the individuals to deal with posture, gestures, and emerging representations and images.

In the children's interactions, gestures that reproduce quite well certain postures, expressions, and verbalizations that occur in the child's environment are frequently seen. In that process, imitation occupies a central position. However, children's imitation does not circumscribe them to already experienced situation as previously pointed out (Stockinger & McCune-Nicolich, 1984). Imitation helps the children liberate themselves from the past and control it by voluntary repetition and created images (see also O'Connell & Bretherton, 1984). Through the imitation of their present or past partners and especially of their caregivers, the children's gestures, linked with increasingly broader semiotic systems (and, therefore, with roles), are diffused and transformed, opening new possibilities for the interactional sequences (Oliveira & Valsiner, 1997).

This involves the use of diverse cognitive-affective psychological instruments to deal with the social antogonist conception structuring the situations. With that, the child's social knowledge and abilities are first supported by a scripted interaction (Haste, 1987; Light, 1987), by the mastery of role-counterrole dynamic structures (Oliveira, 1988), before these become internally appropriated by him or her through polyphonic discourses (Wertsch, 1991). All of this involves not only rational elements that are negotiated in the experiences—as in Mead's (1934) conception of role taking or in Nelson's (1986) notion of script—but also, and mainly, a great deal of affect (Oliveira, in press; Oliveira & Valsiner, 1997).

From the analysis of the episodes, it can be noticed how some parts of the culturally constructed gender role information in object-oriented activities are used by the children as means of achieving some interactional goals as, by using that information interpersonally, they gradually construct their own version of gender's identity. In this manner, they can go beyond historical constructed boundaries and recreate personal meaning.

ACKNOWLEDGMENTS

The author gratefully acknowledges the critical comments of Mary Jane Spink, Tania Sperb, and Maria Clotilde Rosseti-Ferreira to this text and the financial support to the Brazilian finding agencies FAPESP and CNPq.

NOTES

[1] Group A with two boys and four girls of two years of age, and Group B with six boys and two girls of three years of age.
[2] The number in parentheses indicates the age in months of the child at the session.

REFERENCES

Bakhtin, M. (1986). *Marxism and the philosophy of language*. Cambridge, MA: Harvard University Press.

Baldwin, J.M. (1892). Origin of volition in childhood. *Science, 20*(51) 286-287.

Baldwin, J.M. (1895). The origin of a "thing" and its nature. *Psychological Review, 2*(2): 551-572.

Berger, P., & Luckmann, T. (1966). *The social construction of reality: A treatise in the sociology of knowledge*. Harmondsworth, UK: Penguin.

Bergson, H. (1948). *Essai sur les donées immediates de la conscience* [Essay on the immediate data of consciousness]. (original work published 1889). Paris: PUF.

Bretherton, I. (1984). Representing the social world in symbolic play: Reality and fantasy. In I. Bretherton (Ed.), *Symbolic play: The development of social development* (pp. 1-41). London: Academic Press.

Bronckart, J.P. (1992). El discurso como acción. Por un nuevo paradigma psicolinguistico. [Discourse as action: Toward a new psycholinguistic paradigm]. *Annuario de Psicologia, (54)*: 3-48.

Bruner, J. (1975). From communication to language: A psychological perspective. *Cognition, (3)*: 255-287.

Camaioni, L. (1980). *L' interazione tra bambini* [Children's interactions]. Rome: Armando.

Cole, M. (1985). The zone of proximal development: Where culture and cognition create each other. In J.V. Wertsch (Ed.), *Culture, communication and cognition: Vygotskian perspectives*, (pp. 146-161). Cambridge, UK: Cambridge University Press.

Doise, W., & Mugny, G. (1984). *The social development of the intellect*. Exeter, UK: A. Wheaton.

Dubon, D.C., Josse, D., & Lezine, I. (1981). Evolution des échanges entre enfants au cours des deux premières années de la vie. [The evolution of the exchanges among children during the first two years of life]. *Neuropsychiatrie de l'enfance, 29*(6), 273-290.

Du Preez, P. (1991). *A science of mind. The quest for psychological reality*. London: Academic Press.

Duveen, G., & Lloyd, B. (1990a). Introduction. In G. Duveen & B. Lloyd (Eds.), *Social representations and the development of knowledge*, (pp. 1-10). Cambridge, UK: Cambridge University Press.

Duveen, G., & Lloyd, B. (1990b). A semiotic analysis of the development of social representations of gender. In G. Duveen & B. Lloyd (Eds.), *Social representations and the development of knowledge*, (pp. 1-10). Cambridge, UK: Cambridge University Press.

Elbers, E., Maier, R., Hoestra, T., & Hoogsteder, M. (1992). Internalization and adult-child interaction. In R. Maier (Ed.), *Internalization: Conceptual issues and methodological problems* (pp. 5-31). Utrecht: Faculteit der Sociale Welenschappen.

Farr, R.M., & Moscovici, S. (Eds.), (1984). *Social representations*. Cambridge, UK: Cambridge University Press.

Fogel, A. (1992). Movement and communication in human infancy: The social dynamics of development. *Human Movement Science, 11*: 387-423.

Forbes, D., Katz, M.M., & Paul, B. (1986). "Frame talk": A dramatistic analysis of children's fantasy play. In E.E. Mueller & C.R. Cooper (Eds.), *Process and outcome in peer relationships*. New York: Academic Press.

Galifret-Granjon, N. (1981). *Naissance et évolution de la répresentation chez l'enfant* [The origin and the evolution of representation in the child]. Paris: PUF.

Giffin, H. (1984). The coordination of meaning in the creation of shared make-believe reality. In I. Bretherton (Ed.), *Symbolic play* (pp. 73-100). London: Academic Press.

Guillaume, P. (1926). *L'imitation chez l'enfant*. Paris: Felix Alcan.

Haste, H. (1987). Growing into rules. In J. Bruner & H. Haste (Eds.), *Making sense: The child's construction of reality* (pp. 163-195). London: Methuen.

James, W. (1890). *Principles of psychology*. New York: Holt.

Janet, P. (1929). *L'evolution psychologique de la personality* [Psychological evolution of personality]. Paris: A. Chachine.

Lawrence, J.A., Benedikt, R., & Valsiner, J. (1992). Homeless in the mind: A case history of personal life in and out of a close orthodox community. *Journal of Social Distress and the Homeless, 1*(2): 157-176.

Levine, J.M., & Resnick, L.B. (1993). Social foundations of cognition. *Annual Review of Psychology, 44*: 585-612.

Light, P. (1987). Taking roles. In J. Bruner & H. Haste (Eds.), *Making sense: The child's construction of the world* (pp. 41-61). London: Methuen.

Lloyd, B. (1987). Social representations of gender. In Bruner & H. Haste (Eds.), *Making sense: The child's construction of the world*, (pp. 147-162). London: Methuen.

Lloyd, B., & Duveen, G. (1992). *Gender identities and education: The impact of starting school*. London: Harvester Wheatsheaf.

Lyra, M.C., & Roseetti-Ferreira, M.C. (1995). Understanding the co-constructive nature of human development: Role coordination in early peer interaction. In J. Valsiner & H.G. Voss (Eds.), *Structure of the learning processes*, (pp. 51-77). Norwood, NJ: Ablex.

Mead, G.H. (1934). *Mind, self and society*. Chicago: University of Chicago Press.

Moscovici, S. (1990). Social psychology and developmental psychology: Extending the conversation. In G. Duveen & B. Lloyd (Eds.), *Social representations and the development of knowledge*, (pp. 169-185). Cambridge, UK: Cambridge University Press.

Mugny, G., & Carugati, F. (1985). *L'intelligence au pluried: Les répresentations sociales de l'intelligence et son dévelopment* [Social representations of intelligence and its development]. Coussel, France: Delval.

Musatti, T. (1986). Early peer relations: The perspectives of Piaget and Vygotsky, In E.C. Mueller & C.R. Cooper (Eds.), *Process and outcome in peer relationships* (pp. 25-53). New York: Academic Press.

Nadel-Brulfert, J., & Baudonniere, P.M. (1982). The social function of reciprocal imitation in 2-year-old peers. *International Journal of Behavioral Development, 5*, 95-109.

Nelson, K. (1986). *Event Knowledge: Structure and function in development*. Hillsdale, NJ: Earlbaum.

Newman, D., Griffin, P., & Cole, M. (1989). *The construction zone: Working for cognitive change in school*. Cambridge, UK: Cambridge University Press.

O'Connell, B., & Bretherton , L. (1984). Toddler's play alone and with mother: The role of maternal guidance. In I. Bretherton (Ed.), *Symbolic play*, (pp. 337-368). London: Academic Press.

Oliveira, Z.M.R. (1988). *Jogo de papéis: Una perspectiva para análise do desenvolvimento humano* [Role playing: A perspective for the analysis of human development] Unpublished doctoral dissertation, IPUSP, São Paulo.

Oliveira, Z.M.R. (1997). The concept of "role" and the discussion of the internalization process. In B. Cox & c. Lightfoot (Eds.), *Sociogenetic perspectives on internalization*. Mahwah, NJ: Erlbaum.

Oliveira, Z.M.R., & Rossetti-Ferreira, M.C. (1993, March). *Can the concept of "role" help to understand the internalization process?* Paper presented at LX Meeting of SRCD, New Orleans, LA.

Oliveira, Z.M.R., & Rossetti-Ferreira, M.C. (1994). Coordination of roles: A theoretical-methodological perspective for studying human interactions. In N. Mercer & C. Colls (Eds.), *Teaching, learning and interaction* (pp. 217-221). Madrid: Fundación Infancia y Aprendizage.

Oliveira, Z.M.R., & Valsiner, J. (1997). Play and imagination: The psychological construction of novelty. In A. Fogel, M.C. Lyra, & J. Valsiner (Eds.), *Dynamics and indeterminism in developmental and social process*. Mahwah, NJ: Earlbaum.

Ortega, R. (1994). El juego sociodramático como contexto para la compreensión social. [The sociodramatic game as a social understanding context]. In A. Alvarez & P. Del Rio (Eds.), *Education as cultural construction* (pp. 79-88). Madrid: Fundación Infancia y Aprendizaje.

Piaget, J. (1995). *La formation du symbole chez l'enfant* [The child's formation of symbols]. Neuchâtel and Paris: Delachaux and Nietlé.

Rogoff, B. (1990). *Apprenticeship in thinking.* New York: Oxford University Press.

Shotter, J. (1992). *Knowing of the third kind.* Utrecht: Utrecht University.

Stockinger, S.K.S., & McCune-Nicolich, L. (1984). Shared pretend: A sociodramatic play at 3 years of age. In L. Bretherton (Ed.), *Symbolic play,* (pp. 159-191). London: Academic Press.

Tudge, J. (1990). Vygostsky, the zone of proximal developmental, and peer collaboration: Implications for classroom practice. In L.C. Moll (Ed.), *Vygostsky and education: Instructional implications and applications of sociohistorical psychology,* (pp. 155-172). Cambridge, UK: Cambridge University Press.

Valsiner, J. (1987). *Culture and the development of children's action: A cultural historical theory of developmental psychology.* New York: Wiley.

Vygotsky, L.S. (1986). *Thought and language,* (2nd ed.). (Original work published 1935). Cambridge, MA: MIT Press.

Wallon, H. (1942). *De l'acte a la pensée: Essai de psychologie camparée* [From act to thought: Essay on comparative psychology]. Paris: Flammarion.

Wallon, H. (1959). Le role de "l'autre" dans la conscience du "moi" [The role of the "other" in self consciouness] *Enfance, (3-4):* 279-285.

Wertsch, J. (1991). *Voices of the mind: A sociocultural approach to mediated action.* Cambridge, MA: Harvard University Press.

Winegar, T.L. (1994). Investigación evolutiva en contextos naturales: Un estudio descriptivo del periodo de desayuno en una guarderia [Developmental research in natural settings: A descriptive study of mealtime in a daycare center]. *Infancia y Aprendizage, (66):* 105-112.

7

DYNAMIC INTERPLAY BETWEEN PRIVATE AND SOCIAL SPEECH: A MICROGENETIC APPROACH

Sumedha Gupta
University of North Carolina at Chapel Hill

The interest in private speech (PS) as an important developmental phenomenon has been influenced in large part by Vygotsky and his sociogenetic thesis on the development of language and thought (Vygotsky, 1934/1986). Vygotsky based his theoretical formulation on the idea of a dynamic developmental process in which ontogenesis is not an unfolding of behavior but a constant reformulation and intermergence of both the elementary and complex layers of human psychological process (Van der Veer & Valsiner, 1991). This clearly non reductionistic focus formed the background to Vygotsky's formulation of the social origins of all higher mental functioning and provided a framework for conceptualizing the developmental utility of psychological tools. One psychological tool, private speech (PS), was seen by Vygotsky as a linkage between general social speech, from which it originates, and inner speech (IS), into which it eventually transforms. According to Vygotsky, all speech is originally social; in other words, its first function is communication. In the course of development, this general social speech differentiates into a distinct form of communication for the self, termed PS. Originally labeled *egocentric speech* (Piaget, 1923/1962; Vygotsky, 1934/1986), these self-addressed utterances, observed both in the presence and obsence of others, have, in modern-day usage, typically been distinguished from social speech (SS) by either using the Vygotskian criteria of the predicated and subvocalized nature of the PS trajectory or by operationalizing definitions of PS based on inferences of intended audience (self vs. other) and function (task-regulation vs. conversation; Diaz & Berk, 1992). As Diaz and Berk point out, preassumed distinctions between PS and SS based on nonobservable inferences may "ultimately prove futile and theoretically uninteresting." The difficulty in making clear distinction between SS and PS further complicates Vygotsky's theoretical assertion that PS is a developmental path linking the social functions of speech to the internal regulation of thought embodied in words, labeled IS. Although may be useful to distinguish between different characteristic of general speech, possibly by assigning them different labels, care must be taken that labels do not imply rigid distinctions. In this chapter, it is argued that the relationship among SS, PS, and IS may not entail a *clear* differentiation between SS and PS and an internalization of PS into IS. Instead, all forms of expressed verbal and nonverbal (facial expressions and gestures) speech for self and others and IS (mental processes connected to symbols) dynamically interact and through their interactions develop together.

The conceptualization of PS as the one and main developmentally necessary transition point between intermental and intramental functioning is made possible through defining it as a unifunctional construct. Emphasizing the dynamic *process* full of changes and reversals by which tools come to be useful for psychological development, Vygotsky seemed to limit the importance of PS to a taskregulatory, performance-oriented role. Ironically, the emphasis on task-regulatory functions has led to a search for linear, causal relationships between the functional roles PS in hypothesized to play and behavior, which in turn has resulted in overlooking both the applied complexity of the PS phenomena and its theoretical link to thought. Although a few researchers have challenged the hegemony of the task-regulatory function of PS (Berk & Gavin, 1984; Flavell, 1966), much of the PS research has continued to focus on performance variables linking PS to unitary task-related behavioral outcomes (see Diaz & Berk, for examples). Furthermore the tendency to ignore the theoretical implications of a multifunctional perspective has resulted in an implicit assumption of construct stability. Thus, whatever independent functions a researcher ascribes to PS is often tested under the supposition that differences in amount of PS, statistically correlated to specified behavioral outcomes, can be taken as evidence for or against either its internalization into IS or its developmental utility for performance on other cognitive tasks.

As a multifunctional construct, the study of PS would render such standard unidimensional methods incomplete and possibly invalid, varying instead for individual microgenetic and ontogenetic analyses over time. Such a framework may allow an understanding not only of PS's stable functional uses over time but also of the typical variability observed in its functional expressions. There is no dearth of descriptions of the multifunctional quality of PS—for example, regulatory function, emotional expressions, fantasy role play, self-awareness, and communicative role (Diaz & Berk, 1992; Flavell, 1966; Nelson, 1989)—what is lacking is a conceptualization of how these various functions interrelate and coalesce in ongoing action. Likewise, a bridge is needed between this multivariable construct and its dynamic relationship with thought, IS, and SS throughout ontogeny.

In this chapter, it is argued that PS, SS, and IS are intimately linked and the complexity of their interrelations in the developmental process makes inevitable a multifunctional role for PS. It is also argued that a multifunctional construct is compatible with the original theoretical foundations of a sociogenetic psychology. However, part of the sociogenetic foundation has been built on Vygotsky's thesis of the separate development of thought and speech. In order to clarify the evidence for a SS-PS-IS dynamic relationship and the multifunctional role of PS, it is necessary to question the seperability of thought and speech in Vygotsky's formulation. It may be that the social mediation of all higher mental functioning (HMF) is no theoretically compatible with viewing thought and speech as distinct mental faculties that can be described as developing separately and interrelating at some later point in ontogeny. Instead, understanding them as connected and developmentally codependent from the beginning stages of early social interaction may allow a foundation for analyzing the systemic and novelty-producing processes of development.

By positing a dynamic and intimate linkage between thought and speech in their rudimentary premature forms, an avenue is opened not only for the early existence of meaningful and adaptive vocal and non-vocal expressions, but for those expressions to take a variety of functions that become significant for the self, the social other, and future self-other interaction patterns. What may be helpful in clarifying these arguments and furthering our understanding of the PS phenomena is first a theoretical reanalysis of our assumptions of the relationship between thought and speech along with an elaboration of what is meant by PS, SS, and IS. Second, microgenetic analysis of general speech may be a means to document the multifunctional roles of PS and their interplay with SS in ongoing life processes.

THEORETICAL FOUNDATION FOR PS-SS-IS RELATIONSHIP

Missing Links in Vygotsky's Formulation of Thought-Speech Separation

Vygotsky viewed thought and speech as having different genetic roots that, at some point in ontogeny, become inextricably intertwined such that from that point on there is the possibility for thought to become verbal and speech intellectual. Part of the data used to formulate this thesis was work by Köhler, Yerkes, and Bühler on chimpanzee vocalizations and tool use (Vygotsky

1934/1986). According to Vygotsky, chimpanzees show rudiments of both "human-like" intelligence and speech in which the use of primitive tools and simple socially meaningful vocalizations are employed. They are limited, however, to using tools institutions where a direct visual correspondence between task and solution is present, indicating to Vygotsky a reliance not on "true" intellectual operations but on mechanical reactions. Likewise chimpanzee vocalizations are seen to be purely affective vocal reactions that, although serving both biological and psychological functions, are strictly a part of the "total emotional syndrome," and "not connected with intellectual reactions, i.e. with thinking" (Vygotsky, 1934/1986, p. 79). Thus, Vygotsky asserted that in the phylogeny of thought and speech, a prelinguistic and preintellectual state can be discerned. In the terminology of Werner's (1957) orthogenetic principle, there is relatively little systemic differentiation or separation between the developing organism and its environment and thus little hierarchic integration between mental faculties (i.e., thought and speech). Similarly, Köhler's experiments with chimpanzees used on prespeech children resulted in comparable findings, (i.e., the beginnings of "primitive" problem-solving behavior and the existence of the social and emotional phylogenetic functions of speech), and was therefore used as evidence for an ontogenetic separation of thought and speech in humans.

It is the merging of these different curves of development, resulting in the ability to understand the relationship between sign and meaning and to make functional use of signs, that constitutes the turning point in human intellect and is the salient difference between anthropoid and human mental functioning, Although Vygotsky asserted the existence of different genetic roots of thought and speech and their eventual integration, he allowed uncertainty as to whether this merging occurs at one point or many, as a sudden discovery or though slow experiential functional change. What is less clear in his analysis are his thoughts on how, by what process, this merging takes place. One obvious place for clues to this process is in Vygotsky's conceptualization of the relationship among PS, SS, and IS. The social mediation of all HMF is seen in his description of this relationship. (IS branches from general SS simultaneously with the differentiation of the personal and social functions of speech, labeled PS and SS, respectively. In both structure and function, PS is a transitory from between speech for others (SS) and speech for self (IS). It is speech for oneself that originates through differentiation from speech for others. Thus, PS is seen as retaining the social properties of SS while developing in the direction of IS. It is connected to thinking and serves "mental orientation, conscious understanding" (Vygotsky, 1934/1986, p. 228) and thus is essentially involved in seeking and planning solutions to problems. In its evolution, PS connects, with increasing sophistication, semiotic mediating devices or psychological tools to internal mental processes, thereby eventually internalizing into IS; the expression of thoughts in linguistic form.

In conceptualizing IS, it is necessary to understand Vygotsky's distinction between personal-sense or "pure" knowledge and socially shared meaning systems. The different degrees or shades of meaning constructed from individual experience and culturally defined meaning systems form each person's field of personal sense. Although this field has dynamic boundaries that may overlap among people, the variety of forms possible in the field allows unique meaning systems for each individual, independent from standardized senses shared by all members of a society. In IS it is this personal sense that dominates over static definitions. IS, thus, is a dynamic combination of the culturally accepted symbolic system (words) and individual sense knowledge constructed from personal experience and social interaction. It is the process of internalizing words to bring forth thought such that the speech structures come to form the basic structures of the child's thinking.

This evident connection between though and speech found in the form of IS, on the surface, provides an avenue to understand the ontogenetic relationship between thought and speech. However, it is clear that although the development or increasing sophistication of thought merging with words is the nature of IS, the initial rudimentary mergence must already be formed. As mentioned earlier, little explanation is given for the initial merging process. Furthermore, according to Vygotsky (1934/1986), thought and linguistic processes are never fully equated such that, throughout the life-span there can exist areas of thought and speech that have little direct relation to one-another. For example, "no thought process may be involved when a subject recites to himself a poem learned by heart or mentally repeats a sentence supplied to him for experimental purposes. Finally there is lyrical speech prompted by emotion...it can scarcely be classified with intellectual activity in the proper sense of the term" (p. 89). Thus, Vygotsky implied that the unity of thought and speech is limited to a circumscribed area in which forms of nonverbal thought and nonintellectual speech continue to exist in adulthood.

It seems both theoretically and empirically reasonable that all forms of speech activity do not need to be derived from conscious planful thought (as that seems to be the definition used for intellectual activity) or that verbal thought does not need to include *all* types of thought and speech. There are underlying assertions, however, that should be scrutinized. First, thought as "intellectual activity" can be separated into a very specific form of mental functioning. Although intellectual activity must clearly be based on "lower" basic mental functions, that is, affective and reflexive forms of memory and attention, within the realm of thinking there is a qualitative separation between the operations of HMF supported by basic skills and the use of those skills in tasks not clearly employing higher thought processes. Second, though as intellectual activity is genetically and potentially functionally distinct from other major forms of mental activity such as speech. This assumption has its foundations in Vygotsky's assertion that in human ontogeny, thought and speech originally develop along parallel and seemingly unrelated lines. After thought and speech being to intermingle, their continued relationships itself transforms. Later complex forms of verbal thought (i.e., IS) are not simple continuations of the early development of thought and speech seen in animals and humans. Instead the "nature of the development itself changes, from biological to sociohistorical"(Vygotsky, 1934/1986, p. 94). Whereas the idea of transformation of early to later forms of thought and speech follows the developmental assumption of the dynamic, evolving nature of mental processes, the gap created between these forms (biological to historical-cultural) within ontogeny is difficult to reconcile within a framework that is working under the *developmental* supposition of social mediation of meaning systems. The process by which thought and speech develop toward sophisticated forms of mental functioning may be easier to handle theoretically by not fundamentally divorcing intellectual activity from the realm of basic adaptive functioning.

Reformulation of the Ontogenetic Thought-Speech Relationship

If the nature of the development of IS and verbal thought changes from the biological to the sociohistorical, this transformation or linkage from biological to cultural can most easily be seen as occurring through the route of coconstruction of social meaning systems. A basic assumption of sociogenetic theories is that the emergence of complex mental functioning occurs through the active internalization of cultural messages; a process by which the construction of meaning systems takes place. As these meaning systems are seen in very early childhood (Vygotsky, 1934/1986, p. 81, referencing Bühler, Hetzer, & Tudor-Hart, 1927), in the Vygotskian preintellectual, preverbal stage, it seems theoretically plausible to view the linkage between the biological and sociohistorical not as a sudden meeting occurring at some point in ontogeny but as a gradual emergence that has its roots *in the earliest stages of social interaction*. The nature of beginning forms of social interaction clearly involve automatic motor and verbal activity that are suggestive of what Vygotsky termed preintellectual functioning. It is these early or "primitive" forms of intellect that form the continual basis through which mental activity takes complex forms. Thus, the implicit Vygotskian assumption that the developmental fusion of thought and speech can be separate from automated; affective, and instinctual mental functioning may be meaningless and possibly theoretically counterproductive. Basic cognitive processes such as memory, attention and sensations are not only fundamental to all HMF, but theoretically guide and are guided by HMF throughout ontogeny. Likewise the role motivation or affect and instinct in the development of HMF cannot be easily ignored. Yet separating their development from the thought-speech fusion cuts off the main avenue open for the *development* of HMF. Complex developmental processes, based on but going beyond basic survival skills, are formed through the sense meaning constructed through social interaction the only route for sense meaning emergence being the systemic coordination of all functioning mental processes. The implication of this for speech and thought is that the roots of speech and thought exist and develop in tandem from the beginning.

The plausibility of positing (a) an interrelationship between thought and speech from the earliest stage of infant-other meaning construction and (b) a multifunctional role for the speech forms born from that relationship, may be aided by an examination of one of the foundations on which developmental thought was built. The ideas of Baldwin, one of the major contributors to both Vygotsky's and Piaget's theories of development, provide the basis of such an exploration.

EARLY FOUNDATIONS FOR SOCIOGENETIC THOUGHT

Based largely on the writings of Baldwin (1892, 1894, 1895) the co-constructivist perspective has important implications for our understanding of the phylogenetic and ontogenetic roots of thought and language. It useful to outline the aspects of Baldwin's theory relating to the study of speech. Baldwin asserted that development proceeds through three hierarchically ordered levels of imitative capacities; organic, conscious, and volitional. Imitation in Baldwin's theory forms the basis for all simple and complex development. It is these principles of imitation, along with a capacity to form higher controlling centers (centers organizing and integrating developing mental structures—similar to Werner's notion of hierarchic integration) that form the basis through which mental functioning can develop from simple to complex forms. Baldwin (1892, pp. 286–287) divided imitation into simple and persistent reactions. In simple imitation (SI), a stimulus causes a physiological reaction that through the principle of "circular activity" repeated reproduces both the stimulus and the reaction. This form of imitation comes close to physiological habit and can be accounted for without reference to the three elements of voluntary processes; "desire, deliberation, and effort" (p. 286). In contrast, persistent imitation (PI) has the first linkages to HMF by allowing the development of conscious will or volition. The physiological difference in mechanism between persistent and simple imitation is the retention in persistent imitation of the copy produced, which can then be compared to the original reaction. This comparison takes place in what Baldwin termed co-coordinating centers' that develop in increasing complexity as the imitated stimuli also increase in complexity. The existing discrepancy between the different reactions gives rise to a state of motor restlessness or dissatisfaction, which in turn produces effort or "will-stimulus." Thus, through physiologically based circular processes, the representation of the nonexact imitation is further repeated and modified with greater volume and intensity until by sheer number of produced reactions the copy and varieties of the copy are created. According to Baldwin (1895) then the "useless elements fall away...and the successful effort is established" (p. 377).

PI and Social Suggestion: Foundation for Development of Multifunctional Role of PS

The proposed mechanism for not only intentional imitation but *variability* in that imitation opens an avenue for coordinating the process of persistent imitation with social suggestions. All motor activity including vocal activity has a base not only in simple imitation and instinctive reaction but also in the first source of meaningful intentional stimulation. Such stimulations provide a base for forming higher controlling centers and thus a basis for the goals and outcomes (however primitive) that the process of persistent imitation is working towards. The expression of the constructed sense meaning can take both verbal and nonverbal forms (gestures, body movements, and vocalizations). For humans, the verbal form is the most efficient. It emerges out of simple imitation and becomes constructed into sense meaning through persistent imitation and social stimulation. As persistent imitation and social suggestion both inherently allow for novelty, this verbal form of constructed sense meaning can serve, from the beginning, a variety of functions that are linked tightly with both biological lower mental functioning and HMF. What is important to not here is that on some level the antecedents of thought and speech are not separate. Instead it can be shown that all forms of activity (verbal and nonverbal) in organisms that have the capacity to form higher coordinating centers *can* but do not necessarily have to have an intellectual base. These actions can be serving specific preconscious goals that have at their base rudiments of effort, desire, and possibly deliberation; voluntary processes that may incorporate the integration of rudimentary forms of thought and speech.

Baldwin's (1892) 4-month-old daughter, for example, grasped at the "mere sight of fingers extended before her" (p. 286) after having been lifted by clasping her hands around previously extended fingers. Although this is described as simple imitation, falling easily under sensorimotor suggestion and bordering physiological habit it also has a connection to will, possibly involving the "glimmerings of desire" (p. 286). Seemingly such motor activity and its corresponding vocalizations would in Vygotskian (1934/1986) terms be preintellectual and thus evidence for the separate development of thought and speech; "rudimentary intellectual reactions occur independently of speech...crying, babbling...as well as the child's first words are pre-intellectual. They have nothing in common with the development of thinking" (p. 110). On some level, however, these activities have everything to do with the development of thinking—from the basic mental processes to the beginning of "will-effort" in Baldwin's terms. It is the very process of repeatedly and possibly reflexively grasping at extended fingers that not only keeps the avenue for further social interaction open but also allows comparison (or persistent imitation) of the social other's highly variable actions. The repetitive, reflexive, "pre-intellectual" verbal and nonverbal action patterns forming the foundation of simple imitation are the very basis by which persistent imitation and higher order coordination of sense meaning can emerge.

The importance of the idea of simple and persistent imitation being the basis for all motor and verbal activity for analysis of the PS phenomena is the theoretical basis it gives for multifunctional roots of PS. It is being argued that the linkage between basic organic adaptation via simple imitation and higher mental development via persistent imitation can most easily be made by conceptualizing thought and speech as being connected and developmentally codependent from the beginning states of early social interaction. Through the mechanisms of motor excess actions and circular reactions simple and persistent imitation become flexible systems that allow variability of constructed sense meaning in all three levels of imitative capacities (organic, conscious, and volitional). Diversity, therefore, is present not only in action patterns (organic imitation) but in the goals or functions of those actions (conscious and volitional imitation). Thus, because the expression of sense construction can form a variety of meanings, all forms of meaning expression (SS, PS, IS) in all manifestations (verbal and nonverbal) can take on a variety of functions i.e., creative, affective regulatory) in service of those meanings. Furthermore, as the expression of sense construction into sounds and movements can take on a variety of interacting roles at any given time, SS, PS, and IS cannot only be present in tandem but can interrelated and through such interactions influence and canalized their collective development. Thus the development of thought and speech can be thought of as a gradual process that involved, from the very beginning, an interaction between basic mental functions and verbal and nonverbal expressions of those functions. Through processes (admittedly yet to be specified) of social and self-meaning construction, the interaction between thought and speech increases in complexity and thereby develops toward sophisticated forms of HMF.

According to Vygotsky, the epigenesis of HMF takes place through the internalization of semiotic mediating devices (somehow via social interaction). This process would seem to require semistructured mental processes that continuously form intimate linkages with the organism's activity and speech. If PS is a means by which such internalization takes place then it must be able to take a variety of form and expressions in order to account for the great variability and heterogeneity evident in the developmental pathways that lead to the stable and general outcomes of personal meaning systems. As argued earlier, the increasing sophistication of psychological functioning necessitates interdependence and coactions between developing systems. Through their interrelationships, these systems may metamorphize in various ways. They may not only merge to produce new qualitatively different structures but also individually develop, possibly but not necessarily linking to other developing systems.

EMPIRICAL STUDY ILLUSTRATING
MULTIFUNCTIONAL ROLE OF PS

Functional Variety and Ambiguity of Speech Act Expressions

In order to document the various functional roles PS can take and its close interrelationship with other speech forms, transcriptions of adult-child conversation in the course of a vocabulary game are analyzed. The data presented in this chapter were originally collected for a doctoral dissertation (Markel-Fox, 1993). Children were administered a revised version of the Peabody Picture Vocabulary Test (PPVT-R). Standard testing procedures were embedded within the context of a game, allowing for both goal-directed PS and the PS-SS interplay seen during social interactions. Children were presented four stimulus cards with pictures of common objects and were asked to find a particular object. The actual experimental situation (materials, testing procedure), secondary to the purposes of this chapter, provided a source of adult-child conversation in the context of a semistructured game situation. Table 7.1 illustrates the potential outcomes of an interaction between various speech-action patterns and the self-other forms they can take.

Table 7.1 represents all possible PS and SS scenarios, open ended as they are, that can take place during the course of an interaction. The four columns indicate the four possible states of being assuming a baseline frame of activity that entails the minimum requirement needed for engaging in the task at hard. The definition of *action* is clearly one of the most difficult and imprecise to operationalize. Here it is defined as active, overt movement that goes beyond the "passive" state of doing only what is necessary for maintaining the ongoing interaction.

TABLE 7.1.
A Formalized Example of All the Possible
PS SS Forms Taken During the Course of an Interaction

	Speech and Action	Only Action	Only Speech
Intrapersonal	A	a	a'
Interpersonal	B	b	b'
Both	AB	ab	a'b'

The three rows indicate the most concrete differentiation possible between PS (intrapersonal interaction) and SS (interpersonal interaction). It should be noted that the difficulty in specifying what constitutes action forms also exist in distinguishing between the intra-personal and interpersonal functions of action and speech. Although pure forms of PS and SS cannot be discounted, it is posited that the pure forms are rarely expressed as such because of the close interrelated nature of the developmental trajectories of PS and SS; all forms of social action serve the self in some way just as all forms of action for the self can be seen as either emerging out of social interaction and/or moving toward competence in a social world. In specific instances, however, speech acts may be defined as serving *primarily* either form or an observable combination of both forms. Thus, the first two rows are not meant to be interpreted as indicating consistent isolated intra or interpersonal behavior, but instead instances representing the primacy (as reliably interpretable) of either form. The symbols in the table are used to analyze the speech transcriptions.

The denotations in Table 7.1 can be elaborated in the following way:

A— Speech and action are used as a self-regulating device that can include problem-solving stratagem, show of affect awareness of self in activity fantasy and creative word play. For example, the child may point to a stimulus card, repeating the nature of the picture on the card while trying to decide the accuracy of his on her choice. Here, again although it is not possible to ultimately rule out an interpersonal function, it is being classified as intrapersonal due to lack of clear reference to a social other. These symbols are designated more as all the theoretical possibilities Vs as a set indicator of actual inter and intra functions.

B— External social referencing with verbal and non verbal action. The coordination of speech and action for specific social goals (e.g., asking assistance, creating social bond, facilitating the continuance of the social interaction for personal—enjoyment, information seeking)—and/or cultural (—politeness—reasons). For example, the child may tap the experimenter on the arm, raise his eyebrows and smile while saying "I got it right, didn't I?" Here again it is not possible to rule out possibility of intrapersonal functions being played, however, the possibility of purely or primarily interpersonal functioning is being represented.

AB— Speech and action taking on social function, at the same time serving self-functions in some combination of columns A and B. For example, explicitly giving a verbal message (with social reference) and also frowning and taping the card repeatedly. Likewise, a verbal message ay be given without social reference. Thus the child, looking down at the cards may say "this is right?", frowning and tapping the card repeatedly. This second scenario is more ambiguous as an interpersonal reference. Yet empirical data illustrate most adults respond as if the child was socially interacting. Our emphasis is on the functional role of speech, but either action or speech may be used by the child to express a self or other function. In these examples, as in most behavioral examples, simple as they may be, it is not possible to a priori distinguish which form of verbal or nonverbal behavior is creating a self other function.

a— Some aspect of facial or body gesture (frowns, nods, pointing) that can occur either while engaged in a particular task or while simply introspecting. It can be used spontaneously simply as on expression of internal states and as a self-regulatory device. For example, the child may point back and forth between two cards, stare at one, start nodding, and pick it as his choice.

b— Action used to indicate a meaningful message to primarily a social other, for example, pointing or showing, smiling, winking, or raising eyebrows for a specific intelligible purpose. Thus the child may pick up a card, hold it up to the experimenter while looking at the experimenter, and rouse the eyebrows slightly.

ab— Combination of a and b where action is used for other and self. For example, smiling at something internally amusing while also using that act to indicate personal amusement to social others. Or, for example, the child may in irritation roughly handle the stimulus material (even when asked earlier not to) while glancing at the experimenter to see, her reaction.

a'— Variation of A. Speech used to regulate behavior as classic problem-solving technique, expressive functions, show of affect, and so on. In daily activities, speech is rarely divorced from action, yet its functions need not include nonverbal forms of action. Thus the child may repeat the name of an item in order to try and remember it or simply as word play.

b'— Speech used primarily for social interaction.

a'b'— Combination of a' and b'. For example, a particular speech act spoken reflectively for self yet also carrying information for social other. For example, a child saying. "I'm tired," expressing boredom and telling the other he or she wants to stop.

This general table of scenarios can be used to analyze structurally complex conditions in everyday self-other interactions. The following are three examples of child-adult interactions taking place during administration of the PPVT-R game described earlier.

The following transcriptions are analyzed excerpts of the interaction between PS and SS, illustrating the complex and dynamic multifunctional role speech acts play in young children's social and cognitive growth. Although the categorization of speech acts into specific calls of the table is made difficult by the fluid interaction between SS and PS, the categorization process itself helps to indicate the different functions each can serve and the dynamic nature of their interrelationship. Each speech act is followed by one or more symbols, the first being the most likely categorization based on the child's and experimenter's interactions. The necessity in many cases for a second or third symbol illustrates the functional complexity inherent even in simple speech patterns and the difficulty in precisely specifying one category. Experimenter descriptions of behavior are given in parentheses and the child's action is given within brackets.

Segments of Speech Transcriptions

Experimenter (Ex)
Subject #251 (3 years, 9 months)

Ex: Okay find a picture of a fence
251: a fence (in normal voice) [looking at cards]   [a']/[a˚b']
Ex: fence.
251: fence fence fence (soft voice) [looking at cards and picks one with emphasis]
      [a']/[a˚b'] [shows Ex and glances up]   [ab]
Ex: okay.
251: I went fence fence fence (said with same intonation) [looking at cards]   [b']/(a˚b')
Ex: yups, good. okay sit in your chair, good.

This first example already illustrates the complexity and thus ambiguity of speech act functions. The subject's first comment "a fence" is not easily categorized in any straight label of PS or SS. It displays characteristics of both SS (normal voice tone) and PS (no external verbal or nonverbal social references). The subjects' second comment, "fence fence fence," intoned in a soft voice could be taken as a clearer example of PS, especially in light of the accompanying action (looking at cards, choosing one energetically, and only later showing Ex with social references). However, the subjects' next comment illustrates her awareness of the social situation, desire to contribute to it and thus possibility of social functions presiding in any comment.

1.Ex: Find a picture of an accident.
2.251: an accident [frowns slightly looking at cards] (A) (AB)
        accident accident [looking at cards] (a') /(a˚b')
        [picks one shows ex while still looking at cards] (ab).
        But they all, but they crashed (deep breath) on the side [looking at Ex] (b')/[a˚b'].
        You're supposed to crash in on this front (deep breath) [pointing at card looking at Ex] (B).
3. Ex: Ahh.
4.251: not the side the front (with same intonation) [looking at Ex] (b').
5. Ex: Oh on the front not the side. Find a picture of a net.

6.251:   [puts previous card in pile] net [looking at cards] (a')/(a'b')
a a neaat [looking forward and raising eyebrows] A(AB)
a net picks one shows Ex, looking at Ex] [B]/(AB).

Here the second AB, Line 6, marks a possible transition from both a PS act to an SS act as well as from speech as expressive thought to action as expressive thought. "A net" moves from being both a comment to self, expressing the finality of finding a satisfactory card and/or a social comment to becoming a nonverbal social reference towards the Ex. "A a neaat," Line 6, can be an example of a speech act serving different functions simultaneously. It may be a self-regulating comment as well as an expression of affect (impatience, release of energy) and word play. All these possible functions may be serving a self-regulatory role in the sense of influencing the ongoing action and it is harder to see their role as *primarily* task-regulatory—channeling only performance or learning of the task at hard. Instead, this form of PS seems more relevant to ongoing performance as a means of expressing affect and creativity.

1.Ex: okay.
2.251:   I was going a a net louder [looking at cards and Ex and laughing] (B)/(AB)
3.Ex: yups, okay.
4.251:   net [putting card in pile] [a']/[a'b']
5.Ex: find a picture of someone tearing something.
6.251:   [looks for a while] someone tearing something, someone tearing something (speaking softly)
[a'] / [a'b']
[picks one glances at Ex and shows card] (b)
7.Ex: okay.
8.251:   someone tearing paper [turned toward Ex but looking at held up card] [AB]/ [B]
9.Ex: yea, I think you're right.
10.251:   Because they didn't want it [looking at Ex] [b']/[a'b'].

We can see many examples of speech acts, that although categorized with the same symbols, are, of course, expressing very different combinations of speech act function. For example, the first a', Line 4, seems primarily a reflexive speech act expressing finality, whereas the second a', Line 6, seems more indicative of problem, solving, self-questioning behavior. Similarity, comparison of the AB in this segment to the last two AB in the previous segment illustrates very different combinations of PS-SS scenarios.

The first of the two ABs in the previous segment have possible aspects of word-play and affect exaggerated in such a way as to make social reference likely. The second AB, as mentioned earlier, may be a transition between moving from a possibly strong self-reference to a strong social reference, whereas the AB of this segment could be interpreted as more strongly self-reference based. The important point to not is the complex and ambiguous nature of the speech act functions, which at any given point can be serving both social and individual needs while moving through various transitions of those self-social functions.

1.Ex: Okay find a picture of a hook.
2.252:   A hook [looking at cards [a']/[a'b']
         [goes for one hesitates, shakes head slightly, picks another swinging arm] [a]/[ab].

This exchange illustrates as possible nonverbal self-communicative act where head shake could be serving task-regulatory behavior. However, even though there is no obvious social reference it is not far reaching to speculate that the external show of hesitation may also have to do with the presence of the social other. Categorizing such an act as a nonverbal analog of PS, correlating it to task performance and either confirming or negating a PS <——> task-performance relationship overlooks the actual possible functional complexity. Even were the child alone the function of the head shake may not be purely taskregulatory but have aspect of social play where actions are performed for amusement, practice, and so on, as if and audience was present; a form of play-acting. Although this is not to deny the possibility of "pure" forms of PS being expressed, or at least the fact that speech acts may serve primarily one function or the other, it is important to note the close interrelationships between types and functions of speech forms.

Subject # 226 (4 years, 10 months)

226:   I know which one you're going to do [looking at cards] [b']/[a'b']
Ex: You do?
226:   Bow and arrow [glances at Ex] [b']
Ex: Find a picture of an arrow.
226:   [picks it up quickly and puts in pile, smiles] [a]/[ab]
       woah [laughs-thchee hee hee] saw a whip wrip [looking down and laughs again]
       [A/[AB]
Ex: find a picture-
226:   -someone pulling [pointing looking at cards] [B]/[AB]
Ex: find a picture of someone tying something.
226:   [points to one] nope (says it softly) [chooses another and puts in pile] [A]/[AB]
 Ex: okay. Good.
226:   I know which one you're going to say [smiling looking at cards] [b']/[a'b']
       igloo [pointing to it in direction of Ex but looking at cards] [B]/[AB]
 Ex: find a picture of a nest.
226:   [looking-scanning, puts one in pile] SIMPLE TASK COMPLIANCE
 Ex: okay!
226:   a that wasn't right [very softly making a face at cards] [A]/[AB]

In this sequence the subject's comment "saw a whip whip" gives another example of an interaction between social-self-creative functions; it can serve as a social comment, descriptive comment for self, and word play. It is also interesting to not the primarily self-referential comment "nope." Although this seems a clear example of task-regulatory behavior preceding action, it is not unambiguous whether "nope" actually canalizes later action or is a descriptive accompaniment to it. His last comment "a that wasn't right" spoken softly and with facial expressions seems less regulatory than descriptive or affect releasing. In either case the complexity of interacting mental processes is clear. It seems possible that regulatory tools (verbal and nonverbal) are not the domain of one form of speech. Instead, learning or channeling activity toward task-oriented goals involved a close coalition between inter, and intrapersonal action such that task performance cannot rest simply on externalized comments directing behavior in certain directions. Similarly, speech acts taking place in private or public that entail a primarily "nonsocial" character cannot be simply for task-or goal-oriented outcome but instead may also serve the myriad of affective, descriptive, creative functions necessary for adaptation to a highly variable complex existence.

1.Ex: find a picture of someone filing
2.226:   [scans, chooses puts in pile]
3.Ex: okay.
4.226:   [continued to look at chosen picture] it didn't have anybody filing [looking at new cards] [b']/[a'b']
5.Ex: it didn't?
6.226:   no. [raises eyebrows, lifts finger, looking at new cards] [B]/[AB]
         you didn't [looking ahead tchee hee hee, nodding head] [B]/[AB]
7.Ex: find a picture of a clamp
8.226:   gotcha you stupid clamp [puts in pile looking at one he chose [a']/[a'b']
         you almost clamped my fingers [looking at cards] [a']/[a'b']
9.Ex: hmm
10226:   [makes whining noise, turns finger as if screwing a clamp, glances at ex] [ab]

Here the subject's response "no," Line 6, to the experimenter's question "If didn't?" serves as SS while also being linked to nonverbal expressions that may have self-serving functions. These nonverbal expression could be analyzed as linkages that help the movement from one type of speech act to another; that is, the transition between the comment "no" as a social comment to "you didn't" as both a social (referring to ex) comment and possibly private comment (expressing out loud the subjects's feeling that ex was responsible). The latter part of the interaction involves imaginative play that does not directly include the ex but takes into account the ex's presence and perhaps value judgements.

GENERAL CONCLUSIONS

In this chapter, a multifunctional and dynamic role for PS was posited based on the assumptions of a sociogenetic model and a discussion of the relationship between mental processes and their organization into socially meaningful sense construction. As Vygotsky asserted from birth the mental development of the child does not unfold but is actively constructed on the basis of social interaction. The physical stimuli (visual, tactile, auditory) entering the system are made meaningful through the developing sophistication and organization of the cognitive-affective processes used in daily life. Thus from the earliers point in ontogeny, the child's verbal and nonverbal activity is linked to basic mental processes and gradually becomes linked to more complex sense meaning construction through specific and subtle social stimulation. From this base, the development of speech (PS and SS) can be viewed as developmental expressions of a variety of emerging sense meaning constructions. As mental processes are being organized and interpreted via social mediation the ability to conduct motor and verbal activity should take on characteristics of the same meaning being constructed. PS is one form of the externalized expression of the thought-speech interaction and thus it can serve any of the adaptive-creative functions of the activity born from their union. Theoretically, thus, PS cannot be viewed as a unifunctional construct that systematically and uniformly transforms into IS. Instead, the developmental progression of PS can be seen as an interactive mergence with all forms of adaptive, efficient verbal and nonverbal expressions (i.e., SS, IS, body movements). It is this developmental interrelation between thought and speech that provides the basis for the continuing emergence of sense meaning construction.

Thus it was posited that the very earliest socially meaningful behavior seen in child-other interactions constitutes a union between thought and speech. Through the mediation by subtle and specific social stimulation, early activity gradually differentiates into linkages with increasingly complex forms of meaning construction. The sense meaning constructions will likewise be expressed in all forms of verbal and motor activity. As was seen in the transcriptions, there exists a great deal of variety in the functional expression of both PS and SS. Although a multifunctional role for PS has been previously documented, it is necessary to analyze its occurrence in the context of its adaptive uses as well as its dynamic relationships with SS. It is interesting to not that at any given point a specific speech act function can serve a variety of social and individual needs, ambiguously moving through various transitions of those self-social functions. This is not to say it is futile or meaningless to try and define or analyze the obvious multifunctional roles of complex phenomena. Recognizing the inevitability of mental processes being multidimensional construct, it is important to build models that systematically take into account this dynamic developmental nature.

One key issue that has been left relatively unexplored in this text is how to conceptualize the *process* by which knowledge or sense of societal objects and meanings form. The importance of studying the development of sense construction is clear; as its formation seems essential to the very process of ontogeny. The highly heterogeneous nature of meaning systems makes it likely that their development forms through a variety of different mechanisms. Thus the study of sense formation needs to apply theoretical stances that can incorporate a variety of different processes. For example, some meaning systems must be less flexible and thus more directly incorporated and not as easily modifiable. Other meaning systems may be more ambiguous and only over time constructed by the individual with socially acceptable meanings. Still others may be highly flexible or ambiguous and thus open to reorganization at each point of contact or "infection" with various social messages (Valsiner 1994). The multifunctional and complex forms that psychological tools take make it imperative to study HMF or sense meaning construction by crossing the boundaries of levels from basic biological functioning to abstract affect and motivation. Study of the linkages between these planes and of the regulatory systems allowing both hierarchical organization and plasticity of that hierarchy may provide the models needed to more clearly conceptualize the relationship between though and speech.

REFERENCES

Baldwin, J.M. (1892). Origin of volition in childhood. *Science, 20*(511): 286–287.

Baldwin, J.M. (1894). Imitation: A chapter in the natural history of consciousness. *Mind, 3*, 26–55.

Baldwin, J.M. (1895a). Conscious imitation: The origin of memory and imagination. In J.M. Baldwin, *Mental development in the child and the race: Methods and processes* (pp. 291–321; 322–348). New York: Macmillan.

Berk, L.E., & Garvin, R.A. (1984). Development of private speech among low-income Appalachian children. *Developmental Psychology, 20*, 271–286.

Bühler, C., Hetzer, H., & Tudor-Hart, B. (1927). *Sociologische und psychologische Studien Über das erste Lebensjahr* [Sociological and psychological studies over the first year of life]. Jena, Thüringen: Fischer.

Diaz, R.M., & Berk, L.E. (1992). *Private speech.* Hillsdale, NJ: Erlbaum.

Flavell, J.H. (1966). Le Language Prive [The private language]. *Bulletin de Psychologie, 19*, 698–701.

Markel-Fox, S. (1993). The effects of race and poverty on preschoolers' performance in modified testing conditions. (Unpublished doctoral dissertation) North Carolina State University, Raleigh, NC.

Nelson, K. (1989). *Narrative from the crib.* Cambridge, MA: Harvard University Press.

Piaget, J. (1962). *The language and thought of the child.* Cleveland, OH: Meridian. (Original work published 1923).

Valsiner, J. (1994). Bi-directional cultural transmission and conctructive sociogenesis. In R. Maier & de Graaf (Eds.), *Mechanism of sociogenesis*. New York: Springer.

Van der Veer, R., & Valsiner, J. (1991). *Understanding Vygotsky: A quest for synthesis.* Oxford, UK: Basil Blackwell.

Vygotsky, L.S. (1986). *Thought and language.* Cambridge, MA: MIT Press. (Original work published 1934).

8

AMERICAN, ESTONIAN, AND SWEDISH MOTHERS' REGULATION OF THEIR CHILDREN'S DISCOURSE CONSTRUCTION

Karin Junefelt
Stockholm University, Sweden

Tiia Tulviste
University of Tartu, Estonia

In the socialization process, the child is explicitly or implicitly or implicitly taught how to perform a certain activity in certain sociocultural settings, be they verbal or nonverbal. The child is also taught the meaning of that activity. In this process, language is a powerful means in which cultural values and norms are inherent. In this chapter, we study how some mothers form the United States, Estonia, and Sweden construct and regulate their children's discourse development in mealtime and puzzle-solving activities. This is done within the theoretical framework of Rommetveit's notion of intersubjectivity and Vygotsky's notion of semiotic mediation.

INTERSUBJECTIVITY

The notion of intersubjectivity can be defined as an instance when two interlocutors are conscious of each other and share focus, worldview, values, and norms (Rommetveit, 1979) or share the same situation definition (Wertsch, 1984). Intersubjectivity is regarded to be a prerequisite for a symmetric communication. However, early adult-child interaction is not characterized by a high degree of intersubjectivity. In its development, the child has to pass through different primary, secondary, and other forms of intersubjectivity (see Hubley & Trevarthen, 1979; Trevarthen, 1977) before it can share the social and cultural concepts of the adult world. A totally symmetric interaction and communication is hardly ever attained because "human discourse takes place in and deals with a pluralistic, only fragmentarily known and only partially shared world" (Rommetveit, 1985, p. 183). Yet "intersubjectivity has...in some sense to be taken for granted in order to be achieved. It is based on a mutual faith in a shared social world" (Rommetveit, 1979, p. 96). In some sense, the mother takes intersubjectivity for granted in order to attain it (Rommetveit, 1985). She often imputes meaning into the child's bodily expressions, or speaks on behalf of the child. She takes on the responsibility of creating joint attention, construction, and regulation of the discourse. The basic asymmetry is of central concern in Vygotskian and neo-Vygotskian theories, where self-regulation develops out of other regulation in asymmetric interactions.

Semiotic Mediation

Semiotic mediation is the process by which signs are mediated and incorporated in interpsychological (communicative) and intrapsychological (mental) functioning (Vygotsky, 1978, 1987). "A sign is always originally a means used for social purposes, means of influencing others, and only later becomes a means of influencing oneself" (Vygotsky, 1981, p. 157). The use of language is one example of semiotic mediation, which provides the transition from interpsychological to intrapsychological functioning. Vygotsky himself was most concerned with linguistic signs as mediational means, and assumed the word as the basic unit. Wertsch (1985) extended Vygotsky's semiotic analysis to syntax; that is, he took the utterance or sentences as the basic unit. He also incorporated a distinction between the extralinguistic and intralinguistic contextual references in the analysis, a distinction that was absent in Vygostsky's work. In this way, he explained the child's successive mastery of relationships necessary for syntax: a development from extralinguistic prelinguistic cognitive categories to intralinguistic indexical relationships, where ultimately language can serve as its own context.

Mediation is often facilitated by the fact that many communicative activities have developed into genres: "Genres correspond to typical situations of speech communication, typical themes, and, consequently, also to particular contacts between the meanings of words and actual concrete reality under certain typical circumstances" (Bakhtin, 1986, p. 87). However, speech genres are culturally constructed (Wierzbicka, 1991), which means that even activities may have different content with a widespread distribution across cultures. They may be constructed as different genres in various cultures. There is a difference between more rigid genres such as certain games, like chess, and more open genres such as a mealtime ritual, where the genre does not determine the meanings of a certain utterance, but where the meanings created partly is by the cultural context, which in turn has to be interpreted through the cultural genre.

Semiotically Organized Settings

The activities of problem solving and mealtime are well suited for empirical studies of mother's construction and regulation of discourse. Most studies on mothers' regulation of their childrens' behavior, which have been made from a Vygotskian perspective, have only used problem-solving settings (Wertsch, 1979; Wood, 1980; Wood, Bruner, & Ross, 19976). Wertsch (1979) identified four levels in the transition from interpsychological to intrapsychological functioning in the child. These also reflected four levels of intersubjectivity. The first level of intersubjectivity was characterized by such an asymmetric situation definition in adult and child that communication was very difficult. As the second level, the child was beginning to participate appropriately, but communication problems still existed because of asymmetries in mutual understanding. At the third level, the child's situation definition was almost in accord with the adult's. The child could carry out the tasks with minimal assistance from the adult because intraindividual functioning in the child had increased. The fourth level of intersubjectivity was characterized by an almost symmetric situation definition, and the child could carry out the tasks independently. As to mealtime, Valsiner (1987) showed the historical and cultural differences in the design of the mealtime setting, the cultural and technical tools used, what food is eaten, and how it is supposed to be eaten in a "proper" way. He also showed that during meals the child from very early on learns cultural beliefs, values, and norms. All these aspects of mealtimes as semiotically organized settings have been neglected in previous research.

Social and Cultural Differences

Although cross-cultural research on mother-child interaction indicates many similarities in the mothers' construction and regulation of discourse, there are also many differences. These show that the discourse is shaped by values and norms of the particular culture in which the child is socialized. The values and norms are both inherent in language and expressed by language. Blum-Kulka (1990) and Blum-Kulka and Sheffer (1993) demonstrated cultural differences in mealtime socialization. In their comments made at the dinner table, Israeli parent stated more to mealtime behavior than American parents, who focused more on regulation of conversational maxims.

According to Candill and Weinstein (see Clancy, 1986), American mothers talk more to their 3- to 4-month old children than Japanese mothers, who emphasize nonverbal communication. American mothers place more value on fostering physical and verbal independence than Japanese mothers (Bornstein Toda, Azuma, Tamis LeMonda, and Ogino, 1990). These findings reflect that communication is a prominent value in American culture. This has been considered by Bellah, Madsen, Sullivan, Swidler, and Tipton (1986, p. 167): "The USA is a nation of joiners." Therefore, involvement in and creation of social relationships in central to Americans, and the means to create it is communication (see also Tobin, Wu, & Davidson 1990).

In the literature, the individualistic core of the American culture is widely discussed. It is argued that American stress independence from very early on (see Fischer, 1970). "Sometime after the middle of the eighteenth century, according to Daniel Calhoun, child-training practices began to change from an emphasis on peace and order in the family to the development of 'independent self-sufficient individuals'" (Bellah et al., 1986, p. 57). "Anything that violates our right to think for ourselves, judge for ourselves, make our own decisions, live our lives as we see fit, is not only morally wrong, it is sacrilegious" (Bellah et al., 1986, p. 142).

Individualistic and collectivistic sociocultures employ different habits, which "produces individual and collective practices, and hence history, in accordance with the schemes engendered by history" (Bourdieu, 1987, p. 82). Individualism is regarded to be prominent in the United States (Bellah et al., 1986; Triandis, 1993). Schwartz's (see Triandis, 1993) research in 28 countries showed the United States to be in middle on the individualistic side, and revealed high collectivism in Estonia in all investigated groups (teachers, adults, urban and rural). Historically, the differentiation between peasants and the so-called intelligentsia in Estonia is little developed and the traditions of peasant have been preserved. This could explain the collectivist tendencies in Estonia. Sweden is found to be a moderately individualistic culture. However, according to Daun (1991), the Swedes are extremely independent and self-reliant, although they do not want to "stick out."

Our interest in a cross-cultural comparison of seven American, eight Estonian, and seven Swedish mothers' construction and regulation of their children's discourse was motivated by findings and considerations such as those just mentioned. Do the American mothers regulate verbal activity more often than Estonian and Swedish mothers? Are they less regulative than the other mothers? Do they stress independence more than the other mothers?

However, many studies on mother-child interaction that have dealt with the question of how mothers direct their children's attention, behavior, or speech have been made from the perspective of speech act theory. But, in order to conduct cross-cultural comparison, speech acts as the unit of analysis are not appropriate, because they are ethnocentric: "The cultural norms reflected in speech acts differ not only from one language to another, but also from one regional and social variety to another (Wierzbicka, 1991, p. 26).

This study compares the mothers' construction and regulation of their children's attention, verbal activity, and physical activity in two settings, mealtime and joint puzzle solving. The unit of analysis the sentence type: declarative, imperative, and question.

METHOD

Subjects

The subjects were 2-year-olds and their mothers. In the American study, two girls and five boys took part, in the Estonian four girls and four boys, and in the Swedish five girls and two boys. The mothers had similar socioeconomic background by their work area and educational level.

Procedure

Video recordings were made in the children's homes in two settings: mealtime and puzzle solving. The recording of the mealtimes were intended to effect as natural a setting as possible. Therefore the settings varied in the different families and the different cultures; as did the duration of meals.

For the puzzle-solving task, a wooden picture puzzle of an animal farm was used, which none of the children had seen before. The parents were informed only that the children should solve the puzzle. The recordings lasted until the puzzle was solved or the children gave up on the task.

Transcription

The video recordings were transcribed with regard to distribution of turns and utterances. A turn was regarded simply as the time span during which an interlocutor was holding the floor. An utterance was regarded as a unit that was formally, semantically, or prosodically separated from a subsequent utterance. The following is an example of a turn that included three utterances:

M: you have to eat this now
     okay

shall Mom have some (Am:6.1, which indicates that the example is taken from
the American material, mealtime, child 6, page 1).

The transcripts were made using the regular alphabet, but as close to spoken
language as possible. Unintelligible utterance were marked with an X.

Coding

The material was coded with regard to regulative and praising functions. A
regulative utterance was defined as an utterance used:

1. To direct the child's attention; that is, utterances containing attention
    getters like "look," "see," "listen," or the child's name, and so on.
    Example: M: "See where you can get it to go" (Ap:3.3.).
2. To direct the child's physical activity, that is, utterances containing an
    action verb, and aiming at physical or nonphysical activity. Example: M:
    Sitt i stolen och ät (M: Sit in your chair and eat") (Sm:5.5.).
3. To direct the child's verbal activity, that is, utterances used to elicit verbal
    activity.
    Example: M: Who is that (Ap:4.3.). (See also Table 8.1)

The regulative utterances were coded with regard to sentence types. The reasons
for this was the need for a more unambiguous coding system than speech act
types would offer, because speech acts differ with cultures (mentioned earlier).
In contrast, sentence types were similar in the three cultures. So, the regulative
utterances were coded only with regard to the form of the following sentence
types: declarative, question, and imperative (see Table 8.1). The particle "no"
was coded as an imperative, if it was obvious from the context that it was
used an a regulative utterances. Ambiguous sentences types were not coded.

Genre-dependent contextual aspects were taken into consideration in the
coding of physical and verbal activities. Because intersubjectivity is not attained
when adults communicate with young children, because the children have not
yet learned the pragmatic use or function of certain utterance, the mother might
have one opinion as to how an utterance is to be interpreted, the child another.
The regulative function was coded with respect to the mother's interpretation,
as it was clear from the material that the mother would rephrase or reformulate
an utterance if the child responded "incorrectly," that is, to physical regulation
with a verbal utterance or vice versa. This can be seen in the following examples:

1. M: var ä tuppen nånstans Lars (where is the rooster Lars) (Sp:3.5.)
    C: (t)uppen dä (t)uppen (the (r)ooster the(re)(r)ooster)
    M: var ska den ligga då (where does it go then)

TABLE 8.1.
The Coding Procedure, Examples

	Attention	*Physical Activity*	*Verbal Activity*
Declarative	You need to look more carefully	I don't want you to put any of the food on the floor	And you can tell me what his name is
Question	And do you see a bee a bumble bee	Where does the cow go	Who is this
Imperative	See if it fits	Eat this cheese	Say who it is

2. M: do you know where the rooster goes (Ap:1.3)
   C: go there (pointing)
   M: okay
   put it in

Praise was define as an utterance containing eulogistic terms; for example "good," "good job," "that is not bad" and so on. That is, only verbal expressions counted as praise, and prosodic aspects or bodily communications were not taken into consideration.

Reliability

To evaluate the reliability of the coding of regulation and praise, we followed Guetzkow's (1950) procedure. One hundred fifty units of regulative utterances were classified by two independent, trained coders from each country. Interrater reliability for regulating attention by imperatives was 90% in Estonia, 80% in Sweden, and 100% in the United States. Interrater reliability for regulating physical activity was 71% in Estonia, 86% in Sweden, and 88% in the United States for declaratives; 92% in Estonia, 90% in Sweden, and 93% in the United States for questions; and 91% in Estonia, 91% in Sweden, and 97% in the United States for imperatives. Interrater reliability was 84% in Estonia, 92% in Sweden, and 95% in the United States for questions used for regulating verbal activity. The lowest reliability—regulation of physical activity by declaratives in Estonia—was caused by a few disagreements between coders about whether a certain declarative was a regulative utterance or not.

Analysis

The data analysis procedure was both quantitative and qualitative. The number of regulative and praise utterance types were counted per minute. The qualitative analysis described what was focused on by the mothers from the different countries during mealtime and puzzle solving. The small number of children participating in the study and the fact that they were not equally balanced in terms of gender did not allow us to compare mothers' regulation of boys' and girls' attention, physical, and verbal activities.

RESULTS

Regulation of Attention, Physical Activity, and Verbal Activity

Although there are similarities among all the mothers from the different cultures, there are also prominent differences in how they structure their discourse and regulate their children. All the mothers regulated their children more often during puzzle solving than during mealtime. However, the biggest between-settings differences were found in the Estonian data. During mealtime, both the Swedish and the American mothers regulated physical activity as much as verbal activity. In that setting, the Estonian mothers seldom regulated verbal activity. During puzzle solving, the Estonian mothers regulated attention much more than the American and the Swedish mothers, but verbal activity less often (see Table 8.2).

What Was Regulated?

There were both quantitative and qualitative differences with regard to the regulation used in the different cultures. Regulation of attention during mealtime was used by the American and Estonian mothers to make the child eat: "look at this piece of broccoli down here" (Am:3.10), "kuule söö"—"listen eat" (Em:8.3). Both the Swedish and Estonian mothers used it to distract the child from doing something that was regarded as bad behavior: "titta du har

TABLE 8.2.
The Frequency of Regulation of Attention, Physical Activity, and Verbal Activity per Minute During Mealtime and Puzzle Solving

	Attention		Physical Activity		Verbal Activity	
	Mean	SD	Mean	SD	Mean	SD
Mealtime						
Estonia	0.3	0.2	2.3	0.4	0.7	0.3
Sweden	0.3	0.5	1.9	1.7	1.7	0.6
United States	0.2	0.2	2.4	1.4	2.4	1.1
Puzzle solving						
Estonia	3.6	1.1	7.7	2.7	1.6	1.0
Sweden	1.1	1.0	4.6	2.5	3.0	1.2
United States	0.5	0.8	5.3	4.2	3.6	2.6

ju Musse dör"—"look there is Mickey Mouse" (Sm:3.1); "vaata kuidas sa lusikat hoiad"—"look how you are holding the spoon"(Em:3.1). The American mothers also used it to elicit communication at the dinner table: "and do you see a bee a bumble bee" (M pointing at a picture) (Am:4.6).

During puzzle solving, attention was regulated by all mothers to attract attention to the pieces of the puzzle: "look at this puzzle" (Ap:3.6); "do you see a house" (Ap:6.3); "look at the shapes" (Ap:1.2); "Keep looking keep looking"(for the right place) (Ap:7.4). The Swedish and Estonian mothers used it to direct the child's attention to details of the pieces of the puzzle: "har du sett kon har en bjällra runt halsen"—"have you seen the cow has a bell around her neck"(Sp:1.2); "vaata mis siin kasvab akna juures"—"look what is growing here by the window" (Ep:7.1). The Swedish mothers also use it to praise the child indirectly: "titta nu är all bitarna på plats"—"look now are all the pieces put together" (Sp:2.4). The Estonian mothers wanted their children to look before they put the piece in: "vaata aga kelle auk siin on"—"look but who's hole is here" (Ep:4.1).

Regulation of physical activity was used during meals by the American and Swedish mothers mostly to make the child eat: "can you eat your blueberries" (Am:1.1); "now eat something"(Am:6.4). The Estonian mothers used it to make the child eat in the "proper" way: "vôta lusikaga"—"take with spoon"(Em:3.1). The Swedish mothers used physical regulations during mealtime to correct table manners: "Lena när vi äter sitter vi still i stolen"—"Lena when we eat we sit still in the chair" (Sm:5.6); "du år använda gaffeln också"—"you may use you fork too" (Sm:2.1); "sen kan du torka av händerna"—"then you can wipe your hands" (Sm:4.7).

During puzzle solving most of the physical regulations were used by all mothers to assist the child in putting the pieces into the puzzle: "can you put the tractor back in there" (Ap:6.2); "do you know where the rooster goes" (Ap:1.3); "other way turn it around"(Ap:7.1); "var ska grisen vara då"—"where does the pig go" (Sp:2.3); "får vricka lite på den"—"have to twist it a bit" (Sp:6.1); "pööra ümber"—"turn around" (Ep:4.1). The Estonian mothers regulated their children's physical activity very exactly, step by step. The American mothers provided more general suggestions: "try this puzzle sweetie" (Ap3.5); "could you come over here please" (Ap:2.8).

Regulation of verbal activity during mealtime was used by mothers from three cultures to get the child's opinion on food: "you want strawberry yogurt" (Am:1.11); "how is your dinner" (kAm:6.4); "va re gott"—"is it good (Sm:5.2); "va re ett gott ägg idag"—"was the egg good today" (Sm:4.4); "kas on hea progand"—"is the carrot good"(Em:3.2). It was also used in Sweden to regulate the child's table manners: "va brukar du säja efter maten dåa"—"what do you say after dinner then" (Sm:2.2); "tack tack sajäjer man tack tack"—"thank you thank you say thank you" (Sm:5.7). In American it was also used to elicit table conversation: "had a busy day" (Am:6.6); "did you go to the playground today"

(Am:7.2). Talking at meals was sometimes even stopped by Estoninan mothers: " söögi aeg on ju sina siin räägid"—"it's mealtime now you are talking here" (Em:8.4).

During puzle solving, regulation of verbal activity was used in each culture for labeling purposes: "what is that" (Ap:3.7); "what's a rooster say" (Ap:4.5); "va ä de fóör nåt"—"what is that" (Sp:1.6); "va tuppen då"—"what does the rooster say then" (Sp:4.3); "kes see on kes annab lapsele piima"—"who it is who gives the child milk" (Em:7.2). The Estonian mothers elicited less verbal activity than the mothers from Sweden and the United States.

Discussion—Regulation

From our quatative and qualitative analyzes, a pattern emerges as to what the mothers from the different cultures found important to regulate during mealtime and puzzle solving.

In the Estonian informants the most prominent feature was to concentrate on the ongoing activity per se; that is, to perform the physical activity of eating and solving the puzzles and not mixing these activities with verbal activities. Thus, most of the Estonian mothers' regulations concerned the physical activity and details of the activity in order to carry it out "properly" through the regulation of physical activity and attention. Verbal activity was of secondary importance.

In the American informants, the most prominent aspects were to make the child perform the physical activity of eating and solving the puzzle but at the time to encourage verbal activity. This is demonstrated by the quantitative (see Table 8.2) and the qualitative data. It is as if the American mothers were encouraging their children to generate a secondary verbal representation of what they were doing, along with the action required to be carried out. This is socialization of verbalization that seems to go beyond the verbalization absolutely required to solve the task. Thus, most of the American mothers' regulations concerned physical activity and verbal activity. Attention was of less importance.

With regard to the most prominent regulative aspects, the Swedish mothers fall in between the Estonian and American mothers. Regulation of attention was used by Swedish mothers in a way similar to that of Estonian mothers, whereas regulation of verbal activity was used in a manner typical of American mothers.

From very early on, Estonian and Swedish children are taught to pay attention to details by regulation of attention: during mealtime to details of behavior, and during puzzle solving to details of objects. By intense regulation of physical activity and attention, and few regulation of verbal activity, the Estonian children are implicitly taught that verbal activity is of little importance. Interestingly, the same was true in Sweden not long ago. However, the Swedish children in this study were exposed to regulation of verbal activity similar to that of the American children.

TABLE 8.3.

The Frequency of Using Declaratives, Questions, and Imperatives per Minute During Mealtime and Puzzle Solving

	Declarative		Question		Imperative	
	Mean	SD	Mean	SD	Mean	SD
Mealtime						
Estonia	0.2	0.1	0.8	0.4	2.2	0.3
Sweden	1.0	1.0	2.0	0.7	0.9	1.1
United States	0.8	0.4	3.2	1.7	0.9	0.6
Puzzle solving						
Estonia	2.4	1.3	2.6	1.5	7.9	2.3
Sweden	2.6	2.1	4.6	2.7	1.5	1.1
United States	1.3	1.5	5.9	3.8	2.3	3.1

The frequent regulations of verbal made by the American and Swedish mothers show that the American and Swedish children from very early on are taught the importance of communication and verbal representation.

Regulation and Sentence Types

Whereas American and Swedish mothers preferred questions as a regulative means, the Estonian mothers preferred imperatives (see Table 8.3). Across all informants, imperatives are first and foremost used to regulate the children's physical activity and attention. Questions are used to regulate verbal activity and physical activity. Declaratives are used to regulate physical activity. However, many of the declaratives used are probably polite imperatives as are some to the questions, the so-called *whimperatives*.

As to cultural and syntactical differences, the material shows that regulation of physical activity differs between the cultures as to the preferred sentence type: The Estonian mothers were likely to use imperatives, the American mothers to use questions, and the Swedish mothers to use declaratives.

DISCUSSION

Studies conducted from the perspective of speech act theories have shown a frequent use of imperatives in speech to young children. As children mature, directives are used in a more indirect way (Bellinger, 1979; Schneiderman, 1983). But, the frequent use of imperatives in the Estonian data shows that there are also sociocultural differences in the use of them.

A frequent use of imperatives has been connected to working, class verbal behavior (Bernstein, 1965; Edward, 1979; Hoff-Ginsberg, 1991). We are aware of difficulties in separating social classes in other cultures on the same basis as in England and America, especially in countries like Estonia. On the other hand, many studies made in the United States have shown that the way mothers interact with their children depends not so much on the social class they belong to but on the educational level of the mothers (see Cousin, Power, & Olvera-Ezzel, 1993). The Estonian mothers participating in our study had at least a college education. The high frequency of imperatives in the Estonian mothers can therefore not be explained by social class.

The material shows that there are differences in the use of sentence types in the different cultures. It shows that the connection between the linguistic form and regulative function is weak. Children have to learn by prosodic patterns, the genre, and the context what is to be regarded as a specific type of regulative utterance in their culture in a specific activity setting. In the light of these results, we question the empirical results of a distinction between the so-called direct and indirect speech act types (Searle, 1975).

No doubt there are several reasons for the distribution of preferred sentence types for the same regulative function in the mothers of the different cultures. One way of explaining it could be by considering it from the perspectives of different individualistic and collectivistic tendencies in these countries (see earlier). The collectivistic tendencies in Estonia may be a reason for direct regulation by the use of imperatives, and more detailed regulation. The American mothers' preference for more indirect ways of regulating their children by using questions might be related to the individualistic core of the American culture.

Praise

The American children were more often praised than the Estonian and Swedish children, both during mealtime and puzzle solving (see Table 8.4). What was praised during meals differed in the various cultures. In Estonia, the children were praised for table manners (e.g., for saying "thank you" and for wiping their face) but the appearances of the children were also praised (e.g., the children's teeth, shoes, and bibs). In Sweden, the children were also praised for table manners (e.g., for saying "thank you," and for using a spoon). In addition, they were praised for eating with a good appetite. In the United States, the children were also praised for eating well, but they were priased foremost for "correctly" answering questions during what seemed to be a replica of a adult-adult table conversation and for being polite (e.g., saying "excuse me" when doing something regarded to be inappropriate.

There was generally more praise during puzzle solving than mealtime in all three cultures. However, the amount of praise during puzzle solving must be

TABLE 8.4.
The Frequency of Praises per Minute During Mealtime and Puzzle Solving

	Praises	
	Mean	SD
Mealtime		
Estonia	0.07	0.12
Sweden	0.02	0.03
United States	0.15	0.16
Puzzle solving		
Estonia	0.12	0.18
Sweden	0.37	0.61
United States	0.96	0.68

considered in relation to how the puzzle task was carried out. All the Estonian children finished the task. All but one Swedish child completed the task correctly by first taking out all the pieces and then putting them back again. In contrast, only one American child completed the task correctly. Three children took out one piece at a time and put it back. Three other children started but gave up.

The way the task was performed might be regarded in relation to the child's interest in the toy, the mother's expectations, cultural values, and norms. In Estonia, the children are not exposed to toys in the same way as children are in the United States. That may explain the Estonian children's willingness to do the puzzle. On the other hand, the American children are implicitly or explicitly exposed to their culture's highly regarded value of choice. One American mother explicitly states: "you know you don't have to do this if you don't want to" (Ap:2.12.).

What was praised above all by the mothers of the three cultures was the child's physical activity during puzzle solving. Praise could concern a single aspect of the whole act or the whole act. In the Estonian and the Swedish data it was most common that the mothers did not praise their children until they had completed the entire task. In the American material, the mothers often used praise *during* the puzzle solving task, which seemed to be a strategy to encourage and/or to regulate their children to complete it.

The expression of praise varied among the mothers of the three cultures. In Estonia the most common utterances were "good girl/boy" and "that is not bad;" in Sweden "good" and "very good" were most frequently used. In the United States, they ranged from "very good," "good job," to "you did it wow," and "ta daa," accompanied by the intonation pattern like a fanfare, and applause.

DISCUSSION

The Estonian expression "that is not bad" is an understatement, whereby and utterance is reinforced by a slight form of praise. It is similar to the understatements of the old Icelandic sagas, where nothing was praise unless it was regarded to be something extraordinary. The most remarkable American expression for praise in the material was "good job." To work hard and to do a good job is one of the basic concepts in the American culture (see Bellah et al., 1986). This concept seems to be so important that it undoubtedly is transmitted metaphorically from early on to each generation: "The most fundamental values in a culture will be coherent with the metaphorical structure of the most fundamental concepts in the culture" (Lakoff & Johnson, 1980, p. 22).

A comparison between the mothers of the three cultures shows not only differences as to quantity but also as to qualitative aspects of praise. In cross-cultural interactions, different ways of praising may cause misunderstanding. Praise is not a universal phenomenon to be taken for granted in each culture. There are cultures in which praise does not occur at all, as a means of socialization (e.g., the Gusii in East Africa; LeVine et al., 1994). The occurrence or nonoccurrence of praise and its formal and functional realization in different cultures seem to be related to different values and norms dating back in different cultural ideologies (see also Allwood, 1981).

CONCLUSION

Although our study showed that there were differences within each culture as to the mother's construction and regulation of the discourse, these differences were outweighed by cross-cultural differences. Due to an asymmetric intersubjective situation definition, the mothers regulated their children intensively; the Estonian mothers the most, the American mothers less often, and the Swedish mothers the least. However, most striking differences were the regulative aspects and the mediational means used for regulation.

The American mothers used regulative utterances to elicit verbal communication more frequently than the others from Sweden and Estonia. The fact that American mothers expect a lot of verbal activity from their children has also been found by previous comparative studies. This is in accordance with the view that communication is of prominent value in American culture, and that American mothers from very early on start to socialize their children into good conversation partners.

The Estonian mothers used regulative utterances to elicit attention more often than the other mothers. They wanted their children to pay attention to details and concentrate on ongoing activities, not mixing these with verbal activities, especially while eating.

The Swedish mothers regulated verbal activity less than the American mothers, but attention more than them. All mothers paid great attention to regulation of physical activity. The finding that Americans and Swedish mothers preferred questions as mediational means, whereas the Estonian mothers preferred imperatives was striking. So was the finding that declaratives were used more often by the Swedish mothers than by the others. These differences indicate that American and Swedish mothers regulate their children more indirectly than the Estonian mothers. This might indicate that more individualistic cultures use more indirect means to regulate children. Individualistic and collectivistic tendencies, respectively, might also be reflected in how many choices mothers offer their children. The American mothers in our study allowed their children to make lots of choices for instance to choose what food to eat, and if to do the puzzle or not. The Estonian and Swedish mothers did not.

Praise was used more often by the American mothers than by the other mothers. Whereas the Estonian and Swedish mothers praised their children when they had completed a task, the American mothers seemed to use praise as a regulative means to encourage their children to do something that was required.

There were differences between the two semiotically organized settings, mealtime and puzzle solving. Puzzle-solving activities were much more regulated than mealtimes. That could, of course, be explained by the fact that 2-year-old children can manage pretty well to eat independently but not to solve a puzzle. However, the differences in the mothers' regulations of the mealtime and puzzle solving could be explained by differences in socioculturally specific practices, values, and norms, and also beliefs about when and how to start to socialize children into table manners, problem solving, and language use. The socioculturally specific activities of mealtime and puzzle solving reflect typical situations of speech communication. They reflect socioculturally constructed genres. These function as frames for the mothers' discourse and regulation construction with her child. The mother's and child's different definition will be reflected in the regulations.

The differences within and between the cultures as to how the mothers construct and regulate the discourse correspond to the ideas of the sociocultural theory of *mediated action* (Wertsch, 1991), which stresses the situatedness of mediated actions. From this perspective, the differences in regulation and praise mirror differences in sociocultural norms and values rooted in historical and institutional traditions. In the process of socialization, children from different cultures learn to regulate and praise their own and other people's behavior according to their own cultural norms, also in the sense of how detailed different activities are to be regulated and what mediational means are to be used. Each child is socialized into his or her own sociocultural situation.

ACKNOWLEDGMENTS

This work was supported by grants from HSFR, the Swedish Research Council for the Humanities and Social Sciences (Grant No. 296/90), Svenska Institutet, the Swedish Institute, and the Estonian Science Foundation (Grant No. 537). We would like to thank Barbara Welles-Nyström, who initiated and conducted the HSFR project, and initiated and participated in the American and Swedish video recordings.

REFERENCES

Allwood, J. (1981). *Finns det svenska kommunikationsmönster?* [Are there Swedish communication patterns?] *Anthropological Linguistics 9: Vad är svensk kultur?* [What is Swedish Culture?]. Göteborg, Sweden: Institutionen för lingvistik.

Bakhtin, M.M. (1986). *Speech genres and other late essays.* Minneapolis: University of Minnesota Press.

Bellah, R.N., Madsen, R., Sullivan, W.M., Swidler, A., & Tipton, S.M. (1986). *Habits of the heart.* New York: Perennial Library, Harper & Row.

Bellinger, D. (1979). Changes in the explicitness of mothers' directives as children age. *Journal of Child Language, 18,* 41-49.

Bernstein, B. (1965). A socio-lingustic approach to social learning. In J. Gould (Ed.), *Penguin survey of the social sciences* (pp. 144-169). Harmondsworth, UK: Penguin.

Blum-Kulka, S. (1990). You don't touch lettuce with your fingers: Parental politeness in family discourse. *Journal of Pragmatics, 14,* 259-288.

Blum-Kulka, S., & Sheffer, H. (1993). The metapragmetic discourse of American-Israeli familes at dinner. In G. Kasper & S. Blum-Kula (Eds.), *Interlanguage pragmatics* (pp. 196-223). New York: Oxford University Press.

Bornstein, M.H., Toda, S., Azuma, H., Tamis-LeMonda, C., & Ogino, M. (1990). Mother and infant activity and interaction in Japan and in the United States: II. A comparative microanalysis of naturalistic exchanges focused on te organization of infant attention. *International Journal of Behavioral Development, 13,* 289-308.

Bourdieu, P. (1987). *Outline of a theory of practices* (Cambridge Studies in Social Anthropology). Cambridge, UK: Cambridge University Press.

Clancy, P.M. (1986). The acquisition of communicative style in Japanese. In B. B. Schieffelin & E. Ochs (Eds.), *Language socialization across culture* (pp. 213-250). Cambridge, UK: Cambridge University Press.

Cousins, J.H., Power, T.G., & Olvera-Ezzell, N. (1993). Mexican-American mothers' socialization strategies: Effects of education, acculturation, and health locus of control. *Journal of Experimental Child Psychology, 55*(2): 258-276.

Daun, A. (1991). Individualism and collectivity among Swedes. *Ethnos, 56,* 165-172.

Edwards, A.D. (1979). *Language in culture and class: The sociology of language and education.* London: Heinemann.

Fischer, J.L. (1970). Linguistic socialization: Japan and the United States. In R. Hill & R. Konig (Eds.), *Families in East and West: Socialization process and kinship ties* (pp. 107-110). The Hague: Mouton.

Guetzkow, H. (150). Utilizing and categorizing problems in coding qualitative data. *Journal of Clinical Psychology, 6,* 27-58.

Hoff-Ginsberg, E. (1991). Mother-child conversation in different social classes and communicative settings. *Child Development, 62,* 782-796.

Hubley, P., & Trevarthen, C. (1979). Sharing a task in infancy. In I.C. Uzgiris (Ed.), *Social interaction and communication during infancy* (pp. 57-80). San Francisco: Jossey-Bass.

Lakoff, G., & Johnson, M. (1980). *Metaphors we live by.* Chicago: University of Chicago Press.

LeVine, R.A., Dixon, S., LeVine, S.E., Richman, A., Liderman, P.H., & Brazelton, T.B. (1994). *Child care and cultures: Lessons from Africa.* Cambridge, UK: Cambridge University Press.

Rommetveit, R. (1979). On the architecture of intersubjectivity, In R. Rommetiviet & R. Blakar (Eds.), *Studies of language, thought and verbal communication* (pp. 93-107). London: Academic Press.

Rommetveit, R. (1985). Language acquisition as increasing linguistic struturing of experience and symbolic behavior control. In J.V. Wertsch (Ed.), *Culture, communication, and cognition: Vygotskian perspectives* (pp. 183-204). Cambridge, UK: Cambridge University Press.

Schneiderman, M.H. (1983). Do what I mean, not what I say! Changes in mothers action-directives to young children. *Journal of Child Language, 10,* 357-367.

Searle, J. (1975). Indirect speech acts. In P. Cole & J. Morgan (Eds.), *Syntax and semantics 3: Speech Acts* (pp. 59-82). New York: Academic Press.

Tobin, J., Wu, D., & Davidson, D. (1989). *Preschool in three cultures: Japan, China, and the United States.* New Haven, CT: Yale University Press.

Trevarthen, C. (1977). Descriptive analyses of infant communicative behaviour. In H.R. Schaffer (Ed.), *Studies in mothers-infant interaction* (pp. 227-270). London: Academic Press.

Traindis, H.C. (1993). Collectivism and individualism as cultural syndromes. *Cross-cultural Research, 27*(3) 155-180.

Valsiner, J. (1987). *Culture and the development of children's actions. A cultural-historical theory of developmental psychology.* Chichester, UK: Wiley.

Vygotsky, L.S. (1978). *Mind in society: The development of higher psychological processes.* Cambridge, MA: Harvard University Press.

Vygotsky, L.S. (1981). The genesis of higher mental functions. In J.V. Wertsch (Ed.), *The concept of activity in Soviet psychology* (pp. 149-188). Armonk, NY: M.E. Sharpe.

Vygotsky, L.S. (1987). *Thought and language.* Cambridge, MA: Harvard University Press.

Wertsch, J.V. (1979). From social interaction to higher psychological processes: A clarification and application of Vygotsky's theory. *Human Development, 22,* 1-22.

Wertsch, J.V. (1984). The zone of proximal development: Some conceptual issues. In B. Rogoff & J.V. Wertsch (Eds.), *Children's learning in the "zone of proximal development"* (pp. 7-18). San Francisco, CA: Jossey-Bass.

Wertsch, J.V. (1985). *Vygotsky and the social formation of mind.* Cambridge, MA: Harvard University Press.

Wertsch, J.V. (1991). *Voices of the mind. A socio-cultural approach to mediated action.* Cambridge, MA: Harvard University Press.

Wierzbicka, A. (1991). *Cross-cultural pragmatics: The semantics of human interactions: Trends in linguistics* (Studies and Monographs, 53). Berlin: Mouton de Gruyter.

Wood, D. (1980). Teaching the young child: Some relationships between social interaction, language, and thought. In D.R. Olson (Ed.), *The social foundations of language and thought* (pp. 280-296). New York: Norton.

Wood, D. Bruner, J.S., & Ross, G. (1976). The role of tutoring in problem solving. *Journal of Child Pschology and Psychiatry, 17,* 89-100.

part III

Theoretical Elaborations for Sociogenesis

9

INTERACTION, REGULATION, AND CORRELATION IN THE CONTEXT OF HUMAN DEVELOPMENT: CONCEPTUAL DISCUSSION AND EMPIRICAL EXAMPLES

Ana Carvalho
Amélia Império-Hamburger
Universidade de São Paulo, Brazil

Maria Isabel Pedrosa
Universidade Federal de Pernambuco, Brazil

IN
    FORMA
        AÇÃO
FORMA
        INTENÇÃO
AÇÃO

INTENÇÃO
INTENSÃO

IN TENÇÃO TENSÃO
                      LANGUAGE IS A VIRUS
INTENÇÃO IS A VIRUS
EM TENSÃO   IN IS A VIRUS
      UM PRINCIPIO DE AÇÃO

A MENOR FORMA DE VIDA
DE FORMA E DE AÇÃO

IN FORMA AÇÃO
INFORMAÇÃO
VIDA VIS VIRTU VIRUS
EM TENSÇO
INTENÇÃO

Amélia Império-Hamburger
Para Laurie Anderson[1]

The purpose of this chapter is to specify the meanings of some concepts that we have been using in our work on children's social interactions in play groups as a *topos* (i.e., a meaningful space) of development (Carvalho, 1992, 1994; Pedrosa, 1989; Pedrosa & Carvalho, 1995; Pedrosa, Carvalho, & Império-Hamburger, 1996). The theoretical basis of this work involve the assumption that individual development occurs in a social context, in the sense of a context of interpersonal exchanges, in several of the so-called "social species" (Hinde, 1974); and particularly in the human species, where a second emergent and also constitutive meaning of "social" is found: the sociohistorical (Carvalho, 1992; Valsiner, 1991; Vygotsky, 1978). The logical bases are framed within dynamic systems theory (Fogel & Thelen, 1987; Thelen, 1989) and in the logic of simultaneous constitution.[2] Our approach aims at an interdisciplinary articulation for the analysis of natural phenomena—from physics to psychology—that can both integrate them and point out their specific characteristics.[3] We illustrate the fact that all human characteristics constitute themselves within a culturally structured environment. Further, we point out that similar general principles and processes apply to nonhuman phenomena, provided they are framed within their specific levels and functional implications.

This purpose is pursued starting from the concept of *field of interactions*, and going forward through the unfolding of the concepts of *social interaction, regulation/coregulation,* and *correlation*. Along this discussion, the *general law of sociability*, and its fundamental principles—*attention orientation, sharing or shared attribution of meanings, and persistence of meanings* (Pedrosa et al., 1996)—will emerge from the observed phenomena. This conceptual framework is used in, and shown as derived from, the description and analysis of interaction episodes among 2- to 3-year-old children during free play, and is compared with their equivalent uses in the pertinent literature.

Our starting point is the epistemological similarity that can be established between the analysis of the sociopsychological system constituted by a group of children during free play as a dynamic system, and the analysis of a physical system endowed with perennial movement—specifically, the Brownian movement as analyzed by Perrin (1909). The Brownian movement is the movement of suspended particles in a fluid, which presents one and the same characteristic whichever scale is used to observe it (plain eye or microscope): It is irregular and unceasing. This phenomenon was identified by the Greeks: Epicure observed the movement of dust particles in a light beam, and described it in a way that was virtually recovered by Perrin in the 19th century. Perrin defined it as an eternal and spontaneous movement, using concepts that were completely foreign to the causality and the determinism of space-time relations in classical physics theories (Serres, 1977). Epicure deduced from this one and only regularity—the constant irregularity of the movement—the existence of a minimum and unchangeable unit, the atom; in the absence of this sort of unit, no constantly irregular movement would be possible. This is evidently a nonlinear reasoning: It implies a relationship between parts and whole, a system whose components move incessantly but that preserves a stable configuration. The atom concept, thus defined, is analogous to the concept of an individual constituting and being constituted by a social system (Oliveira, 1993).

We look at the play group as a *social* field of interactions—analogous, in a basic sense, to a gravitational field (the field of interactions of particles endowed with mass) or to an electromagnetic field (the field of interactions between electrically charged particles). *Interaction* is understood as the potential of regulation between the components of a field. *Regulation* between the components is said to occur when the movements or the behaviors of one component cannot be understood unless the existence, the presence, or the behavior of other components is considered; regulation operates according to laws that are peculiar to each type of interactional field, for example, the gravitation law in the case of a gravitational field.

An interactional field is thus defined by the nature of the interacting components, and simultaneously defines them. This circularity is what Império-

Hamburger (in preparation) referred to as the logic of simultaneous constitution: The whole that is never the same and the unchangeable unit reciprocally constitute each other. It is also present in Newton's (1704/1979) definition of the Laws of Nature: "*the laws through which things themselves are formed*" (p. 401). The use of this language makes clear that interaction refers to a potential information transit between the components of a system, such that the properties of the components define the nature of the system and are simultaneously constituted in the actualization of the interactional process.

We are thus forced to define what is meant by *social* when referring to a *social field of interactions*, and also to specify the nature of *sociability* as manifested in a particular field of social interactions.

ANALYZING CHILDREN'S PLAY GROUPS AS A FIELD OF INTERACTIONS

The episodes to be described and discussed in this chapter were selected from weekly video recordings, over 12 months, of a group of 2- to 3-year-old children during free play activities in a day-care center in São Paulo, Brazil.

In this situation, the activities of the children are not structured through adult interference or orientation, except in a very loose way (e.g., allowing the children access to the playground or playroom, and supervising the group to avoid accidents or serious fights). At first sight, there are few cues to help the observer to distinguish this type of assembly from other types. What we mean by *assembly* is the joint existence of components that perform movements and/or contacts in a geometrical space, with a seemingly random time sequence. The observer's task is thus to find cues about the nature of these movements, to understand the properties and the mechanisms of this assembly and of its components in order to picture them as a coherent system of meanings (i.e., to place them in a theoretical context).

As pointed out before, our starting point in the search for relationships between the observed actions was the concept of *field*, a concept that still has an enormous heuristic and organizing power in contemporary physics theories. We look at the group of children playing as acting in a field of interactions whose social nature is defined by their species-specific actions and relationships between them.

Regulation and Sociability

Episode 1: Alternating Dyads.   The children are playing in a large outdoor playground, partially covered by a canvas, on which several toys are scattered: rubber animals, wood blocks, dolls, cushions. At one of the corners delimited by the canvas, two children are playing in a seemingly independent way with wood blocks, piling them up and throwing them down. The episode was recorded during 9 minutes. During this time, there are two changes in the

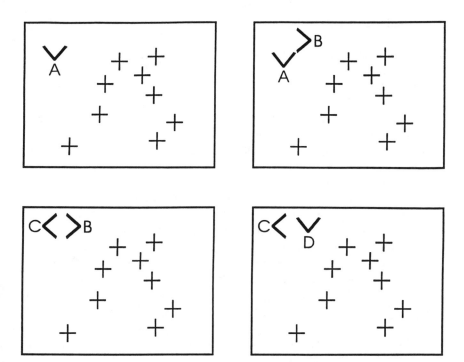

FIGURE 9.1.   "Alternating Dyads." A scheme of the distribution of the children in the playground area covered by the canvas, while the alternation of the dyads in the upper left corner occurs. A, B, C, and D stand, respectively, for Eliane, Viviane, Daniela, and Daniel, and their relative spatial position is represented by the V signs.

composition of the dyad: one of the children leaves, a third child arrives; the child who had stayed leaves, and a fourth child arrives. In every case, the dyads preserve the spatial configuration and the activities that characterized the former dyad, still playing independently (Figure 9.1).

Some aspects were specially remarkable to the observer in this sequence. First, there were very few explicit contacts between the participating children—brief glances as they visually inspected the environment and two short contests over objects and isolated verbalizations, as illustrated in the following description.

Eliane (G, 2;1)[4] is already playing with wood blocks when Viviane (G, 1;8) approaches her and sits by her side. Eliane uses a long wood block to hit her pile of blocks; she scans the surroundings, occasionally looking at Viviane. Viviane chooses another long wood block and uses it to destroy her own pile of blocks, then starts to pile the blocks up again. From a distance, Daniela (G, 2;2) watches Daniel (B, 2;8) who also plays with wood blocks in another place, then looks at Viviane and Eliane, approaches them, and sits down. Eliane leaves and Daniela places herself in front of Viviane.

Second, the replacement of partners is accompanied by a replacement of *roles*, which can be conceived as positions in the interactional field.

When Eliane leaves and Daniela arrives, Viviane starts to play with the wood blocks formerly used by Eliane, and Daniela plays with the blocks that Viviane had been using. There is a contest over one of the blocks, and Viviane leaves. Daniela looks at Daniel, who is nearby, and goes on playing with her blocks. Daniel approaches her, removes some wood pieces, making room to sit beside Daniela, and starts playing with the blocks. Both children alternate their attention between the environment and the toys they are playing with. Daniel leaves.

During the episode, a few nonreciprocated verbalizations occurred: "*me dê*" ("gimme!"), when Daniela tries to hold one of Viviane's blocks; "cadê?" ("where's it?"), when Daniel approaches Daniela; "*caiu*" ("fell down"), when Daniela hits her pile and the blocks fall to the ground while Daniel is sitting beside her; and "*meu*" ("mine") when Daniela holds a block while looking at Daniel.

Space (the proximity between the children and their spatial relations) and time (the sequence of individual actions along the 9-minute period that configures the episode) have oriented the observer's attention to frame this sequence as an episode; there was also an assumption about the possibility of identifying cues about the social nature of the regulations occurring in this interactional field.

It can be useful, at this point of our reasoning, to recall a few aspects of the analysis of social phenomena in other animal species. According to Hinde (1974), the proximity of conspecifics in a given time interval is not a criterion for the definition of sociability. As assembly of moths around a light source is not a social phenomenon, because the mechanism that controls the individual organisms is not the presence of a conspecific, but, instead, the species-specific attraction to light sources. What this reasoning implies is that a mechanism of regulation by the conspecific is a condition for the definition of sociability.

In this episode, there are some cues showing that the children's actions are regulated by other children rather than by other characteristics of the environment: in the choice of a particular spot, where a dyad was playing previously (while there were many places where room and similar toys were available); in the preservation of the dyadic configuration in spatial terms; in the imitation of the use of objects—piling them up and then knocking them down using a particular type of wood block (a long one); in the occurrence of verbalizations, even if not reciprocated. There were practically no explicit social *exchanges*, which would evidence reciprocal regulation or coregulation. The episode is labeled as social because the behavior of the individual (in this particular case, the behavior of at least three individuals—Viviane, Daniela, and Daniel) can only be understood if the presence or the behavior of the other children are taken into account; that is, if it is analyzed in the context of the constitutive social interactional field.

Eliane also belongs to this interactional field: Although her behavior shows no evidence of regulation by the other children, it regulates them, even if she is not aware of this role. This is an important point, because it shows that individual actions are not foreign to the social field; they belong to it even if it is another individual's action that shows this belonging. This is true whether we refer to a short span of present time or to a longer, historical time—a question to which we return later in this chapter.

This analysis also shows that our concept of social and of the process of regulation does not require reciprocity. Child A can imitate Child B without B's awareness; or A can act toward B and no effect of this action is perceptible in B's attention or behavior (Branco, Carvalho, Gil, & Pedrosa, 1989). In both cases, A is socially regulated, even if B is not.

The property of the components in the field of interactions that can be defined as social is, thus, the ability of regulating and being regulated by conspecifics. *Social beings* are those endowed of this property, which we refer to as *sociability* (Carvalho, 1992, 1994; Pedrosa et al., 1996). Just like any other species-specific characteristic, sociability manifests itself differently in different species, and it is the researcher's task to identify their specificity, to formulate the laws or principles required to understand them, and to analyze their functionality in the species life context.

The preceding episode allows a few steps in this direction if a question about the mechanisms of information transit in the system is asked. The answer suggested by the analysis of the episode is that the orientation of attention by the presence or by the behavior of the partners is a first principle of sociability when this particular interactional system is considered: "Viviane looks in turns to Eliane and to her toys," and then holds a long wood block and imitates Eliane's action; "From a distance, Daniela looks at Daniel who is playing with wood blocks, then at Eliane and Viviane." Next, she approaches the two girls.

It may be convenient at this point to hint that two controversial aspects of the concept of regulation are discussed in the final part of this chapter: the potential, but not necessary, connection between regulation and rules; and the relationships between this connection and the biological concept of regulation in homeostatic theories (Ades, 1985; Menna-Barreto & Marques, 1988).

Orientation of Attention and Information

Episode 2: Meetings by the Sofa.   The children (8 girls and 4 boys, mean age 2;3) are in the playroom; no caretakers are present. Many toys are scattered on the ground: wood and plastic pieces, toy cars, rubber animals, a carton box. At one corner of the room there is a sofa where Daniela (G, 2;7) is sitting, playing with a rubber pig head. Other children are nearby—Telma (G, 2;3), João (B, 2;3), and Lucinéia (G, 2;10). Lucinéia gives Daniela a wood ball she brought from another part of the room, and then leaves. Daniela places the ball on the sofa beside other balls that were already there. During the sequence (which lasts about 10 minutes), all but one of the children in the room eventually approach the sofa, play together, leave and return several times. Daniela is a "nuclear" child, who stays on the sofa and takes part successively or simultaneously in all the proposed games: She "feeds" and "bathes" her pig (suggested by Paola [G, 2;6], who gave her a wood block she uses as a "soap"); she accepts and organizes on the sofa the wood balls offered by Lucinéia and later by Telma; he pretends to feed on and to wash the hair of another child; she accepts Paola's make-believe theme when Paola leaves saying "*Vô trabalhá*" ("I'm gonna work"), and later returns saying "*Cheguei!*" ("I'm back!"); she allows Viviane (G, 2;2) to "comb" her hair with a wood block. The other children also engage in similar themes: Eliane (G, 2;6) offers Daniela "water" in a small cup; Alex (B, 2;5) says to Eliane "*Quélo água, quélo água*"

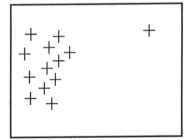

FIGURE 9.2.   "Meetings by the Sofa." The sofa where the children meet is depicted in the photo. The lower half of the figure is a scheme of the distribution of the children in the room, in the first minutes (left), and in the second part of the episode (right).

("I want water, I want water"); after about 40 seconds during which there are interferences by other children, contests, and crying. Eliane offers Alex a small cup from which he pretends to drink. The episode is interrupted when Lucinéia brings a large carton box; Daniela, Viviane, and Lucinéia sit inside the box, wave, and say "tchau" ("bye-bye") to the observer; Lucinéia vocalizes an imitation of a car motor ("brr..."). The other children leave to other parts of the room (Figure 9.2).

Although this description is very synthesized, it can be recognized that the sequence is very complex. At this moment, though, we want to highlight only what it suggests about the question of attention orientation and its meaning and unfolding in the context of our discussion.

From a functional point of view,[5] attention is a particular case of the general phenomena of orientation through which every living being frames the world according to the requirements of its own nature. Orientation mechanisms select parts of the environment and have been described and studied in several different levels by the biological sciences: Some examples are the tropism, the reflex, and the (innate releasing mechanism) (IRM) of classical ethological theories (Hinde, 1970).

It can be said that a sunflower orients itself to the sun, or that a moth orients itself to a light source, even if produced by a flame that will burn it—two examples of phototropism in different natural kingdoms. We would not usually refer to attention in these cases. It is possible, though, to mention attention if a dog raises its ears, stands up in an alert posture, and eventually growls and barks or eventually wags its tail when a certain scent or a certain sound reaches its senses. In the three cases—sunflower, moth, and dog—there is a process of regulation, and the functional requirement of selecting relevant parts of the environment is fulfilled. The difference lies in the potential differentiation among sensation, perception, motivation, and action. In the sunflower and the moth, these processes seem to be tied together in a single observable event. In the dog, it is as if there was a distance that allows alternatives between perception, resulting motivation, and action: a space of information containing the possibility of attribution of meanings to perceptions and to motivations that can regulate the subsequent action.

This approach to attention orientation explicates a further and more specific meaning of the property of sociability, a meaning that goes beyond the general one we proposed before (regulating and being regulated by conspecifics): It leads to the concept of social as a space of information created by the organisms endowed with sociability. This is a more limited concept, but still valid for a large variety of beings.

The "Meetings by the sofa" sequence shows once more that the children's actions are oriented by something more than the strictly physical properties of the environment—these don not have a meanings by themselves, a per se meaning. During the episode, the concentration of the children in the corner of the room where Daniela is initially playing on her own is salient. The lower half of Figure 9.2 depicts this concentration, contrasting the distribution of the children in the room (roughly 25 square meters) in the first and the second parts of the episode.

The meetings by the sofa seem to be oriented by an interest in the other children and in their play activities, rather than in the available toys: Lucinéia repeatedly brings toys, which she offers to Daniela. Paola arrives twice carrying several objects and engages in coordinated games with Daniela. Telma offers Daniela a toy, and then holds it back when Daniela tries to get hold of it. Eliane arrives with a cap and a rattle, which she uses a far, pretends to fill the cap with "water," and offers it to Daniela Alex, who was playing nearby, accepts this script saying "I want water." Viviane arrives with a wood piece and uses it to "comb" Paola.

The attraction that this particular spot in the room exerts suggests that the other child and his or her activities are a privileged focus of attention, an organizer or a framer of the environment. In the previous episode, practically no explicit exchanges occurred, but only *parallel play* (Parten, 1932); in this one, several coordinated actions and games were observed. In both cases, there is evidence of relationships between the group components, through the basic mechanisms of attention orientation (a perceptual mechanism) and attraction (a motivational mechanism).

This episode illustrates also, and clearer than "Alternating dyads." the transformation of information into meanings in the process of regulation that in some cases we can recognize as reciprocal regulation or coregulation. The individual actions are mutually adjusted and create joint or shared activities, as when Alex engages in the script enacted by Eliane and Daniela (offering "water") and is eventually allowed to take part in it. It also illustrates the freedom or the potential for different outcomes (i.e., the unpredictability) that the attribution of meanings introduces in the interactional field, as when Telma seems to offer Daniela a toy, and then holds it back. The attribution of meanings is unpredictable a priori: It is defined on a moment-to-moment basis, which is the essence of a stochastic process.

Once again, before we move to the description of another episode that can illustrate this second principle of sociability—the attribution of meaning, it seems useful to go back to some analogies with the behavior of other animal species as an essay to further understand the functional basis of this concept and the extension, or the limitations, of its applications.

The ability of attributing meanings to the information present in the interactional field emerges in the course of evolution as a functional requirement of the potential ambiguity of the conspecific whose presence (or existence) defines this interactional field (Carvalho, 1989). Examples of this phenomenon are the situations in which divergent motivational states are unchained simultaneously by the perception of a conspecific; for instance, in courtship interactions a rival male elicits both aggressiveness and fear; a potential sexual partner elicits sexual attractions, but also fear and aggressiveness (Hinde, 1974). The signs exchanged by the partners in these situations (i.e., the information dynamics present in the interaction field) will eventually lead to an outcome, not entirely predictable: The information given by the partners' behaviors is interpreted—it has different potential meanings—according to context cues (e.g., whose territory is the scenery of the encounter) and with the partners' present dispositions. Depending on the species, these can include previous experiences in similar situations or with this particular partner, group status, and so on. Our point in this argument is that the ambiguity of the information offered by social partners, and thus the functional requirement of the ability to interpret it (to attribute meaning) are positively correlated with the complexity of social life in nature: As this complexity increases, the potential meanings of the partners—using another language, the potential roles of the partners—are more diversified, and thus require more ability to transform information into meaning.[6] In evolutionary terms, this relationship implies the presence of this ability in many animal species, including some cases of previously unsuspected degrees of sophistication—for instance, the recently recognized deceiving ability (Machievellian intelligence) in primates (de Waal, 1982; Plutchik, 1990; Whiten & Byrne, 1988).

What are the processes or mechanisms through which a sign or information is transformed in a meaning? In the next episode, we look for cues in this direction.

From Information to Meaning

Episode 3: Laughters.   The children are outdoors in the playground. Two girls (Daniela, 2;1, and Lucinéia, 2;4) are standing in a two-seat swing, which is pushed back and forth by Cristiane (G, 1;9). Daniela and Lucinéia are laughing loudly and screaming in a playful mood Eliane (G; 2;0) approaches the swing and starts to push it, too, which makes the swing movement stronger, as Eliane's strength is added to Cristiane's. Cristiane and Eliane leave, the swing movement slows down; Daniela and Lucinéia stop laughing. After a moment, Cristiane comes back with Rafael (B, 2;9) and they start to push the swing again; the movement is now even stronger than before, possibly because Rafael is an older child. As the swing moves higher, Lucinéia starts to laugh loudly, and so does Daniela, who also shakes her body rhythmically. As soon as Rafael stops pushing and the swing slows down, being pushed only by Cristiane, the laughing stops. It bursts again as Rafael gives the swing another strong push. Rafael stops pushing once more, and the laughing stops, although Cristiane is still pushing. Rafael leaves for a brief moment, then comes back and starts to push. Lucinéia starts to laugh and to scream playfully. Daniela looks at her, then at Rafael and also starts to laugh, scream, and shake her legs (Figure 9.3).

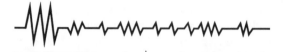

FIGURE 9.3.   "Laughters." Two moments of the episode: The beginning, when the intensity of laughter (schematically indicated in the graphs above the photos) is not related to the intensity of the swing movements, and in the final part of the sequence, when this relation occurs. The moment in which each photo was taken is indicated by the vertical sign in the line above the photos.

Laughter is a frequent expressive behavior in the free play situations we observed. It it also frequently accompanied by body movements and vocalizations such as playful screams (Plutchik, 1990). From the standpoint of an ethological analysis of communication, laughter is considered the product of a phylogenetic process of ritualization that is, the construction of a communication resource through natural selection (Lonrenz, 1966; Otta, 1994; van Hoof, 1972). From intention movements, autonomic responses, or displacement activities elicited by fear, aggressiveness, and other motivational states, and under the pressure of the need of information exchanges relevant to a functional outcome of social encounters, phylogenetic history selects behavior with maximum communication value, through processes such as the reduction of morphological variability, increased conspicuousness of movements, and independence from the variations in the motivational state of the partners. The behavior created through these processes are ritualized gestures or sequences of gesture that inform the partners about each other's behavioral dispositions and regulate their subsequent actions in the interactional field (Hinde, 1974).

From a comparative perspective, it is acceptable to understand part of the regulation processes occurring in human social interactions as mediated by phylogenetically ritualized gestures and behaviors, especially during the first years of life, when there is a limited use of verbal resources. Beside laughter and smiles, a well-known example is the lateral bending of the head presented by young children in appeasing and object-offering contexts (Montagner, 1978). The "Laughters" sequence suggests, though, that the existence of phylogenetically ritualized codes does not imply the absence of a permanent dynamics of transformation and construction of meanings in the history of interactional systems. New codes can be constructed from a ritualized gesture, from an idiosyncratic gesture, and even from linguistic codes that have a sociohistorical origin.[7]

During the "Laughters," sequences, laughs appear at first as expressions of pleasure and excitement elicited by the swinging movement. During the episode, Daniela and Lucinéia turn it into information about a particular aspect of the game that they chose together: the stronger movement resulting from the pushes of a second and/or a stronger child. Having agreed about this choice, the two girls coordinate their actions, adjust them to swing movements, and thus create the possibility of communicating this choice to the other children and of regulating their behavior accordingly. Laughter is operating here as a new code, with a particular meaning in the interactional field constituted by these children.

In our next episode, a similar transformation is observed, suing idiosyncratic gestures and vocalizations to create a new meaning. An initially agonistic encounter, originated from one of the children's refusal of access to a toy to another child, is transformed in an imitation game. Like in the previous episode, this transformation involves the shared creation of new meanings for gestures and sounds, and an increasing rhythmic synchronization of the partner's behaviors.

Episode 4: From Disagreement to a Rhythmic Game.   Viviane (G, 2;1), João (B, 2;3), and Alex (B, 2;4) are playing in the two-seat swing in the playground. Another girl tries to join them and is discouraged with pushes and hair pulling. João participates in this rejection, and immediately after leaves to where the caretake is with some other children. After about 3 minutes, João comes back to the swing, where Viviane and Alex are still playing João looks at Viviane. She pushes him and stands up in the swing seat. João puts his tongue out for her, she kicks him lightly. He says. *"sai"* ("get out!"); she imitates him, putting out her tongue and saying "get out!" Viviane starts to jump and to singsong; "pula, pula, pula… pé pé pé" ("jump, jump, jump…. foot, foot, foot…"). João climbs the swing, looking at Viviane. Viviane pushes him lightly with her foot and says "Get out…" João replies "ai, não…" ("oh, no…"). Viviane jumps three times, singing "te, te, te…" and starts to move her body up and down slowly, synchronizing the movements with the sounds "te, te, te…" João imitates her and coordinates the rhythm of his movements and vocalizations with hers. After a few seconds, João looks away and the game is interrupted.

The last episodes illustrate again the meaning we are attributing to the concept of co-regulation (Fogel, 1992) or reciprocal regulation (Pedrosa, 1989): It is defined as a process of mutual adjustment through which an agreement about meaning, or a shared meaning, is reached. In "Laughters," this agreement is evidenced by the signaling behavior of Lucinéia and Daniela, and the motor behavior of Rafael and Cristiane (pushing the swing again), which are mutually adjusted during the sequence. In Episode 4, the initial disagreement is elaborated and gives origin to an imitation game. Once more, the unpredictability introduced by the attribution of meanings in the interactional field is exemplified.

Coregulation can unchain a more specific process that creates an attractor, in which case refer to it as a correlation (Pedrosa et al., 1996). Similar to the mathematical meaning of correlation, in the case of social interaction systems, the concept implies information reduction or condensation and also more precise information (the same trends that occur in the phylogenetic process of ritualization). How does this reduction occur? In a mathematical sense, an "A.B action" action" contains less meaning than an "[AB] action" (Haken, 1978, 1988). Because A's action is never identical to B's action, their joint expressions eliminates the differences and preserves only the similarities, "throwing out the noise", that is, irrelevant (not meaningful) information for the agreement. Correlations thus involves an economy, an abbreviation (Lyra & Winegar, 1996).

A coregulation process can either constitute or not constitute a correlation. For instance, in the sofa episode, Paola gives Daniela a wood piece, and Daniela uses it to "bathe" the pig, and Daniela allows Viviane to "comb" her hair. In both cases, reciprocal regulations are occurring, but hey do not lead to attractors as implied in a correlation process; the regulation that occurs does not create a collective configuration evidencing convergence and selection of meanings. In this episode, the attractor that represents a convergent selection of actions is the global configuration "meetings by a certain place." The isolated actions, although they may be coregulated, can be considered noise.

When a correlation occurs, it opens the path for the emergence of a third principle of sociability: the persistence of meaning, which we examine through the analysis of the next two episodes.

Abbreviation and the Persistence of Meaning

Episode 5: "Dêta, dêta!" ("Lie down!"). The children are playing in the playground where several toys are scattered. Viviane (G, 1;8) is sitting alone, playing with toy dishes. From a distance, Vania (G, 2;0) looks at Viviane. Viviane lies on the floor and Vania bends over her. Both girls get seated; Vania lies down, but Viviane does not look at her. Vania stands up and leaves, then comes back and lies again. Viviane starts to lie down, but then gets up and looks around. Vania is still looking at Viviane. From a distance, Cristiane (G, 1;9) is looking in the direction of Vania and Viviane. Vania vocalizes a playful scream and looks in the direction of Cristiane.

Cristiane approaches Vania and lies down beside her. Vania gets closer, pulls Cristiane's shirts, and touches her uncovered belly with an object. Cristiane shrinks and Vania laughs. Cristiane gets seated and points to the ground with her hand. Vania lies down and uncovers her belly. Cristiane brings her hand close to Vania; Vania laughs and vocalizes, then gets seated again. Cristiane lies down. Vania says "dêta, dêta!" ("lie down! lie down!"), pulls Cristiane's shirt, and touches her belly. Cristiane screams and gets seated. Vania taps the floor saying "*aqui, dêta!*" ("lie down, here"). Cristiane points to the ground and Vania moves away. Cristiane keeps pointing to the ground and looking at Vania.

The sequence is interrupted by two caretaker who cover the ground with a canvas. After the canvas is placed, Vania is heard saying "*Dêta!*" ("Lie down!") repeatedly while she returns to her former place, now over the canvas. Cristiane approaches her and points to the canvas; Vania keeps saying "lie down, lie down!" Another child (Rafael, B, 2;9) runs toward the girls, whirls, and falls seated near them; the children laugh and Rafael lies and turns over his body, lying on the floor. Cristiane bends over him and touches him and Vania says "lie down, lie down!" From a short distance, another girl (Daniela, 2;2) is watching the three partners; she lies down, moves her legs, and then sits. Rafael stands on all fours, while Vania pulls his shirt and touches his back with a toy saying "lie down!" Daniela lies again. Vania, Rafael, and Crisitiane stand on all fours, Daniela (still from a distance) imitates them and says "*miau, miau!*" ("meow, meow"). The children laugh, run, and crawl on the canvas.

The arrival of a caretake interrupts the game as the children orient themselves toward her. Several minutes later, when the children are already engaged in other activities, Vania is heard repeating "lie down, lie down!" several times. The whole sequence lasted about 6 minutes.

This detailed step-by-step description was presented in order to highlight and to allow us the discussion of some particularly important aspects. Firt, this episode recovers and amplifies the previously discussed concepts of attention orientation, regulation, and coregulation. Viviane's spontaneous action of lying down beside Vania—whose attention was already oriented toward her—seems to be framed by Vania as a starting point of a already oriented toward her—seems to be framed by Vania as a starting point of a possible game: lying down and sitting in turns. Viviane does not engage in this proposal; but the configuration constituted by the dyad of Viviane-Vania attracts the attention of Cristiane, who approaches them and behaves as if she shared the meaning proposed by Vania. Using this shared meaning as a starting point, the game is constructed together by Vania and Cristiane, with added components (touching the body of the lying partner) and including expressive signs of pleasure and playful dispositions (laughs, vocalizations).

A second interesting aspect is the introduction, by Vania, of a verbal explication of an already shared proposal, when she says "lie down" after Cristiane is lying, as if confirming it. It may be useful to state, at this point, that Cristiane is probably a deaf child and does not present articulate speech (it can be noticed, during the description of the episode, that she does not verbalize and uses motor gestures—pointing—to communicate with Vania), a fact that indicates that the agreement between the two girls was not dependent on a previously existent sharing of the linguistic meaning of the word. Despite this, there is evidence of an increasing coregulation in the initial sequences of lying-sitting turns; when Vania fails to use her turn and instead invites Cristiane to lie again, the game is briefly interrupted: Cristiane keeps pointing to the ground, as if a rule of alternating roles had been established between them.

The third interesting point is that the meaning of Vania's repeated verbalization ("lie down") seems to undergo a differentiation process during the episode: It is used initially as a confirmation, then as an invitation and as a marker of the alternating roles; as a new invitation after the caretakers interrupt the game; and as the name of the game itself, when, already configured, it attracts and engages other children (Rafael and Daniela).

Viviane's action of lying down was framed and selected by Vania, when she repeats it, and by Cristiane, when she engages in Vania's proposal. In a similar way, a linguistic selection—matching the gesture—was made by Vania after she says "lie down" for the first time. These words evidently belonged already to Vania's verbal repertoire; she brings them to the situation and uses them in different moments, as if testing, establishing, or specializing them. It is an active construction or reconstruction of the words in the interactional field, where they now stand for a shared action or a particular configuration. The action of lying down is the essence of the game that was created through the shared attribution of meanings to the partners' actions; that is, the action that represents the game, "lie down" is the linguistic expression that represents this action at another level of meaning. Through this relationships, the words acquire an "actualization effect" in this particular interactional field: By saying "lie down," the child increases the probability of the game being maintained and/or started again with other partners. The words "lie down," as well as the whole configuration of the game—the actions of lying, sitting, touching in turns—were transformed, from "suspended" information in the interactional field, into shared meanings.

We believe that some of the regulation and coregulation phenomena that were identified in this episode must be characterized as correlations, meaning the exercise or the actualization of shared potentialities (Pedrosa et al., 1996) leading to the creation of new meanings that can be condensed or abbreviated, and thus allow qualitative changes in the space of information. Lyra and Rossetti-Ferreira (1995) showed how face-to-face exchanges in mother-infant interactions in the first months of life pave the way to the introduction of the object as a mediator of social exchanges (mother-object-baby) as the negotiation involved in the establishment of eye contact is abbreviated.

In an analogous way, during the "Lie down" episode there is a condensation of informations (words, gestures and actions), the word possibly being the best potential representation of what is being shared. It is important, for our argument, to demonstrate that these representations come to be part of the group culture, in the sense of evoking similar episodes in later moments of the group history. Our aim is to point out the nature of the process through which such a possibility can eventually can eventually exist: Abbreviation creates the possibility for the persistence of a meaning—the third principle of sociability in the social field of interactions we are analyzing here.

One more episode can help us to clarify this last statement.

Episode 6: Pretending to Sleep. The children are playing in the playground, where only one toy is available: a two-seat swing. An agonistic sequence occurs when Lucinéia (G, 2;9) tries to join the children who are using the swing (Viviane—G, 2;1/ Joêo—B, 2;3/ Alex—B, 2;4) and is repelled. A similar scene occurs later, and was described in Episode 4. In the meantime, Viviane and Alex, and then Alex and Lucinéia, develop a "pretending to sleep" game, closing their eyes and bending their heads against the seat. Another child (Daniela—G, 2;7) approaches the swing, observes the scene for a moment,

FIGURE 9.4. "Pretending to Sleep." Left: The beginning of the "pretend to sleep" game. Right: The arrival of Daniela while Alex and Lucinéia (sitting on the right side of the swing) "pretend to sleep."

and says "*Eu tambiém quelo* **bincando**" ("Me wanna **playing** too"); she steps into the swing and says to Lucinéia, "*códa! códa!*" ("wake up! wake up!"), thus making explicit the shared meaning of the game. During the sequence the children laugh and vocalize playful screams. The total duration of the episode was 7 minutes (Figure 9.4).

One again, this episode shows the occurrence of shared construction of a meaning that lasts and is diffused. The meaning emerges between two partners and "contaminates" other children, creating a recognizable configuration; this is evidence by Daniela's verbalizations: "Me wanna *playing* too"—where the verb form suggests the perception of an ongoing process—and "wake up! wake up!" which makes explicit the meaning collectively attributed to the configuration."

At first sight, the concept of persistence requires the specification of a temporal criterion. In our view, this specification is arbitrary and does not affect the concept's validity. The meaning can last a few minutes, like in the play episodes that were described here, it can persist for weeks, like in other observations we have described elsewhere (e.g., Carvalho, 1992), or it can be incorporated in a particular play group's culture, in a society's culture or in the culture of several societies, as in the case of traditional games such as kites, marbles, top spinning, and other "ruled games"—in which cases it also becomes a historical phenomenon. It is not the duration, but rather the fact of persistence the qualifies this concept as one of the basic principles of sociability in the situations examined here.

The relationships that we suggest among correlation, phylogenetic ritualization, and ontogenetic abbreviation processes indicate the possibility of an articulation between different levels of natural phenomena. From the attractor in the mathematical sense to animal communication, from animal communication to the construction of linguistic codes, the description and analysis of the relevant processes involve common elements. Concepts such as convergence, synthesis, condensation, and economy can be reported to the physical concept of minimum action, formulated by Maupertuis in the 18th century (Mardegan, 1990). The state-process dynamics—continuous transformation along different time scales, with recognizable moments of stability (attractors)—can also be identified in all these levels: a spatial configuration, the meaning of a ritualized gesture, a ruled game, and the meaning of a word. Persistent meanings, stable configurations, stereotypes, and rituals are necessary moments in the dynamics of interactional fields, like steps of a ladder, from which novelty can emerge again. Wallon (1942/1979) commented:

> A ritual gesture has no meaning except through its relation to a prototype, has no motive except to reach a result which the prototype intermediates, a result whose conditions or possibilities do not belong, at least completely, to the present circumstances. It is less an action than the figure of an action. Its consequences are not contained in it, but rather in the forces that it evokes, that is, in what it represents. The ritual introduces representation, which through it becomes the condensation of an efficiency that is not any more in the simple muscular actions. (p. 129)

It should be clear from this interdisciplinary articulation that our approach to the concepts of attribution and of persistence of meanings does not define them as human specific. They can be found in phylogenetically ritualized behaviors in every species where the conspecific is potentially ambiguous in terms of information and of motivation—in which cases the persistence of meaning, necessarily but not exclusively, involves the transmission of genetic information; and also as products of abbreviation (ontogenetically constructed, which again does not imply the absence of relevant genetic information) at least in the social interactions of nonhuman primates as reported by Hinde (1974), Plutchik (1990), Whiten and Byrne (1988), de Waal (1982), and others. Continuity, though, does not imply nondifferentiation, as should be clear from former statements in this chapter. On the contrary, our reasoning implies mainly that the principle of meaning persistence contains the possibility—or, in a stronger statement, is a necessary condition—for the emergence or differentiation of a specifically human phenomenon: the symbol and its consequences (a symbolic articulated, and later written, language).

It is beyond the possibilities and the purposes of this chapter to explore the unfolding of the phenomena that emerge from the symbol, and the epistemological problems that they have created. However, it is within our scope to suggest a synthesis or an articulation between the concepts we have proposed and similar concepts used in the psychological literature on interactional and developmental processes.

ESSAYING SOME ARTICULATIONS IN
THE ANALYSIS OF INTERACTIONAL PROCESSES

Terminological precision regarding descriptive and theoretical concepts is widely recognized both as a legitimate goal and a necessity of the scientific endeavor. It is also recognized, though, that a certain measure of freedom in the use of terms is not unfrequent when new approaches or new paradigms are being developed, especially when terms are borrowed from other areas or from other sciences where a precise meaning has already been accorded. A classical example is the borrowing of the biological concept of adaptation by psychology, in which it came to mean individual adjustment to environmental change.

In our view, a variable lack of agreement characterizes the use of terms like *interaction* or *regulation* in psychology an neighboring fields such as biology and sociology. For instance, the original meaning of interaction in the scientific terminology (an action occurring between—*inter*—two or more objects, such that the outcome cannot be explained by the individual objects' behaviors, but rather carries their mutual effects) has been enlarged to refer to social events, social exchanges, socially directed behavior (meanings that focus on individual actions), or simply to the context of occurrence of social behaviors. These meanings seem to miss the process idea of information transit, or to reduce it to a linear, time-ordered, and chained effect of individual behaviors (Carvalho, 1988; Fogel, 1992).

In this chapter, we have tried to specify the meaning of interaction as a process of actual or potential information transit in a field whose nature is defined by the nature of its components and of the principles that describe their relationships; the components thus constitute the field, and are at the same time constituted by the actualization of the interactional process. Interaction is both a potential state and a process.

The interactional process can be actualized through regulation among the components of the system. This regulation is identified when the behavior of a component can only be understood if the behavior of other components is considered. Regulation is thus both a process and a product.

Regulation has been used in the literature with two main implications: It implies originally a rule (from the Latin *regula*), an orderliness or law through which conduct is organized. This meaning was incorporated in the embryological concept of regulation as the process through which a structure damaged or partially changed in an early stage of development adjusts to the disturbance and develops normally; in this case, the product (the return to a stable state) is also emphasized. The rule here is stability within a more or less defined range of variation. This same basic meaning—the return to normality— can be found in the use of the concept of self-regulation in classical homeostatic theories (Cannon, 1929):

> The highly developed living being is an *open system* having many relations to its surroundings …. Changes in the surroundings excite reactions in this system, or affect it directly, so that internal *disturbances* in the system are produced. Such disturbances are normally kept within *narrow limits*, because automatic *adjustments* within the system are brought into action, and thereby wide oscillations are prevented and the internal conditions are held fairly constant. The term *equilibrium* might be used to designate these constant conditions. (p. 400, italics added)

In our view, this formulation (especially where italicized) has originated interesting developments of the use of regulation and self-regulation both in psychology and in biology, some of which should be recalled in order to clarify our own use of the term in the analysis of social—inter- rather than intraorganic—phenomena.

One of these developments is the view of the classical homeostasis concept in the recently developed field of chronobiology. According to Menna-Barreto and Marques (1988), the core of biological systems in the classical homeostatic view is the maintenance of stability. The contribution of chronobiology is to point out that variations are also essential components of these systems, and should not be understood as mere disturbances, because they express a process of adjustment to an essentially variable environment; the concepts of time and of rhythmic alterations should thus be incorporated in an enlarged homeostatic view. Ades (1985) argued further that the evidences of rhythmicity in biological systems have led to a dichotomy opposing homeostatic and nonhomeostatic motivational systems, the latter being defined by exclusion; this dichotomy should be surpassed through the definition of the contexts in which mechanisms that do not lead to equilibrium or stable states are prevalent. The activating function of internal and external stimuli, and their role in the apparent spontaneity of motivation processes should be integrated with their "disturbing" effects in a systemic view of the organism and of its relations with the environment, where disturbance of equilibrium is not the only or the main source of actions, and there is more room for novelty in contrast to the return to previously defined stable states.

It is interesting to notice that Piaget's theory—which carries a strong biological influence—assimilates the main implications of the classical homeostasis concept—disturbance, regulation, and equilibrium (in his terms, equilibration)—but also allows for the introduction of novelty (Piaget, 1975).

Piaget's meaning of regulation is that of an active reaction of the subject (organism) to a disturbance, either caused by failures or by lacunas; the rule is the search for equilibrium, understood as a motivational factor and, in both cases (failure or lacuna) and initial state is surpassed, through self-regulation, by a new one, in the direction of a larger and more stable equilibrium. Despite this difference, Piaget's formulation preserves a homeostatic flavor in the concept of a final stable state—the formal-logical reasoning.

In all the former cases, regulation is approached as an intraorganic process. In Wallon (1942/1979), a complementary use is introduced, referring to interindividual processes; for instance, an individual's expressions regulate the other individual's dispositions. This use emphasizes the role of regulation in the construction of communicative systems; that is, at a supra- or interindividual level. This has two important consequences: It introduces the social dimension in the concept of regulation, and it stresses the difference between the meaning of regulation as recovery of equilibrium after disturbances and the creation of novelty activated by other sources.

Finally, novelty or emergent results seem to be the core of the concept of coregulation as defined by Fogel (1992), who also stressed its social dimension: "A social process by which individual dynamically alter their actions with respect to the ongoing or anticipated actions of their partners" (p. 34). Coregulated interactions are "continuous processes, created out of the dynamics of actions, the results of which are emerges, that is, occurring without and explicit plan, without a scheme or program inside each animal's nervous system that guide the action" (p. 31).

We identify two common trends in these developments of the use of the world *regulation:* It moves from an emphasis an stability to an emphasis on variation, flexibility, and novelty; and the notion of adjustment is increasingly dynamic—from the "automatic adjustments" of classical homeostasis to the "dynamic alteration with respect to the partner's behavior" in Fogel's view. These moves are coherent with the general trends in the evolution of our conceptions about nature. Since the Renaissance, the views of nature as essentially stable and permanent (where change is basically a response to disturbance) are being increasingly replaced by a historical conception of nature, with transformation as its care.

In our own use, regulation has very much the same meaning as it does for Fogel: It is a social process, and it involves a dynamic adjustment (alteration) of behavior with respect to the partner's behavior. We keep the distinction between regulation and coregulation (or reciprocal regulation) because we believe it helps to highlight the subtleties of the processes occurring in a social field of interactions: Some of our episodes show that an individual's action can be altered with respect to the partner's without evidence of reciprocity.[12] We also introduce the concept of correlations to designate a particular instance of coregulation involving an abbreviation, and thus creating a condensed meaning with a potential of persistence.

Now we face an apparent contradiction between the dynamic view of interactional fields and the concept of persistence of meanings. However, to include contradiction is the essence of the logic we have assumed (da Costa, 1980): Being and becoming are simultaneous and inseparable states and processes; things simultaneously constitute and are constituted. Persistence is the necessary complement of transformation: In the absence of persistence, no communication (meaningful information transit) is possible. History, in its broader sense, is made of transformation (dynamics, novelty) and stability, regardless of the time scale and the level of natural phenomena an which we are focusing.

We believe that a dynamic view of nature, and the freedom to deal with change and stability with largely different time criteria—from seconds to billions of years—are a contribution, and perhaps a necessary condition, for the integration of the co-called "natural" and "human" sciences in a scientific approach that can replace human phenomena and human beings in the natural world where they belong.

NOTES

[1] IN FORM ACTION/FORM INTENTION ACTION/INTENTION INTENSION/LANGUAGE IS A VIRUS/INTENTION IS A VIRUS/IN IS A VIRUS/A PRINCIPLE OF ACTION/THE SMALLEST FORM OF LIFE/OF FORM AND OF ACTION/IN FORM ACTION/INFORMATION/VTA VIS VIRTU VIRUS/IN TENSION/INTENTION. For Laurie Anderson (The translation misses two poetic analogies between words and mainings; in Portuguese, the word for *information* (informação) preserves its Latin origin from *action,* and *life* (vida) has the same root as vis, virtu, virus).

[2] A similarly dynamic logic is Maturana's autopoeisis (Maturana, 1970; Maturana & Varela, 1972; Morin, 1977).

[3] This articulation is not new: It was essayed in the 1930s by several authors (e.g., Lewin, 1939), but was not consistently pursued in the postwar developments of psychology. In our view, dynamic systems theories have contributed to the revival of this perspective.

[4] Sex and age of the children are shown in brackets with the following conventions: B (boy)/ G (girl). 0,0 (years, months of age).

[5] It is necessary to emphasize the functional point of view in order to make it clear that the following argument does not imply intentionality.

[6] Supposing some readers may not be familiar with the ethological and comparative perspective, it should be noted again (cf, foot note 5) that the present argument is not teleological and carries to implication of intentionality—Two frequent criticisms of the analysis of psychological phenomena with this approach. The absence of these implication is heuristic for the analysis of these phenomena in young children and allows an articulation with the analysis of other natural phenomena (Morin, 1973).

[7] These possibilities are exemplified in Episodes 4, 5, and 6.

[8] The words are part of a song that accompanies a traditional street game.
[9] If random variables are not independent from each other, it is desirable to have a measure for ... the degree of their correlation. Because the expectation value of the product of independent random variables factorizes, a measure for the correlation will be the deviation of E (XY) from E(X)E(Y)" (Haken, 1978, pp. 30-31).
[10] Paraphrasing Laurie Anderson, "meaning is a virus."
[11] Our tanslation, from the 1979 Portuguese edition.
[12] The probability of this type of observation is perhaps enhanced by the homogeneous quality of interactions among children of this age. This is a main reason for the pertinence of our analogy with Brownian motion.

REFERENCES

Ades, C. (1985). Motivação animal: Da equibração clássica à perspectiva etológica [Animal motivation: From the classical equilibration to an ethnological perpective]. Psicologia-Teoria e Pesquisa, 1(2): 147-157.

Branco, A.U.A., Carvalho, A.M.A., Gil, M.S.A., & Pedrosa, M.I. I. (1989). Fluxo de interações entre crianção de brinquedo em grupo [The flow of children's interactions in a free-play group setting]. Psicologia, 15(1): 13-27.

Cannon, W.B. (1929). Organization for physiological homeostasis. Physiological Review, 9(13): 399-431.

Carvalho, A.M.A. (1988). Algumas reflexões sobre a categoria "interação social" [Some thoughts about "social interaction" as a category]. Anais da XVIII Reunião Anual de Psicologia (pp. 111-116). Ribeirão Preto, S.P., Brazil.

Carvalho, A.M.A. (1989). Etologia e comportamento social [Ethology and social behavior]. Psicologia e Sociedade, 5(8): 145-163.

Carvalho, A.M.A. (1992). Seletivadade e vínculo na interação entre crianças [Bonds and selectivity in young children's interactions]. Unpublished postdoctoral dissertation, Universidade de São Paulo, Brazil.

Carvalho, A.M.A. (1994). O que eé "social" para a psicologia? [What does "social" mean in psychology?]. Temas em Psicologia: Questões teórico-metodológicas, 3 1-17.

da Costa, N. (1980). Ensaio sobre os fundamentos da lógica [An essay on the foundation of logic]. São Paulo, Brazil: Hucitec/Edusp.

de Waal, F. (1992). Chimpanzee politics. London: Jonathan Cape.

Fogel, A. (1992). Developing through relationships: Origins of communications, self and culture. New York: Harvester-Wheatsheaf.

Fogel, A., & Thelen, E. (1987). Developing of early expressive and communicative actions: Reinterpreting the evidence from a dynamical systems perspectives. Developmental Psychology, 23(6): 747-761.

Haken, H. (1978). Synergetics: An introduction. Berlin: Springer-Verlag.

Haken, H. (1988). Information and self-organization: A macroscopic approach to complex systems. Berlin: Springer-Verlag.

Hinde, R.A. (1970). Animal behavior: A synthesis of ethology and comparative psychology. Cambridge University Press.

Hinde, R.A. (1974). *Biological bases of human social behavior.* New York: Cambrige University Press.

Lewin, K. (1939). Field theory and experiment in social psychology: Concepts and methods. *The American Journal of Sociology, 34*, 868-896.

Lorenz, K. (1966). Evolution of ritualization in the biological and cultural spheres. In J. Huxley (Ed.), A discussion on ritualization of behavior in animals and man. *Philosophical Transaction of the Royal Society of Britain, 251*: 249-524.

Lyra, M., & Rossetti-Ferreira, M.C. (1995). Transformation and construction in social interaction: A new perspective on analysis of the mother-infant dyad. In J. Valsiner (Ed.), *Child development within culturally structured environments* (Vol. 3). Norwood, NJ: Ablex.

Lyra, M., & Winegar, T. (1996). Processual dynamics of interaction through time: Adult-child interaction and process of development. In A. Fogel, M. Lyra, & J. Valsiner (Eds.), *Dynamics and indeterminism in developmental and social processes.* Manwah, NJ: Erlbaum.

Mardegan, A.L. (1990). *Um estudo das origens conceitual e matemática do Princípio de Mínima Ação* [A study about the conceptual and mathematical origins of the minimum action principle]. Universidade de São Paulo, Brazil.

Maturana, H.R. (1970). *Biology of cognition* (B.C. Rep. No. 9). Urbana: University of Illinois.

Maturana, H.R., & Varela. F. (1972). *Autopoietic system.* Santiago, Chile: Facultad de Ciencias, University of Santiago.

Menna-Barreto, L.C., & Marques. N. (1988). Cronobiologia e homeostasia [Chronobiology and homeostasis]. In J. Cipolla-Neto, N. Marques, & L. Menna-Barreto (Eds.), *Introdução ao estudio da Cronobiologia* [An introduction to the study chronobiology]. São Paulo, Brazil: Cone/Edusp.

Montagner, H. (1978). *L'enfant et la communication: Comment des gestes, des attitudes, des vocalisations devièmment des messages* [Children and communication: How gestures, attitudes and vocalization become messages]. Paris: Stock.

Morin, E. (1973). *O enigma do homem: Para uma nova Antroplogia* [Man's enigma: Toward a new anthropology]. Rio de Janeiro, Brazil: Zahar.

Morin, E. (1977). *La Méthode I: La nature de la nature* [The Method I: On the nature of nature]. Paris: Éditions du Sauil.

Newton, I. (1979). *Optiks.* New York: Dover. (Original work published 1704).

Oliveira, M.M. (1993). O "átomo": Da conceituação indutiva grega à realização quantitative européia [The "atom": From the Greek inductive concept to the European quantitative actualiztion]. *Caderno sobre Ensino de Conceitos em Fisica VI.* São Paulo, Brazil: IFUSP.

Otta, E. (1994). *O sorriso e seus significados* [The smile and its meaning]. Rio de Janeiro, Brazil: Vozes.

Parten, M.B. (1932). Social participation among preschool children. *Journal of Abnormal and Social Psychology, 27*: 243-269.

Pedrosa, M.I. (1989). *Interação criança: Um lugar de construção do sujeito* [Child-child interaction: A topos for the construction of the self]. Unpublished doctoral dissertation, Universidade de São Paulo, Brazil.

Pedrosa, M.I. & Carvalho, A.M.A. (1995). A interação social e a construção da brincadeira. *Cadernos de Pesquisa* [*Social interaction and the construction of play*], (*93*): 60-65.

Pedrosa, M.I., Carvalho, A.M.A., & Império-Hamburger, A. (1996). From disordered to ordered movement: Attractor configuration and development. In A. Fogel, M. Lyra, & J. Valsiner (Eds.), *Dynamics and indeterminism in developmental and social processes*. Mahwah, NJ: Erlbaum.

Perrin, M. (1909). Mouvement brownien et réalité moléculaire [Brownlian an movement and molecular reality]. *Annales de Chimie et de Physique, 18*: 1-14.

Piaget, J. (1975). *A equilibração das estruturas cognitivas: Problema central no desenvolvimento* [The equilibration of cognitived structure: A central problem in development]. Rio de Janeiro, Brazil.

Plutchik, R. (1990). Evolutionay bases of empathy. In N. Eisenberg & J. Strayer (Eds.), *Empathy and its development*. New York: Cambridge University Press.

Serres, M. (1977). *La naissance de la physique dans le texte de Lucrèce* [The birth of physics in Lucrecia]. Paris: Les Éditions de Minuit.

Thelen, E. (1989). Self-organization in developmental processes: Can systems approach work? In M. Gunnar (Ed.), *Systems and development: The Minnesota Symposia on Child Psychology* (Vol. 22). Mahwah, NJ: Erlbaum.

Valsiner, J. (1991). Construction of the mental: From the "cognitive revolution" to the study of development. *Theory and Psychology, 1*(4): 477-494.

van Hoof, J.A.R.M. (1972). A comparative approach to the phylogeny of laughter and smiling. In R.A. Hinde (Ed.), *Non-verbal communication*. Cambridge, UK: Cambridge University Press, p. 209-243.

Vygotsky, L.S. (1978). *Mind in society* (M. Cole, V. John-Steiner, S. Scribner, & E. Souberman, Eds.). Cambridge, MA: Harvard University Press.

Wallon, H. (1979). *Do acto ao pensamento: Ensaio de Psicologia Comparada* [From action to though: An essay on comparative pychology]. Lisbon: Moraes (original work published 1942).

Whiten, A., & Byrne, R.W. (1988). Tactical deception in primates. *Behavioral & Brain Sciences, 11*, 233-273.

10

COOPERATION, COMPETITION, AND RELATED ISSUES: A CO-CONSTRUCTIVE APPROACH

Angela Branco
University of Brasilia, Brazil

Cooperation and competition are probably some of the most ideologically framed concepts used in social and psychological sciences, and their widespread utilization in commonsense language continuously imposes semiotic reconstructions of their meanings, making it difficult to take such terms as useful conceptual tools for the investigation of human social interactions. Nevertheless, they still point to some important relational aspects of social phenomena that deserve a special analysis, due to the relevance of the issue concerning the psychological development of individuals, as well as the organization and the dynamics of social life.

In this chapter I would like to discuss, from a critical standpoint, some of the ways these terms have been conceptualized in scientific research, and present an altenative perspective to approach the phenomena from a co-constructivist framework (Valsiner, 1987, 1994; Winegar, 1988; Wozniak, 1986). If we want to study the processes and mechanisms that participate in the development of human social conduct, we need to approach the phenomena at both an ontongenetic and a microgenetic level of analysis, taking into account the multifaceted and intertwined nature of interactive processes. Coconstructivism does that by analyzing the phenomena of social interaction from a developmental and systemic standpoint, providing a dynamic picture of the complexities involved. A co-constructivist perspective, the basic assumptions of which are outlined here, also demands the utilization of a dynamic terminology. Concepts like goal orientation, convergence, divergence, and negotiation are presented as theoretical tools to approach the study of human social interactions (Branco & Valsiner, 1992, 1997).

On co-constructivist grounds, the issues of cooperation, competition, and related psychological constructs, like prosocial and antisocial behaviors, are here discussed taking as a fundamental theoretical reference the notion of "cultural canalization" processes (Valsiner, 1987, 1994) of convergent and divergent patterns of interactions (Branco & Valsiner, 1992, 1993).

CONCEPTUAL STATUS OF POLYSEMIC CONSTRUCTS

Derived from the Latin *cooperatus* (pp. of *cooperari, or "work together"*), *cooperation* is defined as (a) the act of cooperating, joint effort, or operation; (b) the association of a number of people in an enterprise for mutual beneficial to all those participating. The existence of a common goal is recognized in the definition of cooperative: "to act or work together with another or others for a common purpose" (*Webster's New World Dictionary*, 1991, p. 305).

On the other hand, *competition* (Latin *competitio*) is defined as (a) the act of competing, rivalry; (b) a contest, or match; (c) official participation in organized sport; (d) opposition, or effective opposition in a contest or match; (e) rivalry in business, as for customers or markets; (f) the person, or persons against whom one competes; (g) the struggle among individual organisms for food, water, space and so on when the available supply is limited (competition denotes a striving for the same object position, prize and so on, usually in accordance with certain fixed rules) (*Webster's New World Dictionary*, 1991, p. 284).

The appropriation of concepts such as cooperation and competition by scientific discourse brings about the same problem that arises whenever we try to employ a commonsense terminology—that basically relies on polysemic concepts—to describe or explain psychological phenomena. As such terms are invested of multiple meanings, it is almost impossible to construct scientific knowledge would a well-defined and elaborated terminology. Unfortunately, the connotations of the ordinary language continue in the scientific discourse, and even those who devote some effort to make explicit the conceptual meanings of cooperation and competition within their theoretical framework, do not share the semantic dimension of these constructs (Feger, 1991). For example, Slavin (1991) used the term *cooperation* to describe students' joint efforts to achieve shared goals within the classroom, whereas Boyd and Richerson (1991) applied the concept to designate self-sacrifice; that is, dying for the benefit of the group. Such conceptual pluralism, thus, demands a careful analysis of the constructs involved in the theoretical explanation of the phenomena, making explicit the scope and framework within terms mus be interpreted.

The complexity of the cooperation-competition issue is widely acknowledged by researchers of social phenomena interested in both animal and human scientific domains (e.g., Colman, 1992; Harcourt, 1992; Hinde & Groebel, 1991; Wilson, 1975). Nevertheless, "there exists no theory dominating the field of cooperation research... and even a commonly accepted terminology is in its first stages of development" (Feger, 1991, p. 299).

The topic received a special attention after the ideas of Deutsch (1949) about group processes emerging from different social situations. In the paper entitled "A Theory of Cooperation and Competition," Deutsch defined cooperation as the existence of "promotively interdependent goals" between individuals, in opposition to the occurrence of "contriently interdependent goals" that characterize competition. At the time, he outlined some significant aspects related to these concepts. For instance. Deutsch pointed out to the distinction between *objective interdependence* (featuring the structural aspects of the situation) and the *perceived interdependence* the way the person conceives his or her relation to others. Deutsch also stressed, in his writings, the multifaceted nature of most phenomena involving both cooperation and competition at the same time. It is noteworthy, for example, how competition between groups can induce cooperation among group members (Harcourt, 1992; Triandis, 1991). Few investigators, however, were able to acknowledge these theoretical considerations and further develop relevant ideas concerning the subject.

Despite the multiplicity of definitions and theoretical frameworks in the study of cooperation and competition, the classical criterion employed to describe the main forms of interdependence in social situations still refer to the existence of specific goals among participating individuals (Argyle, 1991; Johnson & Johnson, 1989; Slavin, 1991). Goals can either be objectively structured within the context itself (i.e., by implicit or explicit rules of the activity), or be actively introduced into the context by the person's own goal orientation at that moment (see discussion on the goal-orientation concept later in this chapter). In cooperation, individuals coordinate their conduct to accomplish a common goal, their actions complementing each other in that direction. In competition, the coordination is such that the more one person's efforts drive him or toward the goal, the more the other person is driven away from his or her own objectives. Yet, depending on the theoretical framework adopted, the definition may emphasize perceptual, behavioral, relational, or context-structural components of such coordination (e.g., Hinde & Groebel, 1991; Johnson & Johnson, 1982, 1989; Slavin, 1991).

Feger (1991) argued for instances that "cooperation refers to *intentional behavior* or a *relationship*" (p. 284), whereas Johnson and Johnson (1989) stressed the interdependency *structures* that characterize determined activities, each structure leading to specific perceptions of a conditioned attainment of an individual's goals (in cooperation, one person's goal is accomplished only if others also accomplish their goals; in competition the attainment of the individual's goal is only possible if others fail). No doubt the nature of human social interdependency calls for the consideration of its diverse aspects—from perception and interactions to cultural contexts—but the absence of a systemic approach linking together all parts of the whole certainly lead to an incomplete or even distorted picture of the phenomena.

The complex and multidetermined nature of the social interaction phenomena demands a careful account of the factors involved as well as the multiple dimensions or levels of analysis. As Hinde and Groebel (1991) pointed out, when analyzing a social episode one must consider the different and successive levels of the phenomena, comprising the interaction, the relationship, the group, the society, and the sociocultural structure. Hence, social-interactive events cannot be reducible to any simplistic categorization, where acts motivated by common interests contrast or oppose acts originated by conflicting goals. Example of how the same event can be diversely interpreted from different levels of analysis are discussed by Branco (1992).

One simple episode illustrates this point Joanne notices her younger sister brought home a lot of homework and decides to help her. When Joanne "helps" her sister, doing her homework or assisting her to solve all of her problems, we could say she is being "prosocial" at an interactional level. However, a relationship level, Joanne may be fostering a strong dependence that prevents her sister from standing up for herself. At the same time, Joanne fulfills her own needs to feel powerful and to be the one in control. From this perspective, she is not being prosocial but instead very selfish, even if unaware of her actual motivations. As another example, suppose Greg is saying harsh words to Bob in the midst of a discussion. This might be considered an agonistic episode from an interactional viewpoint, but the event assumes a completely different functional perspective if it is contextualized within a significant friendship relationship between them.

"INCLUSIVE SEPARATION" OF PSYCHOLOGICAL CATEGORIES: THE NEED FOR RECONCEPTUALIZATION

As the scientific endeavor results from and reflects the way our minds cognitively approach the phenomena under investigation, it tends to reproduce the pattern according to which complex expressions of reality and of the continuous flow of experience are converted into discrete categories meant to describe and interpret the observed events. Formal logical reasoning, elaborated and constructed over centuries out of this tendency, has undoubtedly contributed and constructed over centuries out of this tendency, has undoubtedly contributed more than significantly to the scientific knowledge construction about the world of events in which we are embedded. As a natural consequence of this process of scientific development, psychological attempts to analyze human experience have been undertaken, making use of classificatory efforts to build categories that are unambiguous and exclusively well defined, as though the reality of phenomena would fit into separate, nonoverlapping, and noncontradictory sets of events. In the case of psychological phenomena, such expectation are mostly inadequate—reality cannot be analyzed by way of strict distinctions, and is not dividable into nonoverlapping categories. In fact, the dynamic and intertwined nature of developing systems—here represented by the individual subject in relation to his or her environment—calls for an interpretative framework that is based on dialectical principles (Valsiner & Cairns, 1992).

The dialectical perspectives entails explicit consideration of the unity of opposites within a holistic analytic unit (Hermans, Kemper, & van Loon, 1992). A special significance in the relation between apparent opposites was pointed out by Markova (1987, 1982), who has been developing a scheme for dialogical analysis of social interaction. Markova (1987) discussed, for example, the way human languages make use of words with oppositional contrasts of meanings (such as old-young or strong-weak, etc.). These contrasting meanings can be viewed as either irreconcilable opposites located at bipolar ends of a continuum (by way of exclusive partitioning of those from each other), or as mutually interdependent, yet separate opposites within the same whole (by way of inclusive partitioning).

Valsiner and Cairns (1992), discussing conceptual issues related to interpersonal conflicts also criticized the exclusive partitioning of classical logic and suggested the inclusive separation of the partitioned parts of a whole as a way to represent the interdependence of different aspects of a phenomenon, preserving its systemic organization.

From a similar standpoint, we can think of the oppositional relation between "self-interest" (or "self-oriented") and "other-oriented") constructs, which play a central role in the definition of cooperation as opposed to competition, or in the definition of prosocial as opposed to antisocial behavior.

At the core of this conceptual issue lies the construct of *self*. Along the process of differentiation—which constitutes the starting point for the construction of the self—the concepts of self and other are progressively being codefined in a complementary way; that is, the emergence of the self takes place via the establishment of contrasting relations between those parts of the environment that become relevant within specific contexts. The psychological boundaries of what constitutes self and other, nevertheless, are dynamically changing across contexts and over time, as the dynamics of motivational forces driving the individuals within complex situations, also change. Thus, it is almost impossible to set the limits of *what constitutes, for instance, personal goals concerning exclusively the self or exclusively the other.* For example, to make sure that somebody else's goal is achieved may be a central concern or an essential part of an individual's goals, rendering classificatory efforts to separate what pertains to the self or to the other a very difficult task.

This analysis poses a problem for those dedicated to the development of a theory of prosocial behavior (Eisenberg & Mussen, 1989). The opposition between two exclusive categories—self-interest versus other-interest—constitutes here a fundamental assumption, leading to the identification of a prosocial class of behavior or motivation. To argue for the existence of an oppositional relation between the self and the other outside the cultural context within which these psychological categories emerge, however, does not apply from s sociogenetic framework. According to a sociogenetic perspective, the cultural context plays a central role in the construction of self identity, which emerges from the continuous dialogical interaction of the person with the portions of experience qualified as the other. What is part of the self in one culture may not be in another, because the semantic dimension of the self construct fluctuates along specific cultural meanings and value systems. For example, the widespread individualistic ideology of our modern Western society led to the emergence of a self concept described by Lash (1984) as the "minimal self." On the other hand, from a collectivist perspective (Triandis, 1991), which is typical of many social groups, the self construct is differently conceived, other's interests being inclusively inserted in what is considered a self-motivation.

Therefore, to draw a precise distinction between cooperation and competition, as well as between prosocial and antisocial conduct, as stable action strategies, on the basis that "striving together" necessarily opposes to "striving against" other peoples's interests, disregards the complexities and transformational nature of human interactions that are the basic assumptions of a systemic socioecological perspective. Conceptual tools that simultaneously describe contrasting relations between self and other cooperation and competition, and so on within specific contexts, and at the same time preserve the dialectical characteristics of the interactional process would serve the scientific analysis of social interdependence much better.

The study of the structural and the dynamic characteristics of social interactional events demands the development of a methodology in tune with the dialectical nature of the complexities involved (Branco & Valsiner, 1997). Beyond that, social interactive pattens of behavior should be explained from a systemic perspective (Ford & Lerner, 1992) that considers both the canalizing forces enacted by the collective culture and the active role of the individuals. Co-constructivism can provide both.

A CO-CONSTRUCTIVE APPROACH TO HUMAN DEVELOPMENT

The co-constructivist theory (e.g., Valsiner, 1987, 1994; Wozniak, 1986, 1993) is based on the historical roots of the work of Baldwin, Piaget, Vygotsky, and Stern (see Valsiner 1994). Co-constructivism is a kind of *sociogenetic personology*, its sociogenetic approach combining with a special emphasis on the uniqueness of individual persons in their interdependence with culture. In other words, persons are microlevel (personal-cultural) parts of the macrolevel entity ("collective culture"), with the relationship between the two levels describable as that of bidirectional culture transformation. Such interdependence gives rise to a dialectical conceptualization of "culture" itself. On one hand, the *collective culture* consists in the domain of shared meanings of the social group; on the other hand, each individual co-constructs his or her own *personal culture*, actively structuring his or her own version of the collective culture (Litvinovic & Valsiner, 1992).

The collective culture provides the developing child with a pathway of social suggestions, encoded at both physical and semiotic levels. Such constraints, initially present at an external level, are gradually internalized by the child, the whole process being described as a *cultural canalization*. But the structures collective cultural messages. The child is a joint constructor of his or her own personal culture and contributes, even from a subdominant position, to the introduction of novelties into the collective culture.

According the co-constructivism, developmental processes take place in irreversible time (Valsiner, 1994) and are neither deterministic nor indeterministic. Developmental processes are better described by the principle of *bounded indeterminacy* (Valsiner, 1987) occurring at the intersection of the micro and macro cultural levels. The predictability of developmental course is limited, because under some conditions, and at same time, the input from one of the levels (personal or collective cultures) to the other leads to a reconstruction of the latter (with feedback to the former). Yet, a very similar input at another time and under different conditions is rendered ineffective in producing the same kind of transformation within the system.

The developing person is an active, constructive agent who "moves" within the highly heterogeneous landscape provided by collective culture. The heterogeneity of collective culture is particularly found in the semiotic dimension of social reality, but despite the existence of diverse and often contradictory messages, it can be highly redundant both in content and form (Valsiner, 1989), suggesting specific developmental trends.

The semiotic construction of knowledge by an active person with the participation of collective cultural suggestions gives dynamic form to the developmental process. Collective culture sets up a myriad of physical and semiotic forms (both explicitly or implicitly encoded) as the environment of the developing person. Messages from the macrolevel are, however, ambiguous, heterogeneous, overdetermined (redundant), and inconsistent (changing over time). The individual, operating at the microlevel of personal culture, is constantly acting and constructing personal sense, utilizing the semiotic means provided by collective culture. In the process of this co-construction, the person elaborated her or his notion of self, and reconstructs some aspects of the macrolevel environment when the circumstances make it possible.

In the next sections, the development of a goal terminology within the context of a co-constructivist framework is discussed, as a way to approach the issue of cooperation and competition.

APPROACHING THE PROBLEM

Defining cooperation and competition in terms of goals entails a theoretical difficulty. In human actions, goals are constantly being constructed for the immediate future, and can be therefore in a semideterminate state at any time (see Valsiner, 1992). However, defining cooperation and competition via goals requires the assumption that goals are *stable* and *well-defined*. This assumption does not fit with the realities of development, despite serving the needs of everyday communication. The reference to a person's goals constitutes an artificial way through which common language speech as well as psychology try to recognize a stable and well-defined aim that presumably would guide the behavior of the individual toward its accomplishment. Still, the goals terminology can be useful for analytical purposes as an anchor concept that allows the study of the possible range of coordination between people's orientations within a certain context.

The dynamic feature of this particular aspect of human psychological functioning may be better described by the term *orientation*, which frees theoretical reasoning from having to assume the existence of future states, created by persons in the present, but having to assume the existence of future states, created by persons in the present, but having a concrete and stable status. The notion of orientation suggests the direction of the person's actions, which is detected in the present. It serves as a basis to evaluate a significant dimension of the person's motivations. Such orientations continuously emerge, fluctuate, and change, being closely intertwined with the context of the presently ongoing actions. An interesting conceptual reference to the idea of orientation or "intention in behavior" can be found in the work of Allport (1937). Criticizing the excessive emphasis put on the psychological study of "traits." Allport brought the notion of "behavioral trends," that in some way relates to the concept of goal orientation. He said we can describe the individual's trend of behavior ... in terms of the purpose or purposes which he seems to be trying to carry out" (p. 204). However, his idea of purposes does not lie in the future or in the individual's consciousness. It should be found in the act itself by a careful observation:

the teleonomic method makes no use of the notion of consciousness of a purpose imputed to the subject we observe, or of purpose as an agent, motive or force behind his activities. We mean only that if we ourselves were performing the movements made by the individual under observation, we would say that we were doing thus and so... the notion of purpose is used purely as a means of description. (p. 205)

As suggested in the next sections, a co-constructivist analysis intend to go beyond mere descriptions of behavior, by proposing for example, the occurrence of internalization-externalization mechanisms. Nonetheless the point made by Allport is a very important one in order to anchor the idea of orientation in actually observed behaviors.

Having stated that goal orientedness of a dynamically transient kind is a significant characteristic of human motivation, it is necessary to analyze the processes that reflect that feature. The use of terms like goal orientation, convergence, and divergence (Branco & Valsiner, 1992, 1997), in conjunction with the canalization theory (Valsiner, 1987) may facilitate the analysis of cooperation-competition from a co-constructivist perspective. According to co-constructivism, developmental processes are essentially dynamic and dialectical. Therefore, from a co-constructive framework, a useful terminology necessarily needs to reflect this dynamic, processual quality of the phenomena and concept like convergence divergence, and negotiations of individuals' goal orientations within culturally structured contexts may represent a more adequate way to describe and analyze the dynamics of social interactional processes.

CONVERGENCE AND DIVERGENCE IN GOAL ORIENTATIONS

The existence of goals and their role concerning the regulation of individuals' actions has been proposed and discussed within a wide range of theoretical frameworks (Atkinson, 1982; Bandura, 1988; Klein, Whitener, & Ilgen, 1991; Latham & Locke, 1991; Modell, 1990; Oppenheimer, 1987). As stated before, goals should not be considered from a systemic approach as a stable or definable state of expectations, but instead suggest a flexible direction toward a desirable process or outcome. The term *goal orientation* evokes such processual quality, and can be defined as a kind of internal constraining system, semiotically mediated, that, by projecting into the future, constraints the individual's actions, feelings, and thoughts in the present time.

The term goal orientation may refer to behavior itself, as Allport's notion of behavioral trends suggest, or to the accomplishment of a future and state toward which individual efforts are oriented, according to diverse theoretical frameworks. In a co-constructivist approach, the concept lies somewhere in between. On one hand, observable behavior plays a central role as the basis for inferring goal orientations (goals redefined in process along the interactions), instead of stable or well-defined purposes. On the other hand the special consideration given to the functional dimension of behavior—inferred in terms of its meaning within a specific context—goes beyond the mere morphological description of successive actions exhibited by the individual, granting a representational status to the goal orientation concept.

Specific coordinations between individual's goal orientation give rise to processes that can be denominated as *convergence* or *divergence*. In goal orientation convergence, compatibility between the goal orientations is inferred on the basis of the interactors' conduct. The important point here is the existence of compatibility instead of commonality of goal orientations. That means that it is not essential that individuals search the accomplishment of the same unique goal. It is possible, for instance, that two individuals are devoted to different tasks and still are interacting in the sense of shared meanings or reciprocal facilitation of each other's goal. Convergence creates a relatively stable basis for communication efforts, and leads to a certain consistency in interaction that enables the active construction of intersubjectivity between partners.

In goal orientation divergence, goals pertaining to each individual are incompatible, that is, they cannot be accomplished at the same time. For example, two boys are working in a biology project together, but they cannot agree about the best way to present it to the teacher. Divergence may create the conditions for the emergence of novel elements of information and, consequently, a reconstructive activity may follow, resulting in new patterns of interaction.

The movement from divergence to convergence can be described as *negotiation* processes. During a negotiation, conflicting goal orientations can be coordinated to allow the emergence of compatibility. Yet, the degree of convergence or divergence between individuals' goal orientations may vary because compatibility and incompatibility are not exclusively separated categories (Valsiner & Cairns, 1992), and so negotiation processes can occur in distinctive versions, always representing an effort of alignment between different goal orientation.

The dynamic concepts presented here help to analyze the transformational quality of human interactions, but the notion of cultural canalization also plays a fundamental role in the study of the cooperation-competition issue from a co-constructive approach. The investigation of the structures that characterize different cultural contexts, and the way such structures facilitate certain interactive patterns rather than others comprises an important of social interdependence among individuals.

CHILD DEVELOPMENT WITHIN CULTURE

From the moment the developing child enters this world, he or she experiences a flow of successive structured contexts, each specifically structured according

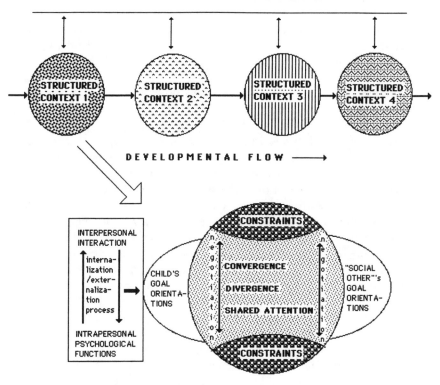

FIGURE 10.1. A Co-constructionist depiction of child's development through structured contexts.

to a different set of rules and expectations. The structures are active even when they cannot be easily identified. The child moves through dynamic interactions with the surrounding environment, particularly through co-constructive interactions with significant others who take care of him or her. As the child grows older, the nature of such contexts as well as the social others that play a fundamental role in the child's emotional-sociocognitive development will change, expanding to a great extent the child's connections with the world. Albeit embedded in a cultural canalization process set forth by structured contexts, the child plays an active role in the process of amplifying his or her specific personal culture. To do so, the child utilizes elements of the shared collective culture as an input on which he or she creates a personal version, now transformed into intrapsychological orientations. The reciprocal coconstruction between personal and collective culture takes place, then, through *internalization-externalization* processes (see Figure 10.1).

Figure 10.1 represents a child's developmental flow, as he or she moves along successive structure contexts. Contexts may or may not overlap, but in some cases they dynamically transform into each other over time. The structure contexts naturally stem from parts of the collective culture, but they are also open to novelties that may be generated by co-constructive processes arising from concrete social interactions. The structure of each specific context sets specific *constraints* deriving from social participation rules and expectations. Participating individuals continuously negotiate their goal orientations, as internalization-externalization processes actively coordinate the persons' conduct at the intersection of individuals' interactions and intrapsychological orientations. Through the dialectical movements that govern such processes, the child co-constructs a synthesis from the perspectives, interests, and meanings that are permanently put into confrontation with each other in the situation.

The negotiation process (as depicted in Figure 10.1) is constantly taking place along the lines of the goal orientations each individual brings into (or creates within) the interaction, and of the constraining conditions that operate on that action. The constraints are not only determined by the way the context is structure, but are also created by interactors' goal orientations.

THE DYNAMICS OF INTERACTIONS AND CULTURAL CANALIZATION PROCESSES

In order to analyze the dynamics of social interactions, it is necessary to take into consideration some basic structural features of social conduct, like the different levels of action coordination. The first level can be labeled preinteractional, and comprises socially oriented attention, imitations, and movements toward interaction. In such cases, one individual displays an act toward the other, be it a look or an invitation to play, but the other does not respond to the act. The second level is the interactional level, and here a true exchange can be observe; that is, both partners display social movements toward each other. Then, by taking, into account the content-meaning dimension of social encounters between individuals, it is possible to differentiate the interactive flow into specific patterns.

The preinteractional level ranges from a diffuse acknowledgment of the social environment to unsuccessful social initiatives, also including observations and imitations in which no participation of the other person is detected. On the other hand, the interactional level comprises a rich variety of convergent or divergent pattern of social exchange, including the occurrence of negotiations between individuals.

Many convergent interactions can be identified during individual's social exchanges. It is possible to observe verbal and nonverbal interactions, which sometimes take the form of imitations or different types of prosocial interaction and cooperation. Divergent interactions can also be categorized into different patterns of social exchange, ranging from interpersonal hostility to game competition. However, the point I want to stress here is the existence of a cultural canalization process that acts on the development of social interactive strategies within specific contexts. Both external and internal constraints play a central role in channeling social conduct according to mechanisms that are explained under the label of *bounded indeterminacy* (Valsiner, 1994).

The collective culture is continuously providing social suggestions, and organizing specific goal-oriented activities for children, derived from a system of values and beliefs that stimulates certain forms of social conduct, inhibiting or suppressing others. The process through which that takes place is cultural canalization. To illustrate the interplay between cultural canalization processes and the dynamics of social interactions, I discuss some interesting data from an experiment we conducted in Brazil (Branco & Valsiner, 1992, 1993).

The experiment goal was to investigate the microgenetic development of social interactions among 3-year-old children in structurally different situations. Two triads (two boys and one girl) we asked to participate in six experimental sessions (each about 25 minutes), followed by a test situation and two additional sessions in which the rules were reversed. The baseline observations of children in their free play context and the all experimental sessions were fully videotaped.

The decision to utilize children's triads (as opposed to dyadic or polyadic social groups) aimed at creating an arrangement both sufficiently noncomplex for the purposes of analysis of social conduct, and rich in opportunities for interpersonal coalitions or confrontations in task-oriented contexts. The selected children did not demonstrate either excessive social inhibition or dominance in the baseline observations. An additional selection criterion was the absence of a history of close interaction among members of the triad.

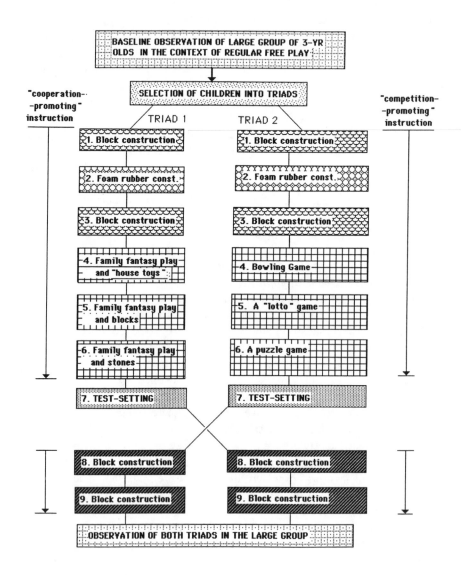

FIGURE 10.2. The general design of the study.

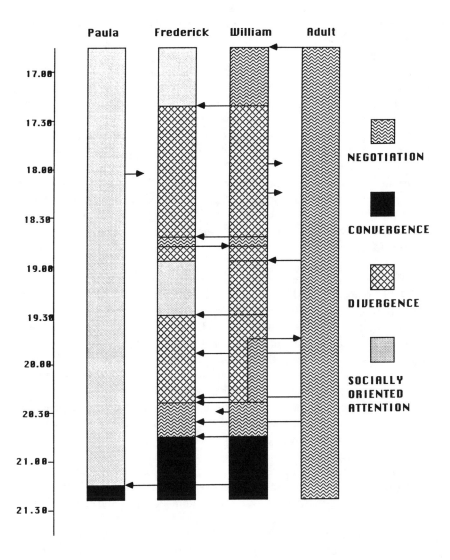

FIGURE 10.3.   Summary of the tetradic interaction sequence described in the text.

The materials used during the sessions were varied to keep up the children's interest, and to provide varied objects that afford coordination of different kinds of structures or play activities, such as wooden blocks, a family doll set, puzzles a bowling game, and other materials.

The basic features of the experimental design are represented in Figure 10.2.

In the cooperation context, children were asked to interact with each other in order to build a unique structure from small pieces of the same material, or they were asked to play together within a fantasy play context. In the competitive context, children were asked to play alone and their performances were then compared. For instance, the adult took photographs of their constructions so people could choose which was the best one, or simply marked on a cardboard their individual scores during competitive games.

During the test situation both triads were instructed to perform the same task: to carry a big doll that was "ill," to undress her to pretend to bathe her, to dry her, to dress her again, to carry her to the "hospital," to examine and medicate her, and bring her back "home." The eighth and ninth sessions constituted the reversal of the experimenter's suggestion for the designated form of joint actions (i.e., cooperation-promoted triad received competitive instructions, and the competition- promoted triad got cooperative instructions).

A fluxogram to compare the development of social interactive strategies used by both triads along the sessions was elaborated in order to represent convergence, divergence, and negotiation (Figure 10.3).

In Figure 10.3, A is the adult, W, F, and P are the children. The bars represent different types of interactions between children; the line represents social oriented attention; and the black bar corresponds to convergence. Whenever convergence takes the form of cooperation, an additional bar is superimposed to the one representing convergence. The main feature of cooperative interactions is complementarity in the coordination of individuals actions, moving them closer to the accomplishment of a shared goal represented by a specifiable product resulting from their activity.

The checkered bar corresponds to divergence and the wavy bar to negotiations. Adult's interventions on ongoing children's behaviors are depicted in the fluxogram by the successive arrows along time flow, allowing the detection of regularities, if any, between adult' behavior and children's social interactive patterns.

Figure 10.4 shows the ratios of socially oriented attention, convergent and divergent interactive patterns, and negotiation for the cooperative and the competitive triads during the first session. Figure 10.5 shows the patterns exhibited by both triads during the seventh session, the test situation.

The evidence presented here clearly indicates the existence of a cultural canalization process. The test situation comprised a task that would be easily accomplished by the adoption of cooperative strategies. The group that

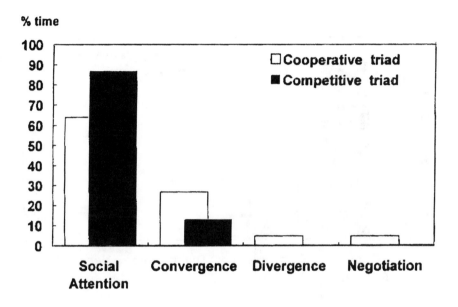

FIGURE 10.4.   Social attention and interactions during the first session.

experienced cooperative rules during six consecutive sessions shows a convergent interactional pattern during 95% of the test time, out of which 81% was spent in cooperation. On the other hand, the group submitted to sucessive competitively structured situations spent 12% of the test time in convergent interactions, only 8% being cooperative. Observing the videos, the way these children regulate their behaviors avoiding true social exchanges is quite amazing. One child, for example, repeatedly waits until the other gives up a certain activity in order to engage in this same activity. The differences detected in the seventh session are strong enough to support the occurrence of channeling tendencies put forward by specifically structured contexts. That is, the results are perfectly aligned with the notion of cultural canalization processes, the constraints for directing behavior found at both the *structural level of activities* and at the *semiotic level of social interactions* with other individuals.

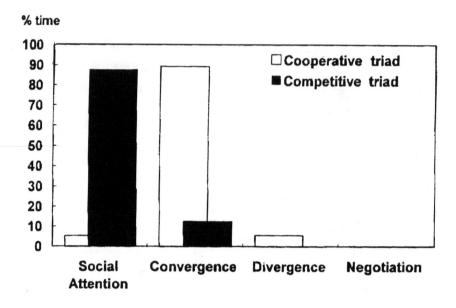

% time

FIGURE 10.5.   Social attention and interactions during the seventh session.

When data are approached at a microgenetic level of analysis, the interplay between convergence-divergence and negotiation demonstrated the intertwined nature of social interactive and negotiation demonstrates the intertwined nature of social interactive processes. This can be illustrated by and interesting episode taken from the first cooperative session. In the episode, the divergent interactions occurring between the two boys over the possession of an object finally resulted in a negotiation process, which gave rise to the emergence of a cooperative coordination of their behavior, including a manifestation of "help" (usually considered as a prosocial behavior).

During the session, the adult (A) is continuously negotiating with the three children to canalize their behavior into "cooperative" rules. William (W), who plays the most active role both interacting with the adult (resisting her efforts to elicit cooperation) and with his peers, initiates divergent interactions with Frederick (F) over the possession of an object. He picks a wooden block he pretends is a "clock" from Frederick. struggles to take the block back, but William threatens Frederick's construction, and the interactional flow goes on with William involved in divergent interactions with both Frederick and the adult. The three children grab a part of the blocks for each of them, and the following conversation takes place.

(A = adult; W = William [boy]; F = Frederick [boy]; P = Paola [girl]
Style: Plain Text= Divergence between W & F
         Bold = Negotiation [W & F] → Convergence
         Bold + Italic = W helps P)

A: Folks, she smiles, what have you done?
W: I won't let him take these from me!
F: Neither will I!
A asks W: But why? Isn't he your friend?
W: No! I'm not his friend because he's taking... he doesn't let me take his clock!
W: Where is the clock?
A picks up PF's clock: What if we have a clock here
and we make a church?
F: takes his block back No!
W: Where is my clock?
A: It's not yours, it belongs to everyone, William!
W: Where is my clock that was here?
A: I don't know... (**and then**) Frederick could help you. He could lend you the clock and then you'd make something very big here!
W to F: So you lend it to me...
F: moves toward P's construction Look what we have here! (**he picks up a block-clock in P's construction and gives it to W**)
W to P: Give it to me! That's what I was looking for, this clock...
A: But this belongs to everybody! (she picks up F's clock) We can use two clocks if we do just one thing!
F: takes his block back immediately OK, but this is mine!
A: Hum...
W: This belongs to him! Nobody should take it, isn't that right, Frederick? This is mine... (holding the block) to build something like this, and nobody will get inside my building, I have to put all here, or they will get lost...
A: Isn't William going to help Paola? She's started to do it, it's turning into a very nice job!
W: moves toward P: Do you want me to help you? (W picks up a different block, which is lying in front of P and puts it in her construction)
A: OK! That's it!
W to A: Like this. That's good ideas, isn't it?
A: Good idea!

It is important to notice here that, before the conflict—or divergence—started, children were not interacting with each other; were oriented to their individual activities. Therefore, we can speculate about the functional role of such conflict interactions for the emergence of the so-called prosocial conduct.

The dynamics between divergence and convergence of goal orientations, represented in the preceding, illustrates the complex mechanisms involved in social interactions claiming a microanalytical approach. Through a continuous negotiation over the rules, the adult succeeds in eliciting active negotiations among children, which ends up in convergent interaction between them. The resistant child, William, who had stated Frederick was not his friend less than a minute ago, now defends Frederick's possessions and helps Paola with her construction, arguing that, indeed, that was a "good idea!"

Many examples of that kind can be identified from the videotaped sequences of peer interactions. The interesting conclusion here is the possibility of identifying and analyzing the functional dimension of episodes of conflict or competition in the coconstruction of convergent and cooperative interactions between children.

In sum, cultural canalization processes occur both at the structural level of activities and at the semiotic level of social interactions. Moreover, the person's active role within structured contexts also indicates the occurrence of a permanent reconstruction or reorganization of the flow of social interactions. That means that within a cooperative context, the emergence of divergence and subsequent negotiations can very likely be observed. In a competitive situation, on the other hand, the agreement over the rules frequently induces some forms of cooperation, in the sense of contributing to the flow of expected actions. This should remind us of the complexities involved in social interactive phenomena, preventing the tendency to create dichotomies and overgeneralize research recommendations. An interesting topic for investigation, for example, may be a functional analysis of divergent and negotiation processes in promoting the introduction of welcomed novelties at both the informational and interactional levels.

CULTURAL ORGANIZATION OF CONTEXTS FOR CHILD DEVELOPMENT: THE SCHOOL SETTING

The analysis of the cooperation-competition issue from a co-constructive approach suggests the need to investigate both the *structural features of the activity contexts* and the *dynamic quality of the interactions* itself. The relationships between social interdependence structures and psychological orientations have been analyzed according to some predetermined categories by Deutsch, in a thoughtful article in which he argued for the bidirectional influences that one aspect exerts on another. Gump (1980), for example, employed the term *eco-behavioral context* as a construct to describe the relationships between both levels. In our study about the teacher's role in promoting and inhibiting specific forms of peer interaction (Branco, 1989), the results show that the teachers behavior, together with the social participation structure (Erickson, 1987) of the activities, does canalize peer social interactions toward what is expected within each context. The structural and the interactional dimensions of the preschool context were working together to facilitate certain types of peer interactions.

Taking the school environment as the principal focus of theory and research, Johnson and others (see Johnson & Johnson, 1989) stress the tremendous impact that cooperative goal structures as contrasted with competitive and individualistic goal structures, have on students' performances, social interactions, self-esteem, and many other aspects of their personalities. The importance of structuring the context itself, for example, is also experienced by preschool teachers who dedicate special attention to the organization of behavioral activity settings. They may not need further efforts to set the appropriate rules through instructional controls, because oral instructions usually seem less effective than structuring the activity setting, in order to capture children's attention, and to promote the necessary understanding of the rules (Wachs & Gruen, 1982).

Concerning educational institutions, once the effectiveness of structuring the activities is well established, teachers and other school staff members of should dedicated special attention to analyzing the *hidden curriculum* (Giroux & Purpel, 1983) embedded in the instructional curriculum, and evaluate possible cultural canalization processes that may be driving the students toward the acquisition and development of very specific ways to relate to each other (Branco, 1992). There is a worldwide call—from politicians to social scientists and educational psychologists—for the promotion of positive social interactions among individuals, under the labels of ethnic integration, solidarity, constructive conflict resolution, and collaboration. All these interactive patterns may be described as forms of prosocial behavior and empathy, concepts that stress the individual's ability and motivation to take into account other people's needs, feelings, and interests. Nevertheless, a naive discourse promoting either cooperation or competition within the classroom, without considering the complexities of human social interactions, does not help in providing schools, or any other institution, with adequate resources to contribute to children's development, according to the values and beliefs of the social community. The study of the characteristics and roles of different types of interpersonal conflict, for instance, represents a relevant research topic. Also, the processes involved in the coconstruction of personal goal orientations within specifically structured settings need to be analyzed. The further investigation of the social interactive phenomena, however, should not prevent schools from immediately drawing benefits from scientific research and applying the available information to better conceptualize and effectively implement social objectives within educational settings.

CONCLUSION

The person's active role within structured contexts indicates the occurrence of a permanent reconstruction or reorganization of the flow of social interactions, as individuals' goal orientations are constantly being coconstructed in irreversible time. Once this premise is assumed, three important points discussed in this chapter should be outlined.

1. Cooperation and competition can be better described in dynamic terms such as the coordination of *convergence and divergence of individuals' goal orientations*.
2. Social interactive patterns of behavior should be explained from a *systemic perspective* that considers both the canalizing forces enacted by the collective culture and the active role of the individuals.
3. The collective culture is continuously providing social suggestions and organizing specific goal-oriented activities for children's development, according to a system of values and beliefs that promotes or stimulates certain forms of social conduct. The process through which that takes place is called *cultural canalization* and it embedded in the notion of the school's hidden curriculum. Educational institutions should, thus, devote special attention to the investigation of the functions and mechanisms of cultural canalization processes, in order to structure contexts to facilitate the development of specific patterns of social interactions.

The main contribution of a *co-constructivist theoretical approach* to the discussion of cooperation, competition, and related issue like prosocial and antisocial interactions can also be summarized as follow: First, co-contructivism offers a systemic and dialectical framework to account for the processual, novelty-promotive nature of interactive phenomena, emphasizing, at the same time, the contextual bounded characteristics of human development. Second, microanalytical methods derived from a co-constructivist approach can be used to identify some of the mechanisms involved in the coordination of individuals' goal orientations (Branco, 1994; Branco & Valsiner, 1992, 1997). Last, but not least, co-constructivism contributes to describing the complex picture of human interactions by providing conceptual tools to approach the issue in its complexity, emphasizing the dynamic movements between social convergence, divergence, the basic function of negotiation processes, and the central role played by interactor's goal orientations.

REFERENCES

Allport, F. (1937). Teleonomic description in the study of personality. *Character & Personality, 5,* 202-214.

Argyle, M. (1991). *Cooperation: The basis of sociability.* London: Routledge.

Atkinson, J.W. (1982). Old and new conceptions of how expected consequences influence actions. In N.T. Feather (Ed.), *Expectations and actions: Expectancy-value models in psychology.* Hillsdale, NJ: Erlbaum.

Bandura, A. (1988). *Self-regulation of motivation and action through goal systems.* Paper presented at the XXIV International Congress of Psychology, Sydney, Australia.

Boyd, R., & Richerson, P.J. (1991). Culture and cooperation. In R.A. Hinde & J. Groebel (Eds.), *Cooperation and prosocial behavioral.* New York: Cambridge University Press.

Branco, A.U. (1989). *Socialização na pré-escola: O papel da professora e da organição das atividades no desenvolvimento de interaçoÛes sociais entre as criançs* [Socialization in preschool: Teachers' and activities' role in the development of child-child interactions]. Unpublished doctoral dissertation, University of São Paulo, Brazil.

Branco, A.U. (1992). Objectivos sociais da educacao: Uma abordagem critica [Social objectives in education: A critical analysis]. *Psicologia Teoria e Pesquisa, 8*(3), 341-350.

Branco, A.U. (1994, June). *Co-constructive analysis of interactive processes: A study of adult-child negotiations.* Paper presented at the 24th Annual Symposium of the Jean Piaget Society, Chicago.

Branco, A.U., & Valsiner, J. (1992, July). *Development of convergence and divergence in joint actions of preschool children: The emergence of cooperations and competition within structured contexts.* Paper presented at the 25th International Congress of Psychology, Brussels, Belgium.

Branco, A.U., & Valsiner, J. (1993, July). *Dynamics of social interaction strategies among young children.* Paper presented at the XII Biennial Meeting of the Society for the Study of Behavioral Development, Recife, Brazil.

Branco, A.U., & Valsiner, J. (1997). Changing methodologies: A co-constructivist study of goal orientations in social interactions. *Psychology in Developing Societies. 9,* (1), 35-64.

Colman, A. (1992). *Cooperation and competition in humans and animals.* Berkshire, UK: Van Nostrand Reinhold.

Deutsch, M. (1949). A theory of cooperation and competition. *Human Relations, 2,* 129-152.

Eisennberg, N., & Mussen, P.H. (1989). *The roots of prosocial behavior in children.* New York: Cambridge University Press.

Erickson, F. (1987). Qualitative methods in research on teaching. In M.C. Wittrock (Ed.), *Handbook of research on teaching* (3rd ed.). New York: Macmillan.

Erickson, F. (1987). Transformation and school success: The politics and culture of educational achievement. *Anthropology and Education Quarterly, 18,* (4), 335-356.

Feger, H. (1991). Cooperation between groups. In R.A. Hinde & J. Groebel (Eds.), *Cooperation and prosocial behavior* (pp. 281-300). New York: Cambridge University Press.

Ford, D.H., & Lerner, R.M. (1992). *Development theory: An integration approach.* London: Sage.

Giroux, H., & Purpel, D. (1983). *The hidden cirriculum and moral education: Deception or discovery?* Berkeley, CA: McCutchan.

Gump, P. (1980). The school as a social situation. *Annual Review of Psychology, 31,* 553-582.

Harcourt, A. (1992). Cooperation in conflicts: Commonalities between humans and other animals. *Politics & the Life Sciences, 11*(2), 251-259.

Hermans, H.J.M., Kemper, H.J.G., & van Loon, R.J.P. (1992). The dialogical self: Beyond individualism and rationalism. *American Psychologist, 47*(1), 23-33.

Hinde, R.A., & Groebel, J. (1991). *Cooperation and prosocial behavior.* New York: Cambridge University Press.

Johnson, D.W., & Johnson, R.T. (1982). *Cooperation and competition: Theory and research.* Edina, MN: Interaction Book Company.

Klein, H.J., Whitener, E.M., & Ilgen, D.R. (1991). The role of goal specificity in the goal-setting process. *Motivation and Emotion, 14*(3), 179-193.

Lash, C. 1984). *The minimal self: Psychic Survival in troubled times.* New York: W.W. Norton.

Latham, G.P., & Locke, E.A. (1991). Self-regulation through goal setting. *Organizational Behavior and Human Decisions Processes, 50.* 212-247.

Litvinovic, G., & Valsiner, J. (1992, July). *Coordination of inductive and deductive processes in parental reasoning.* Paper presented at the XXV International Congress of Psychology. Brussels, Belgium.

Markova, Il (1987). On the interaction of opposites in psychological processes. *Journal for the Theory of Social Behavior, 17,* 279-299.

Markova, I. (1992). On solos, duets, quartets and quintets: A response to Gardner. *New Ideas in Psychology, 10*(2), 215-221.

Modell, A. (1990). *Other times, other realities: Toward a theory of psychoanalytic treatment.* Cambridge, UK: Harvard University Press.

Oppenheimer, L. (1987). Cognitive and social variables in the plan of action. In S.F. Friedman, E.K. Sholnick, & R.R Cocking (Eds.), *Blueprints for thinking: The role of planning in cognitive development.* New York: Cambridge University Press.

Slavin, R. (1991, February). Synthesis of research on cooperatived learning. *Educational Leadership,* 71-82.

Triandis, H.C. (1991). Cross-cultural differences in assertiveness/competition vs. group loyalty/cooperation. In R.A. Hinde & J. Groebel (Eds.), *Cooperation and prosocial behavior* (pp. 78-88). New York: Cambridge University Press.

Valsiner, J. (1987). *Culture and the development of children's action.* Chichester, UK: Wiley.

Valsiner, J. (1989). *Human development and culture.* Lexington, MA: D.C. Heath.

Valsiner, J. (1993). Making of the future: Temporality and the constructive nature of development. In G. Turkewitz & D. Devernney (Eds.), Developmental time and timing (pp. 13-40). Hillsdale, NJ: Erlbaum.

Valsiner, J. (1994). Irreversibility of time and the construction of historical developmental psychology. *Mind, Culture, and Activity, 1,* 1-2, 25-42.

Valsiner, J. (1994). Culture and human development: A co-constructivist perspective. In P. van Geert & L. Mos (Eds.), *Annual of Theoretical Psychology* (Vol. 10) (pp. 247-298). New York: Plenum.

Valsiner, J., & Cairns, R. (1992). Theoretical perspectives on conflict and development. In C.V. Shantz & W.W. Hartup (Eds.), *Conflict in child and adolescent development* (pp. 15-35). New York, NY: Cambridge University Press.

Wachs, T.D., & Gruen, G.E. (1982). *Early experiences and human development.* New York: Plenum.

Webster's New World Dictionary (Third College Edition) (1991). New York: Simon & Schuster.

Wilson, E.O. (1975). *Sociology: The new synthesis.* Cambridge, MA: Belknap Press of Harvard University Press.

Winegar, L.T. (1988). Children's emerging understanding of social events: Co-construction and social process. In J. Valsiner (Ed.), *Child development within culturally structured environments* (pp. 3-29). Norwood, NJ: Ablex.

Wozniak, R.H. (1986). Notes towards a co-constructive theory of the emotion-cognition relationship. In D.J. Bearison & H. Zimiles (Eds.), *Thought and emotion: Developmental perspetives* (pp. 39-64). Hillsdale, NJ: Erlbaum.

Wozniak, R.H. (1993). Co-constructive metatheory for psychology: Implications for an analysis of families as specific social contexts for development. In R.H. Wozniak & K.W. Fisher (Eds.), *Development in context: Acting and thinking in specific environments* (pp. 71-91). Hillsdale, NJ: Erlbaum.

11

A MODEL FOR IDENTITY AND CHANGE IN RELATIONSHIPS FROM A PERSONAL-CULTURAL POINT OF VIEW

Gorjana Litvinovic
University of North Carolina at Chapel Hill

Why should one be interested in relationships? Lives hinge on them. People's relationships with their parents, their peers, their teachers, their children, and their significant others—these all constitute the mobile setting for meaningful life activities. Cognitive-emotional tasks are set within these, and either accomplished or foregone. People's own identities are inextricably bound with the identities of their relationships. So, the process of living is staged against a set of relationships, and certainly uses props and supports drawn from these. Likewise, looking into the past, the very origin of oneself can be seen in relationships (as Vygotsky, 1960, and G.H. Mead, 1934, have taught us).

Relationships are formed and developed within cultural contexts. Collective cultural patterns have been shown to shape the patterns of communication and relating between people (anthropological work continues to show this). On the other hand, relationships have been seen in light of a developing intersubjectivity, a shared unique relationship model that persists through time (Fogel & Lyra, 1997). Besides collective culture and immediate intersubjectivity, yet another plane of analysis may be added to relationship development—that of personal culture (Valsiner, 1987). The development of relationships, thus, may be most fully analyzed as the mutually supporting and transacting functioning of three areas: the collective cultural, the intersubjective, and the personal cultural. In the context of this three-layered model, I analyze the concept of identity and the issue of change as these relate to relationship development.

LEVELS OF OBSERVATION

The analysis of individual development is necessarily observed in the context of relationships; that is, histories of dyadic interactions. The study of relationships, then, is useful from the standpoint of understanding individual development. As we are interested in relationships per se, could we invert this stand, and try out the notion that relationship development must be analyzed in the context of individual subjectivities? Relationships clearly do not exist without participants, and in this simple sense, they are dependent on individual existence. However, the question is whether the development of relationships (their establishment and maintenance) can be observed taking the dyad as the only unit of analysis. It has been argued that methodologies that consider only properties of the individual as indicators of development do not reflect sufficiently faithfully the social nature of human development; that is, the dependence of individual development on contexts of interaction. In order to assess, for example, a child's performance on tasks alone and with an adult, it would be inadequate to use the same measures in both the individual and the social conditions (Ignjatovic-Savič, Kovac-Cerovic, Plut, & Pesikan, 1990). A situation involving dyadic interactions also demands dyadic descriptors; that is, descriptors of those aspects of performance that are irreducible to individual functioning. This methodological lesson, that the study of dyads requires dyadic descriptors, is easily transferable to the study of relationships. However, as the focus of interest shifts to dyadic (relationship) developmental outcomes, there is a risk of losing the individual. In other words, the relationship exists, but the partners in the relationship can become invisible, or they maybe seen as being maintained by the relationship, instead of vice versa. If the individual is lost as we study relationship development, we cannot argue that this is just as well, because the reality of the relationship surpasses that of the individualities and cannot be reduced to them (just as properties of water cannot be reduced to properties of hydrogen and oxygen, to use a famous example, or the meaning of a sentence cannot be reduced to the meaning of the words that make it up). Individuals in fact change in parallel, within, and in spite of their relationships. Besides, dyadic relationships do not exist in a social vacuum. They are, rather, part of a network or, a loose web, the partners being participants in that particular dyadic relationship, as well as many others. Relationship-level developmental effects are certainly related to individual developments, but are not merely a higher level synthesis of these. The "elements" in a relationship, in fact, not only create this "synthesis" by interacting and forming a dyadic unity, but continue functioning as units within and in spite of this (and many other) syntheses.

Two important considerations follow: The level of dyadic development needs to be treated as a separate developmental flow, a separate reality with respect to individual development. Also, individual development, separate from dyadic development, is in fact a part of relationship development.

This distinction (an inclusive one, albeit) again brings up the question of the dichotomizing of human realities. Some authors (e.g., Rogoff, 1990) believe that the goal of research in cultural development is to succeed in overcoming the distinction between the individual and the social. However, this distinction seems to be both analytically and phenomenologically indisputable, as the continued reference to it and struggle to overcome simplistic methodologies (generally unsuccessfully) prove. Besides, human cognition rests on dichotomies and comparisons, the production of distinctions; epistemology demands conceptualization: and analysis rests on the identification of entities. The distinction between the individual and the social is an analytically and pragmatically relevant one. The theory and method that would deal with developments at both of these levels simultaneously (assuming there are only two) needs to cut through their interface, instead of coasting on its surface. An example of the latter approach is Rogoff's notion of *appropriation*, which, by avoiding reference even implicitly to in and out, by universalizing the interface between them rather than cutting through it, essentially reintroduces a "black box" approach into cultural psychology.

In analyzing relationship development, we are actually concerned with a developmental trichotomy. The levels of individual and relationship development have already been mentioned. The third level, which creates a broad context for a variety of relationships, the one under consideration as well as the web of all other contacts that the partners in the relationship are involved in, is that of collective culture (as opposed to personal culture).

The notion of *personal culture* was introduced by Valsiner (1987), but has remained both theoretically unrefined (roughly defined) and methodologically unapproachable. It corresponds to the intuitive understanding that each of us is, ultimately, a very special case of intersecting cultural fields. It also implies a fully social understanding of personality.

In both cases, that of the collective culture and that of the personal culture, we are talking about a set of crystallized, fixed, but essentially arbitrary patterns of phenomena. Thus culture differs from nature. The production of sounds, for example, is natural, but the combination of sounds in a particular word is cultural. Similarly, movements of the human body that are intended to achieve something (e.g., walk from place A to place B) are natural, but the style of the gait, the timing of the action, or the justification for the walk may be cultural. In other words, cultural patterns are those arbitrary patterns in activity that have an established communicational value on the basis of their previous history of employment. Shared culture, or collective culture, provides a broad basis for successful communication among people. It is grounded in semiotic activity.

THEORETICAL FRAMEWORK

It seems reasonable to state that a general metatheoretical principle in psychology demands the developmental and social foundation of this science. The recently emerging theoretical coherence in cultural-historical psychological theory provides an increasingly comprehensive framework for the analysis of developmental phenomena. A number of theoretical tenets about individual psychological development have been proposed and repeatedly highlighted in the context of this approach. These are discussed here from the perspective of their usefulness in relationship analysis. The first axiom, about the critical role of symbolization and semiotic processes, is held up as the most important theoretical assumption. In the second place, the social nature of individual development is reasserted. Third, developmental mechanisms that contribute both to individual and interpersonal development are identified.

The Substantive and Methodological Importance of the Symbol

The symbolic function has been assigned a central role in human development, and the status of the single distinctive feature of the human being. Both Piaget and Vygotsky treated the representational capacity, which emerges out of sensorimotor intelligence, as the single most revolutionary achievement of human development, and as the precondition and building force of human intellectual functioning (Piaget, 1945; Vygotsky, 1929). Within the cultural-historical stream of theorizing, the semiotic aspect of human functioning has been given central importance by, among others, Ivic (1978) and Smolka, Goes, and Pino (1997). This chapter follows their lead.

Ivic based his opinion about the central place of semiosis in human functioning on the analysis of psychological development, both in its phylogenetic and its ontogenetic aspect. In the summary of the contents of the book *Man as Animal Symbolicum* he wrote:

> The study of ontogenetic changes in the behavior of man shows that beside the principle of signalization (in a Pavlovian sense), which is held in common by the higher nervous activity of animals and man, there is also a principle of signification (Vygotsky) which exists only in man. From a psychological standpoint, the principle of signification consists in the ability to create and acquire signs, systems of signs,

and inner and outer symbolic realities. The appearance of these new abilities (i.e., the appearance of the symbolic function) can be recognized on the basis of behaviors which are expressions of the symbolic function and on the basis of the analysis of the products of human activity. The appearance of signs, which are the minimal level of the expression of the symbolic function, can operationally be recognized on the basis of the distinctive features of the semiotic, such as: differentiation between the sign and the signified, symbolic reference (denotation), the signification of at least some absent denotates and at least some classes of denotates. The appearance of semiotic systems, which are the higher level of the expression of the symbolic function, can be recognized on the basis of the existence of grammar, the hierarchical organization of the units of the semiotic system, creativity (productivity), propositionality. The existence of semiotic systems implies the appearance of semiotic operations (denotation, negation, combination of units of the system, transformation of messages). The highest level of the expression of the symbolic function is the process of the creation of inner symbolic realities (inner instances of personality, mental activities) and outer symbolic realities (the creation of culture in the broadest sense). The operational indicators of that level of the symbolic function are processes of internalization (e.g., the internalization of social speech and its metamorphosis into inner speech) and externalization (the creation, keeping, and transmission to new generations of the mindcrafts and handicrafts of previous generations). These distinctive features of the semiotic are neither definitive nor sufficiently operationalized. Further research into the criteria for differentiating the semiotic and the non-semiotic are necessary and are being continued. (Ivic, 1978, pp. 315-316)

He also wrote further:

Arising out of the biological prerequisites which have come to existence in the course of evolution, the symbolic function is the ability of creating systems of signs which appear as the connection between individual nervous systems. The creation of this connection is at the beginning of the process of semiotic communication, in the course of which all the individuals engaged in this communication process change and develop. The results of these changes are translated into semiotic systems and preserved. In this way, a new principle of human development is initiated—that of alloplastic development, i.e. development in the guise of externalization of human abilities in cultural products, those extensions of human ability. The symbolic function is the mechanism through which the connection is actualized between man's biological and his social development, and that is why it is critically important. (Ivic, 1978, p. 322)

In other words, the sign, the symbolic element is instituted as the unit of psychological functioning. Vygotsky (1960) was the first developmental psychologist to point to the word as the appropriate unit of analysis for both linguistic and thinking processes. Without denying that these two kinds of processes are distinctive and might involve entirely different kinds of elements at other hierarchical levels, it is doubtlessly true that the word can be identified as a self-contained unit that belongs to a certain level of analysis in both these processes.

This locus of unity directs us toward certain choices with respect to theory and methodology. For example, a natural consequence is the choice of a systemic view of psychological functioning. Another such consequence is the need—and also the possibility—to use the same approach (semiotic analysis) in studying both individual and social realities. Third, as the word is used polysemically and dynamically in the construction of personal awareness, we find the cognitive-affective breakdown gone. Further, the study of word realities demands the use of an analytical and interpretive method. Finally, without exhausting the list implications, let us still mention that the acceptance of a semiotic approach to psychology calls our attention to and invites a reinterpretation of the unconscious mind.

The methodological importance of instituting the symbol as the basic element of the human psyche cannot be overestimated. This theoretical stand assumes the sign as the analytical element, and the structures, processes, and contents related to the sign as the appropriate topics of analysis in psychology. In taking this stand, we become involved in a true cultural psychology, one that provides anchored access to the meanings involved in human existence.

It is worthwhile to note that the matter of choosing semiotic elements as the common basis both for the theory and the methodology of a cultural psychology has the pragmatically favorable consequence of direct access to phenomena of interest. The sign vehicle is directly observable. It is the visible, intersubjectively verifiable aspect of semiosis. It is a part of the phenomenon of interest, and it is, at the same time, its own "measurement". In other words, in accepting the sign as the bridge between psychological theory and methodology, the issues of measurement and its validity are placed in a new light.

The optimal methodology for the study of development also needs to cut through the internal-external (private-public, individual-social) barrier, the distinction between personal phenomenological worlds and externally observable worlds—both those related to individual functioning and those related to the functioning of groups of people; both those that are events, and those that are structures. Semiosis, in fact, does that. It is a unified and potentially multiple process, aspects of which have simultaneous foci on either side of this barrier.

It should be clear that the choice of symbolic realities as the focus of psychological research does not negate or downplay other levels of psychological functioning. The human symbolic function is not taken to be dissociated from the biological substrate. In fact, biology provides the very basis for the semiotic capacity, as well as for human sociability, which is at the core of communication.

The Person's Social Origin

Cultural-historical theory stresses the social nature of human ontogeny. The development of infants depends on an initial sociability. Survival is enabled by human contact, and hence the special ability to recognize and react to other human beings. However, the primary social contact is also at the basis of the human being becoming human at all. In other words, human nature is actualized and constructed through social interaction and is built of the material of social interaction. In a static outlook, this seems to be circular, because the claim is that man is constituted by that which he himself produces; that is, his existence seems to be the prerequisite for those events that constitute him. Developmentally, however, it is easy to see the ontogeny is couched in a social (and cultural) context, which, in turn, is the accumulated and conglomerated product of many years of many individuals' externalizing activity.

On the other hand, the activity of externalization by individuals remains inherently social and, interactive; it is built on the basis of socially learned assumptions (including needs, values, and goals), using socially sharpened skills (tools and *savoir faire*), and conveys socially interpretable meanings. On the other hand, this activity remains inherently free. It is important to stress this stand, the need for which is, of course, based on a value choice. It is necessary to stress it, because the extreme sociogenetic view, the position that the individual is, in every part, genetically and functionally social, carries the risk of seeing the individual as socially determined.

The issue of determination arises at two levels: One is that of the origin of structures, illustrated by the question—given such a history of interactions— could this person have turned out differently, or could we be seeing something else at this moment? In other words, given this history of interaction, is the next moment in development predictable, or are there multiple possibilities? The other level of determination is related to free will, or the autochthonous character of human actions—is this man's action now the product of "his own mind," or is it the mechanical result of more or less brainwashing?

The first question of social determination—understood developmentally, not situationally—receives a twofold answer in the context of cultural-historical theory. On the one hand, the concept of internalization introduces the possibility of indeterminate individual transformations in mental content (Lawrence & Valsiner, 1993). On the other hand, the *zone of proximal development*, which is the core concept of Vygotskian developmental theory, succinctly synthesizes developmental indeterminacy and developmental propensity.

A positive answer to the second kind of question (man's action is free) leads to a positive answer to the first question (there are multiple developmental possibilities at any moment), but the reverse is not necessarily true. In the history of psychology, the question of free will was most aggressively attacked by behaviorist anthropology (Skinner, 1971). In the quest for a positivist basis for our science, human freedom and dignity had to be sacrificed. A semiotic foundation for psychology would provide a firm methodological alternative that would also, thanks to the characteristics of the sign (such as polysemy, contextuality, etc.), provide a basis for the acceptance of human free will. This choice of theoretical and methodological framework in psychology, therefore, rests on more than purely empirical and epistemological considerations. It is in part driven by the framework's potential implications concerning some basic anthropological values.

Developmental Mechanisms

The developmental mechanisms postulated by cultural-historical theory are the coacting processes of first, internalization-externalization, and second, the generation of a zone of proximal development. The first class of processes works on the redistribution of content (and, as a necessary consequence of the ambiguity of the processes—its transformation). The second consists in the creation of a directed (shaped) motivational field. These concepts remain useful in the analysis of relationships.

The famous Vygotskian dictum states that nothing exists on the intrapsychological plane that has not previously existed on the interpsychological plane. This is not a statement about the isomorphism of the social and individual but rather about the social nature of the process of semiosis—the process of meaningful interaction—which is at the core of learning and development in higher mental processes. It is through immediate interaction with the surrounding world that the individual is shaped. Piaget described the processes of assimilation and accommodation that are involved in the adjustment of psychological structures to evolving realities. From a Vygotskian view, however, this is never devoid of its social aspect, the touch of forces that enter this interaction with the intention of giving and taking. This is not only true in immediate human contact, but also in the interaction of an individual with various products of other humans' activity. The contrast between partners who are never identical (and who are, in any case, asymmetrical in the roles they take) creates novelty in their very contact. Prolonged interaction then involves a negotiating process around this novel contrast. Internalization is based on the process of interpretation of the novelty that arises in interaction with social others. Although inherently social, it is an individual process. Although bound by social realities, it is also shaped by already existing individual structures and is marked by the uncertainty inherent in any process of interpretation.

As far as relationship development is concerned, the understanding of the mechanism of internalization implies that although the basis for a "shared reality" by a dyad is the history of mutual interaction (i.e., the history of "shared experiences" and negotiations about them), the two facets of this reality cannot be identical except by coincidence. This would be true even without the continuous influence throughout development of extraneous internal and external events on both sides of the dyad.

The zone of proximal development (ZPD), it is said, is the difference between what the child can do on his own, and what the child can do with the help of a more competent other. This operational, quantitative understanding of the ZPD is merely one application of a much broader concept. In other words, the notion that a child's individual development can only be adequately assessed with respect to what this child can do with the help of a more competent other is the unidimensional consequence of the ZPD; that is, the consequence of projecting the broader concept onto one dimension of measurement (in this case, success on a task). Starting with this operational, unidimensional definition of the ZPD, we can reconstruct some properties of the original concept.

First of all, the progressive nature of development is assumed. This ensues from the implied possibility of formulating an expected developmental line, along which the current state of the child can be located, with the expectation of progression in a definite direction (what is left variable is the extent of progression, not its nature, or the fact that some of it is expected).

Second, there are two imagined developmental lines involved in this measurement (one is the progression of the "child alone"; the other is the progression of the "child with the help of a more competent other"), and these two developmental lines coincide. If they did not, the measurement of their difference would not make sense as a developmental indicator. The "child's performance with the help of another" is taken as a true marker of the child's potential for future development. The conclusion must be that the direction of development is socially defined, and in fact, that development itself is social in nature.

The definition of the direction of development is social in the sense that the criterion for what is relevant to measuring development is external (e.g., school learning), but it is also social in a more profound sense—the direction of future development, the point toward which the child is headed, is a social datum. This is possible only if the ZPD is more than a frame of measurement. It is the state of potentiality for change within the individual that is opened up by interactive contact. This qualitative understanding of the ZPD is upheld by Vygotsky's notion that symbolic play (not necessarily socially interactive in an immediate sense) creates the ZPD (Vygotsky, 1933/1976).

Qualitatively understood, the ZPD covers the range of developmental possibilities allowed by the current state of the intrapsychological system at any given moment. The system, which contains certain elements (including capacities, knowledge, functions, etc.) structured in a certain way (as a result of previous development), can only change in certain ways, and not others. This is where the limitation and the indeterminacy of development come from.

The ZPD is actualized through action that takes one of the available routes, leading to a new state of the system, and a new state of the ZPD. In other words, the reality of the ZPD changes in the process of activity. Both examples of the ZPD—its operational definition and its creation in play—indicate that this is a dynamic category.

However, its most important characteristic, relevant for relationship development, is that it is also a motivational category. We can think of the action that actualizes the ZPD in one of its possibilities as a vector, whose magnitude is given by the state of the intrapsychological system, and whose direction is suggested by interaction with the environment. The ZPD inherently involves the developmental momentum of the living system; at the same time, it is not just the propensity to lunge forward, but also a shaped propensity—in such a way that it bridges the biological motivational forces of the organism and the leading symbolic social injunctions. The ZPD is what differentiates a developing system from one that is merely working.

IN SUMMARY

The general assumptions adopted at the metatheoretical level are that the approach to meaningful human reality should be developmental, social, and semiotic. The structural elements—identified as signs and their systemic relationships—exist at three different levels: the individual (subjective), the interactional (intersubjective), and the collective (desubjectivized). There may be multiple instances of a level, or multiplicity within each, but the levels are functionally distinct from each other and necessary for each other's functioning.

The crystallized aspect of the semiotic process is referred to as culture. Thus, there is personal culture, collective culture, and the possibility of intersubjective culture. The fluid, dynamic aspects of semiosis, in the place where they span the level of subjective functioning and that of intersubjective functioning, are caught under the umbrella term of internalization-externalization. The model that has been developed in this chapter seems to demand the introduction of a similar processual link with the collective-cultural level. This could perhaps be a process we would call subjectivization-desubjectivization, which would indicate how the patterns constructed in immediate social interaction pass on to be crystallized structures in collective culture.

The interaction of different semiotic systems and/or their subelements creates a future projection of the system(s), limited by the content of the system(s) and inherently motivated by the valuative character of signs; that is, the affective-cognitive synthesis. This future-projecting mechanism, which unites the directing and motivating forces in development, is an interpretation of Vygotsky's ZPD.

The method employed by such a psychology needs to be analytic and interpretive. Its purpose would be to make sense of instances of sense making, by constructing a universalist (nomothetic) schema of human developmental processes.

IDENTITY AND CHANGE IN RELATIONSHIP DEVELOPMENT

The general objective of semiotic construction is the production of sense; that is, humans' meaningful self-orientation. From the standpoint of an individual, sense production is, in fact, identity building. This is identity in the sense close to integrity. It is the seeking of definition—not any kind of definition, but one that expresses a fully understandable unity. The human tendency to create fully understandable unities was argued for at the perceptual level by Gestalt psychologists (Köhler, 1947). At the other end of the process complexity continuum, Bruner (1990) ascribed a constitutive function to the integration achieved through narrative, from early childhood onward.

Identity in the psychological sense is not merely a definition. It is a self-definition. In the context of the present semiotic psychological theory, it has to be a dynamic one. Therefore, it is a narrative definition, because narration is the sequenced, time-framed, organized externalization of the ongoing psychological semiotic process. The narrative about the self is an open one, one that is constantly being told in the effort to integrate its currently available elements. The process of story telling is not only the laying out of a plot of events—in which sense McAdams (1987) would have that the life story is equivalent to a person's identity. It is in part that, of course, and in that case, the narration is a recreated expression of a cognitive schema. In cases of often-told stories, the level of recreation for the purpose of ongoing formulation can actually be minimal. We all know examples for such ossified personal stories (note that the rigidification referred to here is at the level of narration itself, not at the level of the schema). Beside that, any story telling is in fact a struggle to envelop in one explanatory web all the available elements of "truth". This is true even of those fictional stories that emphasize plot. It is an exceptionally important element of the sense-making story telling that involves everyday experience with self and others. The narrative process is then based on the impromptu creation of a conceptual (symbolic) stream, which is hierarchically superior to those elements of the personal semiotic system that constitute knowledge about self in a certain situation or certain frame, such as a relationship, including sentimental and value statements.

Seeing identity, from this standpoint, as a definitional process, we must also see it as a bipolar one. On the one side, there is the definiens: the life story, the self-concept, the self-schema, the Jamesian "Me," and so on. On the other side, there is the definiendum. The most interesting question concerning the self is that of this definiendum: What is it? Where is it? At least roughly, it corresponds to the "I" (James, 1890), to the center of consciousness, to the author of a personal account. It seems that the understanding of identity as a bipolar definitional process could give us some interesting insights into old concepts, but would also provide a clear template for the semantic and structural analysis of narratives.

So, where is identity in relationships? Clearly, each of the persons involved in a relationship lives in a personal world and is developing a personal identity—in fact, probably a number of concurrent identities. However, there is an important new identity emerging in a long-term relationship—that of the dyad.

In the course of relationship development, a dyadic culture comes to regulate the interactions of the dyad, as well as mutual expectations. Picking out two people and their relationship from the matrix of a broader social milieu, however, is artificial and belies the complexity of life. From the very beginning, this dyadic culture is embedded in and supported by collective-cultural assumptions about dyadic relationships. Such assumptions are probably not fully complementary between the partners, as they are based on personal versions of collective culture; however, they are initially assumed to be complementary, for communicational purposes. Collective culture also exerts a direct external influence on the relationship by providing interactive templates within organized spaces, occasions, and so on (as relationships develop in a real and concrete world and not at all in isolation).

Collective culture likewise exerts a mediated external influence, through the expectations that shape interactions of the partners with people outside of this particular relationship. Although these influences are always mediated by the personal cultures and concrete interpretations of the people in question, such third parties will always understand the roles in a relationship in terms closer to the collective-cultural than people who are immediately involved in a relationship. This is partly due to the relative lack of information, and the need to use assumptions in creating global interpretations. On the other hand, such third parties are usually personally and emotionally disinterested (up to a point only, because the very activity of interpreting others' relationships draws on personal schemas and the need to affirm them; sometimes, other people's relationships, just like the examples of other people's behavior in general, may be a symbol that binds very important personal values).

The collective-cultural assumptions (in personal rendering) that are applied by each of the partners inside the relationship, as well as by other people in touch with the relationship, are reworked gradually, through the negotiation of particular points and the exposure of an increasing number of elements of the other's (in the relationship) individual personality. The identity of a relationship is thus created, as the shared within-interaction dialogical narrative about the relationship itself. It is established at the dyadic level and supported by its structures, including a dyadic culture and affective bonds (e.g., attachment; Zazzo, 1974).

Relationship identity is not just another label for the dyad, or for the individual's understanding of it. It is meant to designate the fact that interactional patterns that take place dyadically over time exert the pressure for the creation of a shared account of the relationship. The structures that form the relationship now are not any longer just individual in character. In the light of the dyadic culture, and considering constantly newly arising elements (events in interaction), an ongoing account of the relationship—its definiens—is being constructed by the dyad. This account, just like the personal self-narrative, has a constitutional function.

The process of relationship identity construction, however, is different from the stream of consciousness that creates personal identity. It is externally dialogical and it is intermittent. Because of that, a gap exists between the identity of a dyadic relationship and the personal understanding of it by each of the partners.

In any dyadic relationship, there are three main types of developmental change: that of the relationship itself, and the personal development of each of the two partners. The previous discussion of the discrepancy between these levels of accounting indicates that these developments take place with different rhythms. They are also of different complexity. Personal development consists in the constant reconstruction under the influx of elements that may have nothing to do with the particular relationship under consideration. The two partners, in this sense, may develop at different speeds (i.e., experience developmental transitions at different times) and in different directions (i.e., experience developmental transitions of different types). Their development, off course, is not totally independent of the other person and of the relationship. This is all the more true the closer the relationship is. A close relationship in this sense is one in which the other is a frequent and essential element in the sense making of one's personal life. In Allport's (1961) personology, this particular other is close to the *proprium*. Changes in the life, feelings, and activities of the other affect one's own identity; that is, the meaning of one's own life. Even so, individual development remains personal, these relevant interpretations about the other being personal.

On the other hand, the relationship itself, which is based on the dyadic culture, which encompasses the dyadic relationship identity as well as crystallized interactional patterns, develops under its own impetus. This is extremely important to stress. The dialogical narrative about the relationship creates its own future at least in two ways. First, it does so declaratively. The actual content of self-awareness is in part reflective of the future; it is prophetic. The future, symbolically constituted in the present, directs its own self-fulfillment. Second, the continuously open negotiation process sets up a need for resolution at every step of the way. The statements and counterstatements in the dialogical narrative, coupled with the inherent uncertainty in symbolization, constantly reproblematize the relationship. Once again, in symbolic terms, the future of the relationship demands to be actualized; that is, the dialogical narrative must continue to be reformulated (and, thus, the relationship reconstituted). In other words, the relationship has its own ZPD, which provides both direction and the very expectation of a relationship future.

In terms of rhythm, relationship development is complex: It involves at least two scales of event succession that must be taken into consideration. Just like individual development, the basis for meaning formation is events in microprocess; that is, in real time. Every meeting of a dyad consists in an interactive sequence, where certain contents are exchanged, and in which the dyadic (relationship) identity may be affirmed, refined, and transformed. Meetings are, however, intermittent, in contrast to the doubtless phenomeno-logical continuity of an individual mind. Therefore, the event sequence that treats particular meetings of the dyad as units becomes a necessary scale of relationship analysis, in addition to the meaning-juggling microprocess.

A PROBLEM AND AN EXPLANATION

In order to provide a link between conceptualization and empathetic understanding, we problematize one point of human relationship development. The paradox in question is that, in common experience, the tightest relationships, those that endure, that are maintained through personal effort (and therefore needed, treasured), also involve the most self-centered gestures on the part of either partner in the relationship. Another way to formulate this paradox is through the notion of egocentrism (in the Piagetian sense). Beyond the level of immediately established intersubjectivity and short-term interaction, the establishment of enduring relationships in which both partners have a responsibility for its maintenance requires of each of the partners a degree of decentration; that is, the ability to consider the viewpoint of the other and maintain this consideration in the absence of the other. This is a prerequisite for relationship maintenance. However, it is also true that in these very relationships, partners often fail to take the other's point of view in surprising ways, sometimes demonstrating a blatant inability to see and consider the other's reality (symbolic, of course). For examples, I ask the reader to draw on personal experience. Counterexamples, and there are plenty of those as well, do not essentially harm the nature of the paradox or the need to explain how it is at all possible that two contradictory processes—that of decentration and that of increasing egocentrism—take place simultaneously within a single relationship. A simple solution to this paradox would be to call this "misunderstanding" and state that a long-lasting relationship simply gives enough time for such things to emerge, but it is more fruitful to see this fact as a consequence of the nature of relationship development.

The model explored here tells the following story. Sense in relationships or individual development is achieved through the construction of a coherent account of it. The development of any particular relationship is only one of the many developmental lines that envelop the individual, who is faced with the task of making sense of the many parallel changes and incorporating the interactional events of the relationship into personal development. At the same time, the maintenance of a relationship depends on the successful integration into an ongoing "shared" account of these elements: initial impositions and changes in collective-cultural and social-beyond-the-relationship constraints, the controlled choices of each of the partners, uncontrolled changes in each partner's personal sphere, and emerging elements of the increasingly dependent personal cultures. The sense-creating task is, then, twofold—individual and shared.

However, in close relationships, this task is complicated by the progressive accumulation of inconsistency that is inherent in their nature: On the one hand, there is progressive disclosure of the necessarily different personal systems and hence progressive interpsychological disequilibrium; on the other hand, there is the construction of a shared dyadic culture and a concomitant growing dependency. The impersonal terms of system and element in this context apply to a human living system. As the discussion of the nature and sources of semiosis in humans indicates, the elements under negotiation are not only meaningful in a purely cognitive sense, but are also emotionally charged. The dependency created within a dyadic system, then, is not just a matter of maintaining the balance of mutually supporting structures, but is also based on the symbolic rootedness of human needs and drives.

The problem of the discrepancy between the increasing disequilibrium and the increasing dependency must find a twofold resolution, as the sense-making task is twofold—personal and dyadic. The dyadic culture must then involve mechanisms for resolving the standing interpsychological disequilibrium. In other words, priority in shared interpretation (within interaction) must be given to those elements that establish the continuity of the relationship in the face of differences. On the other hand, each individual must reconstruct the relationship in a way that meets personal needs—and this includes the highlighting of specifics, the purposeful ignoring or misinterpretation of other specifics, the identification of self with relationship, and so on.

CONCLUSION

The aim of this chapter was to synthesize the theoretical points of interest that have emerged from cultural-historical theorizing in the past years that are highly relevant for the analysis of relationship development, providing one view of the general theory of individual development in social context. This view affirms that the study of the sense-bearing aspects of human existence (i.e., the study of human development in the sense of the conduct of lives), may fruitfully rest on the study of the symbolic substrate of both the individual psyche and social relationships. The symbol acts as the appropriate anchor for the method of empirical investigation of human lives for multiple reasons: On the one side, it is the necessary tool of investigation, and hence the necessary tool of the self-conscientiation of the researcher's own position with respect to the subject of inquiry; on the other hand, it is in fact the locus of the spanning and integration of differences between all sides in a social relationship.

The study of relationships, which was sketched out in this chapter creates an appropriate view for the study of individual psychology as well. Although the very viability of an individual psychology may be questioned from the standpoint of a cultural-historical (i.e., sociogenetic) point of view, a phenomenological emphasis leads one to believe that the field of individual consciousness should be treated separately from the field of social interaction. In addition, I would like to stress the distinction between both of these and the collective-cultural level of symbol and meaning transmission. However, these three levels are not mutually independent. On the contrary, they continuously reconstitute and affect each other. They function as a set of mutually dependent open systems. The point to be emphasized is that not one of the levels can be analyzed in isolation from the others.

Further, I wish to point out that, in spite of the fluidity of relationship events and the fragmentary nature of semiotic development (when analyzed in cross-section), individual semiotic structures of a relatively permanent nature need to be considered in the explanation of relationship establishment, maintenance, and dissolution. In trying to understand the nexus of individual structures as the sources of agency, reinterpretation, and internal change in relationships, on the one side, and ongoing external change caused by various events, on the other, we are faced with the problem of the integration of parallel trajectories of developmental change.

This chapter focused on the analysis of dyadic relationships, although, clearly, this model can be generalized to the analysis of multiple-partner relationships (e.g., families). In fact, a consequence of this model is that no relationship can be considered to be a dyadic one, except in its reduced analytic form. Any dyadic relationship includes a chorus of assorted social others, which affect the relationship by their implicit or explicit presence, with or without the awareness of one or both of the partners in the relationship. At the same time, every dyadic relationship is one developmental strand in the total unfolding massive movement of life.

REFERENCES

Allport, G.W. (1961). *Pattern and growth in personality.* New York: Holt, Rinehart & Winston.

Bruner, J. (1990). *Acts of meaning.* Cambridge, MA: Harvard University Press.

Fogel, A., & Lyra, M.C.D.P. (1997). Dynamics of development in relationships. In F. Masterpasqua & P. Perna (Eds.), *The psychological meaning of chaos: Self-organization in human development and psychotherapy.* Washington, DC: American Psychological Association.

Ignjatovic-Savic, N., Kovac-Cerovic, T., Plut, D., & Pesikan, A. (1990). Socijalna interakcija u ranom detinjstvu i njeni razvojni ucinci [Social interaction in early childhood and its developmental effect]. *Psiholoska istrazivanja, 4,* 9-70.

Ivic, I.D. (1978). *Covek kao animal symbolicum.* Beograd: Nolit.

James, W. (1890). *The principles of psychology.* New York: Dover.

Köhler, W. (1947). *Gestalt psychology: An introduction to new concepts in modern psychology.* New York: Liveright.

Lawrence, J., & Valsiner, J. (1993). Social determinacy of human development: An analysis of the conceptual roots of the internalization process. *Human Development, 36,* 150-167.

McAdams, D.P. (1987). A life-story model of identity. In R. Hogan & W.H. Jones (Eds.), *Perspectives in personality* (Vol. 2, pp. 15-50). Greenwich, CT: JAI.

Mead, G.H. (1934). *Mind, self and society from the standpoint of a social behaviorist.* Chicago: University of Chicago Press.

Piaget, J. (1945). La formation du symbole chez l'enfant [Formation of symbol in the child]. Neuchatel, Switzerland: Delachaux et Niestle.

Rogoff, B. (1990). *Apprenticeship in thinking: Cognitive development in social context.* New York: Oxford University.

Skinner, B.F. (1971). *Beyond freedom and dignity.* Harmondsworth, UK: Penguin.

Smolka, A.L.B., Goes, M.C.R., & Pino, A. (1997). (In)determinacy and semiotic constitution of subjectivity. In A. Fogel, M. Lyra, & J. Valsiner (Eds.), *Dynamics and indeterminism in developmental and social processes.* Mahwah, NJ: Erlbaum.

Valsiner, J. (1987). *Culture and the development of children's action.* Chichester, UK: Wiley.

Valsiner, J. (1993). Bi-directional cultural transmission and constructive sociogenesis. In R. Maier & W. de Graaf (Eds.), *Mechanisms of sociogenesis* (pp. 47-70). New York: Springer.

Vygotsky, L.S. (1929). The problem of the cultural development of the child. *Journal of Genetic Psychology, 36,* 415-434.

Vygotsky, L.S. (1933/1976). Play and its role in the mental development of the child. In J.S. Bruner, A. Jolly, & K. Sylva (Eds.), *Play* (pp. 537-554). Harmondsworth: Penguin.

Vygotsky, L.S. (1962). *Thought and language.* Cambridge, MA: M.I.T. Press.

Zazzo, R. (Ed.). (1974). *L'attachement* (Attachment). Neuchatel, Switzerland: Delachaux et Niestle.

12

REFLECTIONS ON THE DYNAMICS OF MEANING MAKING: COMMUNICATION PROCESS AT THE BEGINNING OF LIFE

Maria C. D. P. Lyra
Federal University of Pernambuco, Brazil

This chapter takes a historical, epigenetic perspective of the dynamics of the interpersonal process of communication. Thus the process is understood as the locus of the emergence and construction of meaning. The focus of this chapter is analyzing the origin of this process starting at the beginning of the infant's life.

Communication is assumed to be a relational and continuous process from which novelty is created (Fogel, 1993). This conception is more clearly defined if it is opposed to the conception of communication as a discrete process in which bits of information are assigned to a sender and a receiver and analyzed as distinct contributions to novelty making. Communication as a relational and continuous process means that the unit of analysis includes both the partners and the process of communication (Lyra & Rossetti-Ferreira, 1995). From this point of view, we cannot separate the information that comes from each partners' contributions as autonomous elements of the process of communication. On the contrary, we should grasp the dynamics of this process as a whole system of mutual and interdependent interactions (Boulding, 1956;

Fogel, 1993; Fogel & Thelen, 1987; Laszlo, 1972; Lyra & Rossetti-Ferreira, 1987, 1995, Sameroff, 1982; Thelen & Smith, 1994). However, this dynamic system of communication needs to be analyzed with regard to the specific context in which the human social partners establish and develop their process of communication; in other words, the semiotic-cultural environment in which this process takes place.

A second aspect considered in this chapter deals with the integration of the communication process in the semiotic-cultural world in which it is embedded. In other words, it is assumed that the emergence and construction of meanings requires a theoretical and methodological framework that can guide the investigation of the dynamics of communication as a process that relates individual and cultural environment (Bakhtin, 1973, 1981, 1993; Cole, 1995; Fogel, 1992, 1997a; Rogoff, 1990; Valsiner, 1987, 1994; Wertsch, 1995).

The third aspect to be considered in this chapter refers to the meaning of action as it is embedded in a specific cultural-semiotic environment in the system of communicational development. Focusing on early infancy, it is assumed that the process through which meaning emerges occurs through the exchange of dialogical actions in the sense used by Hermans and Kempen (1995). According to their argument, dialogical actions bypass individualism and collectivism, as does the concept of mediated actions elaborated by Wertsch (1995). Additionally, dialogical actions add the role of the body and, in doing so, dialogical actions become an excellent conceptual tool for analyzing the constitutive dimension of culture at the beginning of life (see also Fogel, 1993). This conception assumes that the dialogue established between a newborn and his or her adult partner can be conceived of as a mutual and interdependent process of negotiation where the actions "talk" like words. In this sense, actions as dialogical action can integrate the internal (intersubjective) and external (intrasubjective) dimensions of communication.

I have chosen to take a dialogical position as the main theoretical and methodological framework in order to discuss the nature of the dynamics of communication as the process through which meaning emerges. I first discuss the consequences of assuming a dialogical position as an epistemological assumption by focusing on the choice of the unit of analysis. Second, I propose that one possible way of relating the cultural-semiotic world and dialogical action in the process of communication is through use of Bakhtin's idea of the evaluative character of answerable deeds in the historical and unique event of being (Bakhtin, 1993). Next, I discuss some of the points raised by dialogical approaches in dealing with the process of communication at the beginning of life; for example, the conception of dialogical actions and the role of language in facilitating the analysis of dialogue as embedded in a semiotic-cultural world. Finally, concentrating on the beginning of life, I propose that we can analyze at least some instances of the dynamics of communication as involving a relational choice within possibilities. This choice carries an evaluative character for both partners that is constructed through the history of their relationship development. This conception can be taken as a theoretical and methodological guide in relating at least some instances of the process of communication between the individual and semiotic-cultural world.

DIALOGUE AS AN EPISTEMOLOGICAL ASSUMPTION: THE CHOICE OF UNITS OF ANALYSIS

When considering development within the social process of communication, the interdependent and mutually transforming characteristics of the exchanges make it necessary to consider this phenomenon as a bidirectional, nonlinear exchange of actions embedded in the cultural and semiotic world (Bakhtin, 1973, 1981, 1983; Marková, 1990a, 1990b). The dialogical logic, which guides the dialogue, has been called dialectical, cogenetic (Rommetveit, 1990; Spencer-Brown, 1969) or the logic of simultaneous constitution (Carvalho, Império-Hamburger, & Pedrosa, Chapter 9, this volume). Each partner is involved in a task that belongs, at the same time, to himself or herself, to the other, and to the semiotic-cultural world in which the communication takes place. Novelty emerges from the historical dynamics of the dialogue. Therefore, this process creates a history that constitutes relationships. At the same time, this process also creates the partners themselves as relational and distinguished subjectivities. Both relationships and subjectivities are created inside a semiotic and cultural time and space context in which communication develops. These inclusive dynamics, which takes place within a specific, concrete, and sociohistorical context, should be understood as an epistemological point of view, as Marková (1990b) proposed. Dialogism is thus understood as "an epistemological approach to the study of mind and language as historical and cultural phenomena" (Marková, 1990b, p. 4). Therefore, this position carries the basic assumption of communication as inserted in a contextual and sociohistorical moment.

In considering the dialogue as the unit of analysis, the central meaning of assuming dialogism as an epistemological approach relies on the fact that the physical units of partners' turns (which compose the dialogue) must be understood from the point of view of a relational and dynamic perspective, which Marková (1990a) called internal relationships. In other words, she proposed that the minimal unit of analysis of the dialogue is a three-step process composed by the first partner's turn, the second partner's turn, and again the first partner's answer in reaction to the second turn. Even in extremes cases of a dialogue that seems composed of two steps as, for example, in a greeting (first partner: "Hi"; second partner: "Fine"), we must assume a reaction from the first partner to the answer "Fine," which will compose the third step (Marková, 1990a).

Even the conception of a three-step process is an arbitrary one and, therefore, a concrete and elective decision by the researcher toward analyzing the dialogue as a unit. Mukarovsky (1977) suggested that the turns may not be considered as delimiting the boundaries of each partner's contribution, therefore, the physical and conceptual boundaries of the turns may not coincide. He proposed the concept of dialogical quality of speech, which means that the dialogical quality, exceeding the frontiers of the physical turns, may spread to all dialogue. For instance, the insistence on getting a positive answer from the partner can be part of successive turns of one of the partners throughout one complete hour of dialogue. Consequently, the quality of each turn may not be homogenous. This does not mean that the partners are not co-regulated, as Fogel proposed (Fogel, 1993; Fogel & Lyra, 1997), but that we have to consider the possibility that the physical and conceptual boundaries of the turns may not coincide. Therefore, it seems that, in any case, the delimitation of turns in the dialogue is a choice made by the researcher. What guides this option?

One consequence of assuming dialogism as an epistemological position is the assumption that all human production has a dialogical character. The dynamic nature that this position carries leads to the conclusion that all scientific contributions must have a relativistic scope. In this direction, the ideas proposed by Rommetveit (1990), based on co-genetic logic, state that what we have established as categories of reality is a shared understanding of the world around us. It is the convergence of perspectives that gives to use the idea of truth and stability. Therefore, searching for a conceptual and methodological option for understanding the dialogue as a unit of analysis carries, in the utmost instance, a search for a convergence of perspectives in the present moment of scientific contributions. Assuming as an axiomatic principle the mutuality and interdependence of partners' dialogical contributions and the embeddedness of them in a specific sociohistorical context, our task should be guided by the heuristic value of our choice. Moreover, this heuristic value will result from the careful analysis of the specific domain in which we are using the dialogical approach, at a specific moment in time. From this perspective, I am not claiming that we must subscribe to an extreme relativistic position, but that the phenomena of our converging perspectives on scientific knowledge should be considered in relation to a specific time-context moment.

Focusing on the dialogical process of communication, the next section considers the problem of integrating the individual and the semiotic-cultural world in which communication is embedded.

EVALUATIVE CHARACTER OF DIALOGUE IN THE HISTORICAL-UNIQUE EVENT OF BEING

In this section, I analyze some of Bakhtin's ideas on the dialogical act of communication as meaning making. I aim to propose a method for assuming a comprehensive bridge between individual action and the semiotic world.

Bakhtin (1973, 1981, 1993) has been considered one of the major proponents of dialogism as conceived from an epistemological standpoint. It is in his earlier works, particularly in his unfinished philosophical essay published under the title, *Toward a Philosophy of the Act* (1993), that Bakhtin expressed the core of his conception dealing with the dynamics that relates the individual's unique deed with the cultural-semiotic objective reality. He stressed the reality of the

unitary and once-occurrent event of Being through the mediation of an answerable consciousness in an actual deed. But that once-occurred event of Being is no longer something that is thought of, but something that *is*, something that is being actually and inescapably accomplished through me and others (accomplished, inter alia, also in my deed of cognizing); it is actually experienced, affirmed in an emotional-volitional manner, and cognition constitutes merely a moment in this experiencing-affirming. (p. 13)

So, for Bakhtin, the core event of Being is the phenomenological dynamics (conceived as an embodied subjectivity) that creates meaning. The meaning of life comes through the answerability of those deeds (each action being a relational-evaluation) that constitute the possibility of connecting culture and the unique event of Being. It is only through answerable deeds that we can create and feel our meaning as participative human beings. Therefore, the connection between these two separate worlds—the one of objective culture and symbols and the one of our experience of life as an ongoing event—lies in the answer-deed. This communion gives us the unity of life experience.

Bakhtin highlighted the historical nature that gives this event is uniqueness. It is not an abstract historicity. The experiencing of life is put in an irreversible historical scale of a processual nature and one that happens in a concrete moment of our embodied subjectivity. So, the theoretical subject only exists in the light of an embodied subjectivity.

But, of course, this theoretical *subjectum* had to be embodied each time in some real, actual, thinking human being, in order to enter (along with the whole world immanent to him *qua* object of his cognition) into communion with the actual, historical event of Being as just a moment within it. (Bakhtin, 1993, p. 6)

Meaning Making: Relational-Evaluative and Historical Constitution

Bakhtin's (particularly 1993) phenomenological conception of the act of Being recognizes the functioning of two different worlds. One is theoretical and disembodied, composing the intellectual-cognitive side of symbolic-abstract cultural constructions. The other is the subjective moment of experiencing life or life-in-process-of-becoming. Moreover, the need to interconnect those two worlds makes Bakhtin unique in his devotion to understand subjective and objective dimensions of life as unitary phenomenon. Trying to relate both sides,

Bakhtin dealt with the core dilemma of action and semiotic functioning. He proposed that this communion can only be done through the assumption of each action as a meaningful evaluative answer in the context of a relational self-others duality. Bakhtin's conception integrates the uniqueness of the historical subjective moment of the experience of Being and the semiotic-cultural environment through the relational character of those answerable deeds. Each time we act, we assume one position or perspective in relation to the others, which are the embodied cultural heritage toward which we act. This can mean a real person in front of us or a cultural construction (for instance, a conceptual scientific framework) toward which we establish an internal dialogue. I would like to emphasize our relational and historical status of being as the essential aspect of the communion between individual and culture. Moreover, in agreement with a dialogical position, the relational nature of our actions guarantee to those actions a character of answerability; being an option within other possible actions (present as possibilities at the same time). This choice comprises a moral choice because it affects the other and ourselves as an evaluation. Those actualized choices and evaluations progressively construct a relationship history.

It is my understanding that the inclusion of the evaluative character of the actual historical deed carries the possibility of grasping the merging nature of culture and individual in the unit of life experience. Furthermore, the creative dimension of those answerable deeds, which emerge from the dynamic context of dialogue, carries the subjective meaning of life experience as participative human beings.

A dynamic and creative world of meaning making emerges from this communion between individual and culture. The real existence and transforming characteristic of this world happens at the level of the embodied and concrete experience of Being in a specific historical-processual time and context. The investigation of the emergence of relationships and subjects as meaning making, from the beginning of life, seems to be a fundamental starting point. What is the nature of the dynamics that give rise to the emergence of novelty as meaning making? From the ontogenetic point of view, how can this dynamic be grasped? How does the exchange of actions comprise a dialogue between an emergent subject, at the beginning of life, with his or her adult partner? How is the semiotic-cultural heritage blended in the dynamics of the dialogue for embracing the early beginning of the process of communication?

DIALOGICAL ACTIONS AND MEANING MAKING AT THE BEGINNING OF LIFE

Considering the dialogical perspective and focusing on the investigation of the communication process at the beginning of life, I discuss two aspects. One deals with the dialogical origins of the individual mind and the comprehension and inclusion of dialogical actions, which include a body, in the process of meaning making. The other deals with the role of language as facilitating the task of relating meaning making with the semiotic-cultural environment in which communication is embedded.

Dialogical Origins of Individual Mind

The dialogical origins of the individual mind can be considered as an axiomatic starting point (Bräten, 1984; Rommetveit, 1990). The dialogical individual comes into being in a self-other duality (Rommetveit, 1990). Studies in early interactions supported this perspective. A number of studies have suggested that the newborn and his or her mother engage in a kind of dialogue either through the use of biological rhythms—like pauses and bursts of sucking during meals (Fogel, 1977; Kaye, 1977) or using vocalizations or other actions of the baby as composing the baby's turns in a type of "pseudodialogue" with a conversationlike structure (Clarke-Stewart, Perlmutter, & Friedman, 1988; Newson 1977; Stern, 1977; Trevarthen, 1977). Furthermore, the inclusion of the body to dialogical actions, highlighting its role before language development occurs (emphasized by Hermans & Kempen, 1995), opens up possibilities to search for the origins of the process through which meaning emerges, grounded in a dialogical, interpersonal context. Moreover, the dialogical nature of a prelinguistic self has been pointed out by Fogel (1993), based on the analysis of perception-action systems of the baby (see also Butterworth, 1992; Kravitz, Goldenberg, & Neyhus, 1978), conceived as a dialectical self-other relationship (Fogel, 1997b). Nevertheless, the question of how the dynamics of the self-other duality allow the emergence of meaning and the symbolic domain through the process of communication and relationship development needs to be further explored. Particularly, how can we approach these dynamics as integrating the semiotic-cultural world in the process of communication since the beginning of life?

A general difficulty exists in broadening the conception of dialogical negotiations toward including the role of embodied dialogical actions. Hermans and Kempen (1995), referring to the notion of pseudodialogues in early infancy, pointed out that this notion involves the presupposition that infants are not able to engage in real dialogues. They interpret this fact by saying that, "this presupposition is an expression of the traditional view that equalizes dialogue with verbal conversation and, consequently, there can be no dialogue preceding the maturation of language" (p. 110). The idea of assuming those dialogues as pseudodialogues and not as real dialogues seems to be based on a twofold assumption. One assumption, more methodological, considers partners' turns as always physically distinguished or objectively separated in the dialogical exchanges. (The boundaries between the physical and conceptual nature of the turns in a concrete dialogue may not coincide, as already pointed out in a previous section of this chapter.) The other assumes that the embeddedness of the dialogue in the semiotic-cultural environment can only be approached through language expertise. In other words, it is language—more specifically speech—that introduces the possibility of dialogue. Those two assumptions are supported by the fact that speech facilities both the separability of partners' turns and the elaboration of a connection between dialogical exchanges and the semiotic-cultural environment. However, dialogical actions, considered as bypassing individualism and collectivism, add the role of the body and, in doing so, allow the analysis of the constitutive dimension of culture from the beginning of life.

Speech as Facilitating a Conceptual and Methodological Linkage With Semiotic-Cultural Environments

Dialogism emerged as a perspective to deal with the dynamics inherent to the exchanges with and within a social world. The dialogical position had grown as a reflection on the domain of language as a symbolic human way of functioning (Marková, 1990b). The task of conceiving dialogical actions, at the beginning of life, as constructing meaning embedded in a semiotic-cultural environment faces the problem of how to attribute to action a similar role in the context of dialogue at the beginning of life. Having language, (particularly speech) to support the analysis of dialogical exchanges—and, therefore, its inherent reflexive characteristic—provides the means to identify, in a more clear-cut way, the dimension of dialogue as embedded in a semiotic-cultural world. Even in the beginning, language expertise facilitates establishing the connection of dialogical exchanges and the semiotic-cultural domain. Let us consider an example taken from the work of Smolka and da Cruz (Chapter 4, this volume) that focuses on the interactive exchanges established between an adult and a group of six children in a day-care center in Brazil. "Assuming that signifying processes emerge in cultural practices" (Smolka & da Cruz, Chapter 4, this volume, p. 7), the following example exhibits the emergence of meaning, its diversity, the fluidity of those meanings, and the interdependence of the interactive dynamics. I have chosen to analyze this example because it refers to very young children (from 13 months and 23 days to 15 months and 17 days) and because the process of meaning construction is done in relation to a kind of flexible word that seems to carry a fluid and emotional meaning more than an explicit object-referent meaning: the word *ai*. As Smolka and da Cruz argue, the word *ai* does not have an explicit object relatedness or referent. Otherwise, in Portuguese, *ai* can be an interjection, expressing pain or discomfort, reproach, or protest within other meanings. Also, *ai* can mean assertions or reflections in conversation. However, the word *ai* facilitates the analysis of the transformations and constructions of this word, in the context of dialogical exchanges (interactive dynamics as Smolka and da Cruz call it), as reflecting instances of the semiotic-cultural environment (a Brazilian day-care center). For instance, some uses of the word *ai* can be interpreted as "instances of appropriation of cultural experiences as she (one of the children) makes or transforms into her own, the *words* of others in different positions" (Smolka & da Cruz, Chapter 4, this volume, p. 14; italics added). Therefore, the word—even though flexible and fluid—helps to guide the analysis that exhibits the relationship of the ongoing dialogue with the semiotic-cultural world in which communication is embedded.

However, even in analyses that highlight the role of the word as delimiting the partners' turn and relating them to the semiotic-cultural ambience, the dialogic nature of the body and action has a role. Focusing on early infancy, a conceptual and methodological approach that integrates the mutuality and interdependence of partners' actions in the dialogical process of communication and the constitutive dimension of culture in those early dialogues seems to be a necessity.

Thus, investigating the process of communication as meaning making from the beginning of life requires a conceptual framework that integrates the role of dialogically embodied actions as reflecting the relationship between the historical-unique dialogical event and the semiotic-cultural environment.

In the next section I discuss the conception of relational choice within possibilities. This conception is proposed as a theoretical and methodological framework for analyzing at least some instances of the dynamics of dialogue as meaning making, embedded in a semiotic-cultural environment.

RELATIONAL CHOICE WITHIN POSSIBILITIES

The process of communication as a history of dialogical actions that realizes a relational choice within possibilities is exemplified based on a twofold assumption.

One assumption consists of the conception of dialogue as dialogical actions that occur in an embodied experiencing moment and that focus on the microprocess of ontogenetic development of communication at the beginning of life. This means that even when one considers different levels that can be assigned to the concept of action, included in all dialogical contexts, empirically they happen together in a single act (Eckensberger, 1995). As Eckensberger (1995) proposed, action can be analytically differentiated as (a) actions toward "the world," (b) actions as action oriented and subject to regulations or reflections, and (c) actions as agency oriented. However, from an epigenetic viewpoint, even considering these different levels, they should emerge through a process of differentiation from earlier undifferentiated units of acting. The concept of relational choice within possibilities focuses on how these earlier unitary dialogical actions construct meaning through relating the partners' relational, mutual, and interdependent contributions (Fogel, 1993; Lyra & Rossetti-Ferreira, 1995; Lyra & Winegar, 1997) and the semiotic-cultural environment in which communication is embedded.

The second assumption takes the idea of cultural niches (Super & Harkness, 1982) as reflecting cross-cultural differences, or cultural specificities in dealing with the infant. The conception of cultural niches integrates all aspects of the cultural life: economic activities, family structures, physical ecology, and the system of values and beliefs, which includes ways of feeding and dressing the babies, and so on (Super & Harkness, 1982). The authors also referred to the dynamic nature of those niches in terms of promoting mutual adaptability of the caregivers and the infant. They also attributed a role to both the structured nature of those niches and the infant. In approaching the dynamic aspects of the relationship between those niches and the infant, Super and Harkness suggested points of pressure and flexibilities guided by the niche and by the infant. So, a mechanism of relational choice within possibilities seems compatible with their ideas. It is also compatible with the conception of *bounded indeterminacy* (Valsiner, 1987, 1994) and the elaboration of this conception as differentiations or partitions of the action and semiotic fields that provide a dynamic direction for the developmental phenomena (Valsiner, in press). This conception and its elaboration describe the conditions for the emergence of developmental phenomena, their co-constructed and creative nature embedded in a specific culture.

The relational choice within possibilities is conceived as a dialogical mechanism that highlights part of the range of possibilities provided by the culture (structured and determined boundaries) and uses this highlighted action in an empirical concrete moment in order to establish and maintain the partners' process of communication in which novelty emerges.

The idea that action comprises (a) a dynamic interface or "link" between the individual and the situational context, an idea also developed by Cairns [1993] regarding biological endowment and social environment, (b) a "choice" from alternatives within the limits of a predetermined context, and (c) the reconstruction or understanding of the changes that result from acting by the individual, was proposed by Eckensberger (1995). The concept of relational choice within possibilities, therefore, is coherent with this general position. However, when applied to the dynamics of dialogical actions, the relational choice within possibilities aims to highlight the role of the dynamics of partners' exchanges in constructing communication as a process of meaning making. Therefore, the present focus is on the flow of partners' action in a concrete and embodied dialogical situation. The focal point, hence, is the embodied nature of dialogical actions, discussed in a previous section of this chapter.

The concept of relational choice within possibilities can be taken as an elaboration of the dialogical perspective in dealing with the dynamics that constitute the early process of meaning making in the dialogue of the infant with his or her caregiver. The embodied, relational, interdependent nature of these dynamics, the evaluative character of the process of choice within possibilities, and the historical nature of relationship development need to be included in the analysis and comprehension of dialogical constructions.

Let us examine, through examples of early communication, the dynamics of relational choice within possibilities as functioning at two related and inclusive levels: (a) the one that relates the individual with the semiotic-cultural environment, at a specific time moment, and (b) the other, which describes the partners' choice to focus on some part of the other partner's flow of actions.

Consider an instance of face-to-face exchanges between a mother and her 3-month-old baby:

> Eye contact is maintained and a mutual repetition of vocal exchanges happen together with some smiles and some movements of the mother's head. The mother is more consistent in "repeating" the baby's vocal production than the baby. But, the baby also repeats approximately the vocal sounds produced by his or her mother. The dyad maintains these vocal "repetitions" for some time; for instance, until the baby continues "repeating" mother's vocalizations or keeps looking at her. If the baby starts smiling very often (or he or she stops smiling), the mother can stop "repeating" baby's vocalizations and start doing face movements or just smiling. If one of the partners gaze away, it can happen that the baby will concentrate on vocalizing more of whimpering. The mother can start to talk more, changing her position or the baby's position, trying to reestablish eye contact.

Aiming to exemplify the functioning of the mechanism of choice within possibilities from the point of view of relating the individual, as a dialogical partner, with the semiotic-cultural environment at a specific time moment, let us imagine some hypothetical cross-cultural differences regarding face-to-face dialogues. Let us consider the issue of tactile contact between the caregiver and the infant. In fact, a comparison between Anglo-American and !Kung cultures (Konner, 1978) exhibits dramatic differences in the amount of physical contact. !Kung mothers maintain a much greater physical contact then do Anglo-American mothers. Considering the role of touching in fact-to-face dialogues, I focus on some aspects that compose a niche (Super & Harkness, 1982). Regarding a face-to-face dialogue, it is possible to consider (a) where the baby is placed (for instance, a crib or a hammock), and (b) some features of the system of values and beliefs that include, among others, ways of holding the baby in order to establish a face-to-face moment (for instance, holding the baby in mother's arms, placing the baby in her lap, or keeping the baby in the crib or hammock). I use the name *rules* to refer to these systems of values and beliefs provided by the semiotic-cultural environment. Let us regard only aspects (a) and (b).

Suppose that some culture assigns a hammock as the right place for a 3-month-old baby. This physical condition sets some instances of the range of possibilities for establishing a face-to-face moment of exchanges. For instance, in a hammock, more than in a crib, it is required from the mother to be closer to the baby's face, leaning her body toward the infant. Moreover, the dynamics that will comprise the actual actions of the partners also relies on the *rules* about what is *right* or *wrong* in dealing with a 3-month-old infant. For instance, the baby can be taken from the hammock and placed on mother's lap more often, raising, therefore, the amount of touching above what appears in a culture in which babies are placed in cribs. Let us imagine that the same culture that assigns a hammock also establishes that it is *wrong* to have the baby in the lap. So, considering face-to-face dialogues, the amount of leaning toward the baby will increase, but not physical contact. However, let us make another supposition: We are dealing with an overexcited baby that cries more often than is normally expected, or even, an extreme case of a blind baby. Regarding physical contact, it could be imagined that considering the physical constraints set by the hammock and given respect for the *rule* of not taking the baby in one's lap, a great amount of touching can still develop in face-to-face dialogues in this specific dyad. For instance, the mother may keep the baby in the hammock, but may touch the baby's face and body in order to encourage eye contact, or in the case of a blind baby, to have his or her face oriented toward her (probably also using vocal production). This task is accomplished through choosing, from within the range of possibilities set by the semiotic-cultural environment, one possibility regarding the flow of the baby's actions in the dialogical situation. This last part integrates the second level proposed in this chapter, dealing with the embodied nature of dialogical actions: the partners' choice to focus on some part of the (available) flow of the partner's actions.

In other words, the dynamic choice within a range of possibilities established as physical and abstract *rules* of a semiotic-cultural environment goes together with the partners' choice to focus on some part of the (available) flow of the other partner's actions. These two levels of the mechanism of relational choice within possibilities aim to relate individual and semiotic-cultural environment in the same process of developmental change. The point I stress here is the possibility of an empirical analysis of the dynamics of the dialogue that, integrating the role of the semiotic-cultural world in the dialogical partners' exchanges, will contribute to the understanding of the social-cultural embeddedness of the process of communication and meaning making.

The second level consists of the partners' relational choice within possibilities available in the present flow of the other partner's actions. It consists of the dynamics that separate, cut, and highlight some part of the flow of the other partner's actions in order to preserve the ongoing flow of the dialogue. This could be understood, in an analogous way, as involving a figure background movement. It means that part of the flow of the other partner's actions becomes a figure and other parts become the background. This analogy with the movement of figure background illustrates the mechanism of choice of one possibility within others in a relational and dynamic way. I have called this mechanism *dynamics of highlighting* (Lyra & Rossetti-Ferreira, 1995; Lyra & Winegar, 1997) or *dialogical-highlighting-dynamics*.

Considering the example just described, the dyadic choice to highlight the vocal sounds as the main figure is made against a background of other actions also present at the same time; for instance, smiles, facial movements, and touching. Also, the maintenance of eye contact functions as a background. If one of the partners gazes away, there will be changes in the movement of figure background. Other actions of the flow of the other partner's actions can become figures in order to reestablish face-to-face exchanges. For instance, if the baby starts whimpering, the mother can change the baby's position in order to try to reestablish eye contact. At this moment, the gaze toward each other becomes the figure.

It is important to make clear that those two levels of the dynamics of relational choice within possibilities—the one that relates the individual with the semiotic-cultural environment and another that describes the partners' choice to focus on some part of the other partners' flow of actions—are differentiated analytically. Empirically, they are synchronously present in a concrete dialogical dynamics of partners' relational actions.

Summary

The mechanism of relational choice within possibilities is proposed as a conceptual and methodological approach that allows access to the process of meaning making through affiliating this process to the semiotic-cultural environment and the specific context of dialogical actions through the history of a dyadic relationship. Thus, meaning making emerges as a linkage between individual and culture in a relational and mutually interdependent dynamics of dialogical exchange of actions.

We can assume that the mechanism of relational choice within possibilities relates to the dynamics that create different forms but the same function, as pointed out by Bornstein (1995) in dealing with cross-cultural differences. However, thinking in terms of relational choice within possibilities as a possible general mechanism of integrating the semiotic-cultural environment in the dynamics of dialogical flow of partners' actions seems to contribute to understanding the nature of the "developmental processes at a closer level of observation" (Thelen & Smith, 1994, p. vi), allowing us "to reconcile global regularities with local variability, complexity, and context-specificity" (p. xviii). The concept of relational choice within possibilities, focusing on the processual dynamic nature of meaning making and relationship development, supports the idea expressed by Kojima (1995): "At a more abstract level of analysis, especially when one considers adaptive functions of psychological phenomena in diverse historical and cultural contexts, a world view of universalism without uniformity [I would say, may emerge]" (p. 144).

Two final points must be raised: the choice of the units of analysis in the dialogue affiliated to the dyadic history of meaning making, and the evaluative character of the relational choice within possibilities that relates individual unique history and the semiotic-cultural environment. These two points are considered in the concluding remarks.

CONCLUDING REMARKS

Historical Character of the Unit of Analysis in the Dialogue

Regarding the process of meaning making as a historical construction, the choice of units of analysis in the dialogical exchanges will be guided by the history of construction of the emergent meanings. The dialogical turns need to be conceived as reflecting the history of choices within possibilities related to (a) the semiotic-cultural environment and (b) the particular flow of dyadic actions in a particular dyad. In other words, this means that the boundaries between the physical units of the turns in the dialogue are dependent on how the emergent meaning can be related to both (a) and (b). For example, consider touching as a meaningful element that emerges in face-to-face exchanges: We need to look at the history of its construction, focusing on the physical conditions set by the hammock, the *rules* of the specific cultural environment, and the dyadic specificities. As a consequence, the physical and conceptual boundaries of the turns may or may not overlap. For example, regarding the construction of the meaning of touching discussed before, the conceptual boundaries of touching as comprising a dialogical turn can be conceived as spreading to a period of time that does not correspond to the time boundaries of each physical unit of turn taking. For instance, touching can happen at the beginning of the face-to-face moments and in moments of great enjoyment, overlapping with the baby's turns; in this case, the physical separability of partners' turns is not clear cut. Thus, the dialogical quality of the dialogue, as proposed by Mukařovsky (1977), should be considered. For instance, those turns can be analyzed together in terms of meaning construction of touching for this dyad. This means that the conceptual guide for analyzing the dialogical actions as partners' turns should consider the history of successive dialogical exchanges through a period of time. Moreover, this history should reflect its relations to the semiotic-cultural environment as integrating the mutual and interdependent partners' exchanges in a particular dyad.

Evaluative Character of the Relational Choice Within Possibilities

In choosing one possibility among others, the dyad accomplishes a mutual and relational evaluation. This evaluation emerges as meaning making through the construction of the history of their relationship. This evaluation is guided by the choice within the options set by the semiotic-cultural environment and guided by the choice related to the actual flow of partners' actions. For instance, in the previously discussed context of face-to-face dialogue, to choose to touch the baby's face carries a mutual evaluation that is constructed through the history of a particular dyad. The emergent meaning of touching includes its *acceptability* or *approval* as an element of face-to-face dialogues.

The evaluative character of each dialogical action as a relational choice based on Bakhtin's conception of answerable deeds in the unique moment of experiencing of Being, has, in my view, significant importance. The embeddedness of individual dialogical actions in the semiotic-cultural world emerges through evaluations contained in each relational action. These relational actions and evaluations create a history that involves an emotional and volitional dimension that integrates this process of choice. However, these evaluations result from the dynamics of the partners' actual exchanges in the concrete and once-occurred context of the dialogue. Relying on the historical and relational character of those actions and evaluations, this conception contributes to a dynamic, mutual, and interdependent view of the ontogenetic process of meaning making, relating culture and the uniqueness of individual dialogical constructions.

Summary

This chapter proposes a mechanism of relational choice within possibilities functioning at two interconnected and interdependent levels: One that relates the individual and the semiotic-cultural environment, and the other that is applicable to the partners' dialogical flow of actions, which relates both partners in the dialogical process of communication. This mechanism concentrates on the dynamics of the process of meaning making as a relational, evaluative, and historical process that constitutes relationship development.

ACKNOWLEDGMENTS

This work was supported by a grant from the Conselho Nacional de Desenvolvimento Científico e Tecnológico (CNPq), Brazil. The author would especially like to thank Gorjana Litvinovic for helping in the construction of the ideas in this chapter. Andrea Pantoja, Sumedha Gupta, Jaan Valsiner, and Terry Winegar are also gratefully acknowledged for their contributing comments on earlier drafts of this chapter. I am grateful to the Department of Psychology at the University of North Carolina at Chapel Hill, USA, for the support provided during my stay as a visiting scholar.

REFERENCES

Bakhtin, M.M. (1973). *Problems of Dostoevsky's poetics* (2nd ed; R.W. Rotsel, Trans.). Ann Arbor, MI: Ardis.

Bakhtin, M.M. (1981). *The dialogical imagination: Four essays by M. M. Bakhtin* (M. Holquist, ed., C. Emerson & M. Holquist, Trans.). Austin: University of Texas Press.

Bakhtin, M.M. (1993). *Toward a philosophy of the act* (M. Holquist & V. Liapunov, eds., V. Liapunov, Trans.). Austin: University of Texas Press.

Bornstein, M.H. (1995). Form and function: Implications for studies of culture and human development. *Culture & Psychology, 1(1)*, 123-137.

Boulding, K. (1956). General systems theory—The skeleton of science. *Management Science, 2*, 197-208.

Bräten, S. (1984). The third position: Beyond artificial and autopoietic reduction. *Kybernetes, 13*, 157-163.

Butterworth, G.E. (1992). Origins of self-perception in infancy. *Psychological Inquiry, 3(2)*, 103-111.

Cairns, R.B. (1993). Belated but bedazzling: Timing and genetic influence in social development. In G. Turkewitz & D.A. Devenny (Eds.), *Developmental time and timing* (pp. 61-84). Hillsdale, NJ: Erlbaum.

Clarke-Stewart, A., Perlmutter, M., & Friedman, S. (1988). *Lifelong human development.* New York: Wiley.

Cole, M. (1995). Culture and cognitive development: From cross-cultural research to creating systems of cultural mediation. *Culture & Psychology, 1(1)*, 25-54.

Eckensberger, L.H. (1995). Activity or action: Two different roads towards an integration of culture into psychology. *Culture & Psychology, 1(1)*, 67-80.

Fogel, A. (1977). Temporal organization in mother-infant face-to-face interaction. In H.R. Schaffer (Ed.), *Studies in mother-infant interaction* (pp. 119-152). London: Academic Press.

Fogel, A. (1992). Co-regulation, perception and action. *Human Movement Science, 11*, 505-523.

Fogel, A. (1993). *Developing through relationships: Origins of communicatio, self, and culture.* Chicago: University of Chicago Press.

Fogel, A. (1997a). Information, creativity, and culture. In C. Dent-Read & P. Zukow-Goldring (Eds.), *Changing ecological approaches to development: Organism-environment mutualities.* Washington, DC: APA Publications.

Fogel, A. (1997b). Relational narratives of the pre-linguistic self. In P. Rochat (Ed.), *The self in early infancy: Theory and research.* Amsterdam: Elsevier North-Holland.

Fogel, A., & Lyra, M.C.D.P. (1997). Dynamics of development in relationships. In F. Masterpasqua & P. Perna (Eds.), *The psychological meaning of chaos: Self-organization in human development and psychotherapy.* Washington, DC: American Psychological Association.

Fogel, A., & Thelen, E. (1987). Development of early expressive and communicative action: Reintepreting the evidence from a dynamic system perspective. *Developmental Psychology, 23,* 747-761.

Hermans, J.M., & Kempen, H.J.G. (1995). Body, mind and culture: The dialogical nature of mediated action. *Culture & Psychology, 1(1),* 103-114.

Kaye, K. (1977). Toward the origin of dialogue. In H.R. Schaffer (Ed.), *Studies in mother-infant interaction* (pp. 89-117). London: Academic Press.

Kojima, H. (1995). Form and function as categories of comparison. *Culture & Psychology, 1(1),* 139-145.

Konner, M. (1978). Maternal care, infant behavior and development among the !Kung. In R.E. Lee & I. DeVore (Eds.), *Kalahari hunters-gatherers* (pp. 218-245). Cambridge, MA: Harvard University Press.

Kravitz, H., Goldenberg, D., & Neyhus. A. (1978). Tactual exploration by normal infants. *Developmental Medicine and Child, 20,* 720-726.

Laszlo, E. (1972). *Introduction to systems philosophy: Toward a new paradigm of contemporary thought.* New York: Harper & Row.

Lyra, M.C.D.P., & Rossetti-Ferreira, M.C. (1987, July). *Dialogue and the construction of the mother-infant dyad.* Ninth Biennial Meetings of the ISSBD, Abstracts and Poster Presentations, Tokyo, Japan.

Lyra, M.C.D.P., & Rossetti-Ferreira, M.C. (1995). Transformation and construction in social interaction: A new perspective on analysis of the mother-infant dyad. In J. Valsiner (Ed.), *Child development within cultural environments: Vol. 3. Comparative cultural-constructivist perspective* (pp. 51-77). Norwood, NJ: Ablex.

Lyra, M.C.D.P., & Winegar, L.T. (1997). Processual dynamics of interactions through time: Adult-child interactions and process of development. In A. Fogel, M.C.D.P. Lyra, & J. Valsiner, (Eds.), *Dynamics and indeterminism in developmental and social processes.* Mahwah, NJ: Erlbaum.

Markovà, I. (1990a). A three-step process as a unit of analysis in dialogue. In I. Markovà & K. Foppa (Eds.), *The dynamics of dialogue* (pp. 129-146). New York: Springer-Verlag.

Markovà, I. (1990b). Why the dynamics of dialogue? In I. Markovà & K. Foppa (Eds.), *The dynamics of dialogue* (pp. 1-22). New York: Springer-Verlag.

Mukařovsky, J. (1977). On poetic language. In J. Burbank & P. Steiner (Eds.), *The word and verbal art.* New Haven, CT: Yale University Press.

Newson, J. (1977). An intersubjective approach to the systemic description of mother-infant interaction. In H.R. Schaffer (Ed.), *Studies in mother-infant interaction* (pp. 47-61). London: Academic Press.

Rogoff, B. (1990). *Apprenticeship in thinking: Cognitive development in social context.* New York: Oxford University Press.

Rommetveit, R. (1990). On axiomatic features of a dialogical approach to language and mind. In I. Markovà & K. Foppa (Eds.), *The dynamics of dialogue* (pp. 83-104). New York: Springer-Verlag.

Sameroff, A. (1982). Development and the dialectic: The need for a systems approach. In W.A. Collins (Ed.), *Minnesota symposium on child psychology* (Vol. 15, pp. 83-103). Hillsdale, NJ: Erlbaum.

Spencer-Brown, L. (1969). *Laws of form.* London: George Allen & Unwin.

Stern, D.N. (1977). *The first relationship: Infant and mother.* Cambridge, MA: Harvard University Press.

Super, W., & Harkness, S. (1982). The infant's niche in rural Kenya and metropolitan America. In L.L. Adler (Ed.), *Cross-cultural research at issue* (pp. 47-55). New York: Academic Press.

Thelen, E., & Smith, L.B. (1994). *A dynamic system approach to the development of cognition and action.* Cambridge, MA: MIT Press.

Trevarthen, C. (1977). Descriptive analysis of infant communicative behavior. In H.R. Schaffer (Ed.), *Studies in mother-infant interaction* (pp. 227-270). New York: Plenum.

Trevarthen, C. (1980). The foundations of intersubjectivity: Development of interpersonal and cooperative understanding. In D. Olson (Ed.), *The social foundation of language and thought: Essays in honor of Jerome Bruner* (pp. 316-342). New York: Norton.

Valsiner, J. (1987). *Culture and the development of children's actions.* New York: Wiley.

Valsiner, J. (1994). Bidirectional cultural transmision and constructive sociogenesis. In W. De Graff & R. Maier (Eds.), *Sociogenesis reexamined* (pp. 47-70). New York: Springer-Verlag.

Valsiner, J. (1998). *The guided mind: A sociogenetic approach to personality.* Cambridge, MA: Harvard University Press.

Wertsch, J. (1995). Sociocultural research in the copyright age. *Culture & Psychology, 1(1),* 81-102.

AUTHOR INDEX

SUBJECT INDEX[*]

[*]The editors would like to thank Monica Amaral, Leticia Araujo, Emmanuelle Christine, Sinesia
Gois-Pedrosa, Daniela Lima, Ana Paula Melo, Karina Moutinho, Micheline Souza, and Pompeia
Villachan-Lyra for their help in the preparation of the Index.